CHRISTINE BROOKE-ROSE
AND
CONTEMPORARY FICTION

Christine Brooke-Rose
and
Contemporary Fiction

SARAH BIRCH

CLARENDON PRESS · OXFORD
1994

Oxford University Press, Walton Street, Oxford OX2 6DP

Oxford New York Toronto
Delhi Bombay Calcutta Madras Karachi
Kuala Lumpur Singapore Hong Kong Tokyo
Nairobi Dar es Salaam Cape Town
Melbourne Auckland Madrid
and associated companies in
Berlin Ibadan

Oxford is a trade mark of Oxford University Press

Published in the United States
by Oxford University Press Inc. New York

British Library Cataloguing in Publication Data
Data available

Library of Congress Cataloging in Publication Data
Birch, Sarah.
Christine Brooke-Rose and contemporary fiction / Sarah Birch.
Includes bibliographical references.
1. Brooke-Rose, Christine, 1923– Criticism and interpretation.
I. Title.
PR6003.R412Z56   1994
823'.914—dc20   93–24543
ISBN 0–19–812375–2

Typeset by Pentacor PLC, High Wycombe, Bucks.
Printed in Great Britain
on acid-free paper by
Bookcraft Ltd.
Midsomer Norton, Bath

TO MY MOTHER AND MY FATHER
FOR THEIR LOVE AND PATIENCE

Acknowledgements

I SHOULD like to extend my thanks first and foremost to Ann Jefferson, who supervised the thesis on which this book is based, for the uncommon care with which she read and commented on my work. I am also indebted to Helen Atkinson, Christopher Butler, Elizabeth Fallaize, and Sir Frank Kermode, who read the text at various stages of its genesis and whose remarks proved most useful. I should like to thank Michael Schmidt of Carcanet Press for permitting me to consult Carcanet's files, and the librarians of the John Rylands Library and the Bristol University Library for granting me access to their archives. Finally, I am deeply grateful to Christine Brooke-Rose for her encouragement, her generosity, and her inspiration.

Contents

Introduction

This book is the first full-length study of the novels of Christine Brooke-Rose. It aims to provide a coherent overview of her fictional *œuvre* and to map her place in the field of contemporary literature. Brooke-Rose has been widely recognized as one of Britain's most innovative contemporary writers. The dismantling of systems, conventions, and readers' expectations is at the heart of all her fiction; the goal of her novels is to teach people to see things anew, to look behind the discursive and social systems which naturalize convention, and to question this process of naturalization. It is not surprising, then, that she should be a difficult novelist to categorize. Indeed, despite the fact that she is a British writer, Brooke-Rose has been consistently identified with the *nouveau roman* and subsequent movements in the French novel since she began writing criticism of contemporary French fiction in the 1960s. I shall examine why this has been so, to what extent it is a relevant classification, and what an alternative approach might entail.

The cross-cultural dimension of Brooke-Rose's work and her position between languages can be traced in her name which, unlike most, proclaims a dual parentage. Born in Geneva in 1923 to a Swiss-American mother, Evelyn Blanche Brooke, and a British father, Alfred Northbrook Rose, Christine Frances E. Brooke-Rose grew up speaking French, English, and German. During her childhood she moved several times between Switzerland, Belgium, and England before finally going to Folkestone at the age of 13 to attend school. She studied English and philology at Somerville College, Oxford, and went on to London to do her Ph.D. Shortly after completing a dissertation on medieval French and English literature she began writing her first novel, *The Languages of Love*, as a form of therapy to counteract the stress induced by a near-fatal illness her husband suffered in 1956. This novel was followed by three more which, like the first, are amusing but relatively conventional. In 1962 she herself suffered a serious illness during which she was convinced she would die. Upon recovery she claimed to have attained a different level of consciousness which she has described as 'a sense of being in touch with something else—death perhaps' (cit. Hall 1976: 183). This experience was a major factor in the change in style and approach evident in her subsequent work. From 1962 to 1968 she wrote literary journalism and fiction in London, but in 1968 Brooke-Rose left her husband and accepted a post at the newly created Université de Paris VIII at Vincennes, where she taught for twenty years before retiring in 1988 to the south of France to concentrate her energy on her novels.[1]

Her literary career can thus be divided at two points: 1962 and 1968. The first break was the direct result of illness, but it also coincided roughly with her discovery of the *nouveau roman* and her growing dissatisfaction with the fiction that was being written in Britain at the time. The second break was precipitated by the collapse of her marriage and her arrival in Paris during the aftermath of the 'events' of 1968. In each case a major alteration in her personal life led to a change of direction in her fiction which was guided by recent 'radical' developments in French literary culture. Not surprisingly, it is the experimental literature and the theoretical constructs developed in France since the Second World War which have had the greatest impact on her approach to fiction and her use of language. But because she writes in English, her work is at one remove from French fiction as well. This distance affords her a critical perspective on both camps; her novels cannot be situated wholly within the literary tradition of either country, nor can they be regarded as entirely rootless.

It is not insignificant that the 'other' through whose perspective Brooke-Rose originally learned to see was a national other. In an interview given in 1986, she claimed that she was 'created . . . as a novelist' at the age of 18 when she served in the WAAF reading German messages during the war (1987*d*). Though she did not begin writing fiction until fifteen years later, the experience of witnessing a war from the enemy point of view gave her the 'ability to imagine what it's like to be the other' (1987*d*). A possible approach to her work is a bifocal view in which she would be seen to have a place within both the French and the English traditions. But by maintaining the division of the

---

[1] For more complete details, see the brief biography in the Appendix.

field of literature into discrete national domains, this tactic precludes comparison between them and ignores the ways in which they interact. For this reason I shall be advocating instead what could be termed a 'transfocal' strategy which parallels techniques employed in the novels themselves. As I shall demonstrate, the common denominator of all Brooke-Rose's fiction is the prismatic effect of viewing one field of knowledge, one language, or one culture through the discursive lens of another, and the idea of crossing between cultural domains is manifest in her novels as a structural principle.

In this sense her novels are more realistic, if not more realist, than those of many of her contemporaries.[2] It is fair to say that the majority of fiction represents the day-to-day discourses of human interaction. Yet in our ever-more complex world, this common or ordinary language is becoming increasingly suffused with the specialized vocabularies of the various environments in which people live and work: there is no longer a single common or ordinary language, but a multitude of overlapping fields of language use, each of which blends a number of highly codified vocabularies with more traditional lexical material. In the vast majority of contemporary fiction there is a resistance to incorporating such jargons, perhaps for fear that they will be incomprehensible to a large portion of a novel's potential audience, and that this will have the effect of limiting readership. Hence the language of most fiction today is somewhere between the language of fiction fifty years ago and the language people actually use. Christine Brooke-Rose goes to the opposite extreme. Recognizing the prevalence of specialized discourses in everyday speech and the effect they have on the paradigms we employ to make sense of the world, she takes them in their purest form, the form in which they are used by those who manipulate them professionally. Her novels work on these languages to reveal the assumptions that underlie them and to show that they too can be used to generate 'a kind of poetry' (1987*d*).

In an article published in 1988 Brooke-Rose describes her fictional project as follows:

---

[2] By 'realist' I mean that which conforms to a set of literary conventions derived from 19th-cent. Realism. See Stern 1973 and Nash 1987 for definition and discussion of these conventions.

I deal in discourses, in the discourses of the world, political, technological, scientific, psychoanalytical, philosophical, ideological, social, emotional, and all the rest, so that knowledge to me is not an extraneous element I can put in or withhold at will, it *is* discourse, it *is* language . . . the source of most of my comic effects is the grafting together, or onto each other, of all these different discourses . . . Discourse comes from Latin *discurrere, to run here and there*. It has today become whole sets of rigid uses, and I am trying to make it run here and there again. (1988*a*: 129; italics in the original)

Breaking down the 'rigid uses' of language by making specialized discourses 'run here and there again' is the principal technical device of Brooke-Rose's fiction. Her novels question the systematicity of theoretical discursive constructs from physics to psychoanalysis by forcing them to interact in such a way as to undermine their claims to convey absolute truths. This 'mobilization' of abstract constructs makes the reader aware of the inherent mutability of even the most formal language, its propensity to yield multiple associations, and the capacity of meaning to go in many directions at once.

The grafting together of discourses could be seen to betray a nostalgic desire to return to a time when the various domains of what we now call the physical sciences were not yet fully distinguished from the arts. Indeed Brooke-Rose praises Milton's use of scientific metaphor which she sees as prefiguring the modern notion of the space–time continuum (1967*a*: 296). But viewed in the context of what J.-F. Lyotard (1979) terms 'la science postmoderne', the desire to forge links between disparate domains can also be understood as a forward-looking attempt to come to terms with the conceptual postulates on which the discursive apparatuses of post-industrial society are based. In what follows I shall indicate several of the most significant intellectual currents on which Brooke-Rose's fiction draws. These include contemporary science, post-Saussurian theories of language and discourse, the technical achievements of Ezra Pound, Samuel Beckett, and the *nouveaux romanciers*, and Mikhail Bakhtin's theory of the novel.

In the 1950s and 1960s there was widespread interest in bringing together disparate domains of enquiry. This was a period in which science was actively engaged in redefining its aims and examining the means it employed to achieve them. The possibility that science and the arts might learn from one another became a touchstone for many contemporary polemics, including the 'two cultures' debate instigated by C. P. Snow's Reed Lectures at Cambridge in 1959. In the 1960s French structuralist criticism attempted to bring the two fields together by establishing a science of literature; toward the end of the decade post-structuralism sought instead to demonstrate the 'literariness' of science. Brooke-Rose began her literary career just prior to the 'two cultures' debate in England, and she moved to France at the height of the structuralist controversy there. It is therefore not surprising that the relation between different fields of knowledge should be of primary importance to her work.

One of the abiding concerns of Brooke-Rose's fiction is the relation of language to 'truth'—scientific or otherwise—and to reality. She holds the view held by many structuralists and post-structuralists that 'reality *is* language' (1973*b*: 614), that our apprehension of the world, of ourselves, and of others passes through a variety of systematized forms of language use, each of which has its own conventions. What we label 'true' will thus only be true relative to the specific conditions for truth established within each domain, and the 'truth' will always be in some senses a fiction outside of the system within which it has been established. According to this view, the claim to formal rigour of the 'exact' sciences is valid only within those disciplines, not in any absolute sense. Consequently, scientific knowledge and poetic knowledge are not different in kind: 'All our systems are fictions . . . Right up to, I suppose, the Second World War, people still believed in the "truth". Poetry was not the same truth as science, but it was poetic truth, and so on. That position is absolutely untenable now' (1987*d*). Brooke-Rose works on the jargons of specialized discourses to demonstrate that truth claims will always be subject to linguistic constraints, but she is aware that this concept is one which has its roots in the very discourses which make those claims.

It is a commonplace that our experience of the material world is rendered intelligible in the *formulation* of observed phenomena, their coding both in formulae and in the forms and figures of language, and it has become evident over the course of this century that the discourse of science is in part a metaphoric restructuring of the world by our minds. This idea is discussed by

Werner Heisenberg in *Physics and Philosophy*. Heisenberg maintains that the language which scientists use to describe phenomena is a specialized use of natural language, one that 'produces pictures in our mind, but together with them the notion that the pictures have only a vague connection with reality, that they represent only a tendency toward reality' (1958: 181). This implies a radical reversal of our traditional conception of the relation between scientific language and everyday language. Scientific language is here recognized as a figurative language, one conscious of its distance from its object. Like the specialized discourse of poetry, it sets itself off from day-to-day language not by the use of different words, but by a different use of the same words. This reconception of the status of scientific discourse threatens the status of science as a discipline, for if scientists no longer claim to describe the world but only the representations they themselves make of it, they are in fact describing an aspect of themselves. This altered view of the relation between science as a discourse and the physical world makes it possible for typically 'literary' uses of language such as metaphor and narrative to gain prominence as forms of knowledge.[3]

In an article published in 1965 entitled 'Dynamic Gradients' Brooke-Rose discusses the relationship between the new science and experimental literature. She takes as her point of reference Alfred Korzybski's semantic theories, semantics being 'the bridge between science and literature' (Brooke-Rose 1965*a*: 89–90). She agrees with Korzybski's basic premiss that 'we must evolve a new way of thinking and reject the old universalistic and absolutist concepts, especially our habit of identification, just as the scientists have done' (90), and she goes on to cite Heisenberg's 'uncertainty principle' (according to which a statement is neither true nor false in any absolute sense but has a certain degree of probability of being true) as the source of the multivalent logic which 'has indirectly affected all our philosophy and all our attitudes' (93). Elsewhere, she points out that, unlike other artistic media, language can be used to denote the non-existent and the impossible (1976*k*: 19–21). In her fiction she uses

---

[3] To a certain extent science has accommodated this threat by altering its discourse, so that now it often refers to the models it proposes as 'metaphors' or 'stories'. The use of rhetorical and narrative paradigms in science has been well documented: see especially Black 1962, Lyotard 1979, and Nash 1990.

this potential to explore the implications of the uncertainty principle for our relation to the world.

Brooke-Rose was, of course, not alone in taking this position. In an article for the *Times Literary Supplement* in 1967 Raymond Queneau speculates as to the consequences for literature of the conceptual revolution in science:

it is all the time becoming more evident that the system that comprises the sciences is not linear (Mathematics—Physics—Biology—Anthropology), but that it is indeed circular, and that the social sciences are intimately linked to mathematics. It is quite clear, therefore, that there is nothing to stop Poetry taking its place in the centre, without thereby losing anything of its specificity. (1967: 864)

The role of literature which would take on board its new-found centrality is then twofold. Literature is in a position first to explore the consequences of modern science for the individual's relation to the world and to other individuals, and second, by pointing to the linguistic constraints under which scientific discourse operates, to contest the efforts of any discipline to defend itself against the encroachment of the arts.

In the late 1960s many French critics saw the role of literature in this light. In the same issue of the *Times Literary Supplement* Roland Barthes writes:

To resort to scientific discourse as if to an instrument of thought is to postulate that there exists a neutral state of language, from which a certain number of specialized languages, the literary or poetic languages for example, have derived, as so many deviants or embellishments. It is held that this neutral state would be the referential code for all the 'excentric' languages, which themselves would be merely its sub-codes. By identifying itself with this referential code, as the basis of normality, scientific discourse is arrogating to itself a right which it is writing's duty precisely to contest . . . the role of literature is actively to *represent* to the scientific establishment what the latter denies, to wit the sovereignty of language. (1967: 898; italics in the original)

It is with a similar task in view that Brooke-Rose's experimental fiction took root in the 1960s, and in this sense her approach to the 'crossing' of science and fiction prefigured her 'crossing' of French and English conceptions of literature.

But this is not to say that her fiction can easily be fitted into the category of science fiction. Science fiction is an inescapably generic term in that it refers to an established and self-consciously maintained set of thematic, narrative, and stylistic conventions. In *A Rhetoric of the Unreal* Brooke-Rose discusses science fiction at some length and demonstrates how the genre has subverted itself in the work of 'new wave' writers such as Stanislaw Lem, Joseph McElroy, and Kurt Vonnegut (1981: 206–88).[4] While her novels *Out* and *Such* could potentially be situated within this counter-tradition, their engagement with science *per se* is minimal, and in cases such as this the term 'science fiction' becomes less than adequate.[5] The majority of Brooke-Rose's writing is 'science fiction' only in a special sense of the term: it addresses the implications of the 'new sciences'—including psychoanalysis and semiotics—for fiction and for our understanding of our relation to the world. According to science-fiction critics such as Robert Scholes (1975: 102) and Darko Suvin (1979: 10), science fiction mimics the cognitive processes of science. Brooke-Rose's fiction complements these processes by elaborating their consequences in other domains, and by reminding us that the discourses of science are, like all discourses, elaborate constructs.

Bringing the role of discursive systems and constructs to our attention is also the goal of much contemporary discourse analysis, however, and it is necessary to specify the ways in which Brooke-Rose's novelistic enterprise differs from a critical analysis of the discourses of conceptual knowledge. The literary counter-part of mediation through analysis is the prismatic effect of shattering a conceptual language into its component parts. A prism refracts light, thus it too functions as a tool for making visible what would otherwise be transparent and pass unnoticed. But a prism also creates a dazzling display of colour, it turns aesthetically neutral light into a pleasing image. Like a prism,

---

[4] References to articles collected in *A Rhetoric of the Unreal* (Brooke-Rose 1981) and *Stories, Theories and Things* (Brooke-Rose 1991a) will be to the revised versions of these articles found in the collections, except in those cases where the passages referred to have been omitted or significantly altered.

[5] Brooke-Rose herself says of *Such* that 'it's not really science fiction, it's more a poetic fantasy' (1990c: 32). Furthermore, though Brian McHale claims with reference to two of Brooke-Rose's later novels that 'looking back at *Amalgamemnon* from the perspective of *Verbivore* . . . we are compelled to see *Amalgamemnon*, retrospectively, as somehow potentially compatible with SF, "as if SF" ' (n.d.: 25), this category is so marginal to conventional science fiction as to put the relevance of the term further in doubt.

Brooke-Rose's novels refract language in such a way as to create an aesthetically pleasing or 'poetic' effect. This effect most often takes the form of mis-representation: linguistic distortions, 'bad copies', or mis-readings. From the point of view of 'neutral' or 'transparent' language these appear to be falsifications, but just as a prism makes us see light in a way that is unfamiliar but equally 'true', so Brooke-Rose's use of language transforms it such that we become aware of its inherent mutability and the tenuousness of its claim to referential validity.[6]

Brooke-Rose views words as essentially 'strange' (1976*k*: 20), and the techniques she employs in her novels work to reveal this strangeness, to defamiliarize the various domains of language use which we have grown accustomed to treating as mere tools. If scientists use language as a tool to represent or express the findings of their experiments, Brooke-Rose experiments with this tool itself. She believes that though the method of the artist 'is not basically a scientific one', still, 'in his own way he also tests his hunches about the reality behind the appearances' (1965*a*: 96). But she maintains that 'the essential function of literary discourse is to perform what it says rather than to prove it' (1976*a*: 67), and her novels can be read as performances of the linguistic drama inherent in any rigorous discursive system, be it scientific or philosophical.

In the foregoing discussion, the 'literary', the 'poetic', and the 'novelistic' have been taken to be synonymous. This is because Brooke-Rose describes the goal of her work on language as 'a kind of poetry', though she chooses the novel as her medium. She disputes the idea that literary discourse can be divided into the poetic and the novelistic based on the techniques used in each genre. Like many of her contemporaries in France, she began her experimentation with novelistic convention by rejecting the linear structure of narrative as a principle of organization. She cites as her two major influences Pound and Beckett, with

---

[6] The metaphor of the prism is not used here merely for heuristic purposes; in fact it is a metaphor foregrounded in Brooke-Rose's first 'experimental' novel, *Out*. The main character of this novel is fascinated both with the capacity of language to represent indeterminacy and the similar effects of light: 'In daylight the stone is blue. At dusk the stone is green. In the electric light the stone is mauve. At the moment it is possible to take one's choice . . . ' (164/166; page references to *Out*, *Such*, *Between*, and *Thru* will be to the original edition, followed by the *Omnibus* edition).

whom she shares a 'passionate concern with language' (1976*k*: 10) and a taste for combining high seriousness with humour (11). To Pound she also acknowledges a considerable technical debt. In an article published in 1961 she shows how in Pound's *Cantos* key words, phrases, and themes are repeated in different contexts, so that with each occurrence they accrue new meanings. This pattern of repetition with variation creates 'a giant agglutinative metaphor' (1961*a*: 83), for it is a matter of juxtaposing the disparate elements of a sequence in a non-linear, non-causal structure. Extended in the temporal dimension necessary to language use, the ring of the metaphor becomes a coil, creating what Brooke-Rose calls a 'spiral' of echoes which reverberate throughout the entire work (1965*a*: 91; 1961*a*: 80). She finds parallels for this technique in Langland's *Piers Plowman* (1961*a*: 80) as well as in the novels of Beckett and the *nouveau roman* (1965*a*: 91–9).

Brooke-Rose's novels of the 1960s manifest a similar move away from diachronic structuring toward metaphoric composition: *Out* unfolds as a succession of descriptions in the present tense which are frequently repeated, often with minor variations, so that it becomes impossible to determine whether they are, in Genette's terms, singulative or repetitive.[7] The only viable time scheme is a rhythm of recurrence which she describes as a 'technique of repetition and echoes' (1976*k*: 10). In her eyes the desire to integrate typically poetic effects into a basically narrative genre represents an attempt to heal the rift between poetry and narrative (1977*a*: 136; cf. 1991*a*: 178). But if her reconception of what a novel is and what it is capable of doing has parallels with the work of Beckett and many of the French writers who followed in his wake, it also harks back to what Mikhail Bakhtin sees as the origins of the novel.

Brooke-Rose refers frequently to Bakhtin in her critical writings, and it is evident that he had a major impact on her thinking about the novel as a genre. Though she did not discover him until the late 1960s, his theories can be retroactively applied to her earlier work which, like its post-1968 counterpart,

---

[7] The abundance of 'repetitive' descriptions (describing *n* times what happens once) contrasts sharply with the more conventional novelistic strategy of 'iterative' description, i.e. describing once what happens *n* times (see Genette 1972: 147–8,153).

manifests the novel's defining features with remarkable fidelity to Bakhtin's characterization of the genre. From Bakhtin's analyses of the history of the novel two main elements stand out: polyglossia and contemporaneity. The polyglot nature of the novel is for Bakhtin a consequence of its genesis between two cultures. The Latin literary language in which the novel first developed viewed itself *'through the eyes* of the Greek word' (1981: 61; italics in the original), and vestiges of this duality have remained throughout the novel's history:

During its germination and early development, the novelistic word reflected a primordial struggle between tribes, peoples, cultures and languages—it is still full of echoes of this ancient struggle. In essence this discourse always developed on the boundary line between cultures and languages. (50)

Because of the novel's sensitivity to linguistic variety, it is also by nature heteroglot: it does not have a discourse of its own but represents other discourses. It is therefore eclectic, incorporating and parodying such diverse forms as dialogue, poetry, sacred texts, and epic, as well as extra-literary genres: 'The language of the novel is a *system* of languages that mutually and ideologically interanimate each other' (47; italics in the original). It is clear from this description that linear narrative is by no means the only tool the novel has at its disposal, and that if certain narrative conventions have come to be considered attributes of the genre, this is a function of the novel's recent history.

For Bakhtin, the novel is a quintessentially contemporary genre in that it mediates between the sacred texts of the past and the culture of the present. The novel looks toward the future and refuses to glorify the past; instead it constantly questions the rigidity of received discursive conventions by setting them in motion: 'the novel inserts into these other genres an indeterminacy, a certain semantic openendedness, a living contact with unfinished, still-evolving contemporary reality' (7). According to Bakhtin, Dostoevsky inaugurated an important variation in the genre, the 'polyphonic' or 'dialogic' novel (1984: 270). Bakhtin posits a link between the dialogic vision and Einstein's theory of relativity because dialogic discourse refuses to subordinate the voices within it to a supreme authority (272). Rather, one voice is made to speak through another and the drama of their interaction is allowed to play itself out in their internal dialogue (185–99).

Christine Brooke-Rose's fiction is highly novelistic in Bakhtin's sense. It employs limited polyglossia, but more significantly, it combines the specialized 'languages' of our secular scriptures: the discourses of knowledge and of theory. She integrates these with the common idiom by means of slips, puns, and double meanings which bring them to life and demonstrate the relevance of the concepts they incorporate for our day-to-day lives. The technique of articulating one discourse through another renders her novels truly polyphonic. They stage the interaction of the languages of diverse disciplines which they inflect with varying degrees of ludic incredulity, but by no means do they subordinate them to a master-discourse of their own. Like Bakhtin, Brooke-Rose sees an awareness of epistemological relativism as the specific contribution of the novel which, unlike other discourses, is self-consciously double-voiced: 'we've got to reach a stage when we can be interested in someone else's "truth", which is what the novelist does' (1987d).

In returning to the historical origin of the novel, Brooke-Rose challenges our identification of the genre with its realist incarnation and invites us to reconsider its 'poetic' possibilities. She has expressed her desire to do with the novel what only the novel can do (1981: 322; 1988a: 129; 1991a: 178), and this can be summed up in one task: work on and with the written word. Yet, contrary to the commonly held conception of her fiction, this does not entail an endless self-reflexive meditation on the nature of writing. There is a self-reflexive dimension to all her novels, as there is to most works which attempt to re-orient a genre, but this is neither their most interesting nor their most significant aspect.

Brooke-Rose has made several speculations as to the future of the novel, one of which merits particular attention, for it is revealing with regard to her own aims: 'Here, perhaps, lies our hope: starting again, *ex* almost *nihilo*, so that narrative can again, as it once did, aspire to the condition of poetry . . . The impetus may come from two apparently contradictory sources, the electronic revolution and the feminist revolution' (1991a: 178). She observes that both feminism and cybernetic technology are based on a paradigm of non-hierarchical oppositions between contrasting elements, and she sees the act of de-privileging the 'positive' term in pairs such as man/woman, presence/absence, or conscious/unconscious as the first step toward a renewal of fiction.

In her own novels she has made considerable progress toward realizing this hope. Her main technique is indeed the 'poetic' use of metaphor to bring together two or more disparate languages, cultures, or fields of knowledge, and there is abundant evidence that her fiction has been inspired by both feminist theory and the cognitive implications of technological innovation. These three elements: the poetic technique of metaphor, feminism, and technology thus provide apposite lenses through which to read her work.

In the chapters that follow these concepts will be used as the principal foci for my discussion of Brooke-Rose's fictional *œuvre*, and a set of reference points by means of which this *œuvre* can be placed in context. In Part 1 her novels will be analysed sequentially from the point of view of the development of fictional technique and the discursive intertext which each work invokes. This will involve an examination of the internal relation of her novels to the non-fictional discourses they incorporate. The chapters will be structured around the major turning-points in Brooke-Rose's literary career. Chapter 1 will treat the early novels: *The Languages of Love* (1957), *The Sycamore Tree* (1959), *The Dear Deceit* (1960), and *The Middlemen* (1961). In these works discourses such as philology and philosophy are thematized but not integrated technically or structurally. I shall argue that this represents a traditional novelistic approach to the use of other fields of knowledge, and that it proves inadequate. Chapter 2 will trace the development in *Out* (1964), *Such* (1966), and *Between* (1968) of a particular kind of metaphor which causes specialized discourses to interact in such a way as to question their authority, their autonomy, and their claim to refer simply or directly to the object of their investigations. In Chapter 3 I shall examine the ways in which *Between*, *Thru* (1975), and *Amalgamemnon* (1984) use this type of metaphor to bring discourses together in a parodic conjunction by means of a strategy of mimicry inspired by feminist theory. Here Brooke-Rose experiments with the rhetorical power of the technique she developed in the first two novels and uses it to examine the notions of culture on which Western civilization is based. *Amalgamemnon* is the first volume of a recently completed quartet, analysed in Chapter 4, which includes *Xorandor* (1986), *Verbivore* (1990), and *Textermination* (1991). The quartet explores the cognitive and cultural consequences of advances in technology and their relation to narrative fiction as a mode of knowledge and communication.

It will have been remarked that there is an overlap in this section at two points: both *Between* and *Amalgamemnon* are dealt with twice in consecutive chapters. There are several reasons for this slightly unusual format. First, *Between* and *Amalgamemnon* are the two novels I consider to be Brooke-Rose's finest achievements. Secondly, I do not want to suggest that the approach I have adopted in each chapter is the only possible one, and by discussing two of the novels from different angles I hope to demonstrate the richness and variety of the interpretations they inspire. Finally, while the turnings in Brooke-Rose's literary career can be pin-pointed with a fair degree of precision, her interests and goals during any one period necessarily overlap. The novels of the 1960s culminate naturally in *Between*, whereas *Thru* quite obviously represents a change of direction. Nevertheless, *Between* is the first novel in which Brooke-Rose makes explicit use of post-Saussurian French theories of language. Similarly, *Amalgamemnon* is the first volume of what Brooke-Rose has designated as a quartet, but stylistically and technically it is much closer to her previous work. The structure I have chosen thus represents a compromise between the advantages of treating each novel in isolation and those of grouping the novels together under conceptual headings which provide a sense of continuity.

While this presentation will lay the necessary groundwork for further discussion of Brooke-Rose's writing, it is not in itself sufficient to account for her novels as literary phenomena. In Part 2 the focus will be shifted from conceptual intertext to literary context in an attempt to situate the novels in terms of the frameworks of the literary and intellectual institutions which have been determining factors in both their production and their reception. Brooke-Rose is integrated into two national contexts in two radically different ways. Her writing gestates within the matrix of the French intellectual arena, whereas in Britain it is a product. For this reason a preliminary account of her publishing history and her reception in Britain will be undertaken in Chapter 5 in order to try to understand why the reading public has reacted to her fiction as it has.

Chapter 6 will attempt to place Brooke-Rose's novels in relation to the dominant critical paradigms of contemporary French and British fiction. It will address the issue of the influence of the *nouveau roman* on her fiction and her conception of literature, as well as indicating certain similarities between her work and writing in the 1960s by novelists such as Alan Burns and Ann Quin who have also been marginalized from the canon of contemporary literature as a result of the categories critics have imposed on the novel in this period. I shall then go on to assess the impact of the intellectual atmosphere of post-1968 Paris on Brooke-Rose's writing. Because she was teaching and writing in Paris at this time, Brooke-Rose had contact with members of a number of influential literary circles, including the *Tel Quel* group, various 'feminist' circles, and OuLiPo. While both her fiction and her critical writing of the 1970s and the early 1980s bear the marks of the ideas these groups generated, I shall show that she was still working very much on her own, and that her writing cannot easily be assimilated to any of the movements these groups led. Finally, I shall consider the question of what has come to be called 'international postmodernism'. Though the label 'postmodernist' has often been applied to Brooke-Rose, especially in more recent writing about her work, it is not altogether clear that this is an accurate characterization. Yet because it allows her fiction to be read in a non-nationalist context, the concept and its alternatives demand close examination.

For the purposes of this study I have intentionally limited my analysis mainly to the two cultures in which Christine Brooke-Rose has lived and worked for most of her life. One reason for this is pragmatic: to attempt both to give a coherent account of her fiction and to situate it in a larger context would be an undertaking beyond the scope of a work of this length. But the primary reason for imposing this limit is that Brooke-Rose has acquired a reputation for writing 'the *nouveau roman* in English'. One of my main goals is to show that this label is misconceived and to try to explain why it has been so persistently attached to her work.

Though informed by French literary and philosophical movements, Brooke-Rose's fiction is distinct from that of her French contemporaries in several important respects. Far from being self-reflexive meditations on the nature of writing, her novels engage in a poetic and playful way with the languages of the various branches of knowledge which pervade our lives. While the relation between the inner workings of the mind and the public sphere is at the heart of all her writing, she approaches this typically English subject from the point of view of the linguistic and discursive processes in which the individual is implicated, an angle conditioned by her immersion in French theory and fiction. No matter which tradition we try to incorporate her into, there is an effect of *dépaysement*, for her novels exploit their position on the borders between cultures. They are English novels which nevertheless benefit from being read through the context of post-war French literature and thought.

Part 1

1. The Early Novels: A Prologue to Experiment

Flying reputations can be dangerous.

(Brooke-Rose 1977*a*: 132)

The direction the English novel was to take in the post-war era was the subject of much discussion in the late 1950s when Christine Brooke-Rose began her career as a novelist. But while her novels of this period—*The Languages of Love* (1957), *The Sycamore Tree* (1958), *The Dear Deceit* (1960), and *The Middlemen* (1961)—are in many respects typical products of their generation, they raise a number of issues which it was not possible to articulate within the parameters of the contemporary debate. The novels enjoyed a limited success, but because most novelists were concerned at the time to redefine the relation of the individual to society in terms of changing values, it was all too easy for readers to focus on the social dimension of Brooke-Rose's fiction and to overlook those aspects which can in retrospect be seen to prefigure the problems and techniques of her later work. This was possible mainly because the capacity for viewing personal identity in terms of language and 'languages', which was to become the hallmark of her work from the 1960s onward, is integrated in the early novels into a realist narrative mode. Thus, despite the fact that they exhibit an increasing frustration with the novelistic discourse of the period, her first four novels did not succeed in significantly altering fictional convention.

They are, for the most part, light entertainments enlivened by mysterious foreigners, odd situations, and an abundance of documentary detail deftly manipulated to appear at once familiar and slightly absurd or ominous.[1] The familiarity of their London setting accounted, perhaps, both for their easy assimilation into the literary world and for their contemporary readers' lack of genuine interest in the more esoteric themes they raise. Reviewers eagerly

---

[1] The majority of the stories in the collection *Go When You See the Green Man Walking* (1970) are also written in this style.

praised the mild satire of their own territory, delighting in the wit with which Brooke-Rose vividly portrayed its types. Like a novel about the television industry described in *The Middlemen*, her early works fall easily into the category of 'professional joke novels, the lid off the law' (110). But her characters are just a bit too typical in their social habits, their tastes, and their personal dilemmas. Indeed, when Bernard Bergonzi complains of the uniformity of the novels he is obliged as a reviewer to read, he gives as a sample situation a scenario that could well be based on *The Languages of Love*: 'a very sensitive, rather neurotic girl, living in an Earls Court bedsitter and having sexual difficulties' (1979: 24). One of Brooke-Rose's reviewers pin-points the problem: 'I have the feeling that young married intellectual Chelsea . . . has been rather overworked, simply because so many of its inhabitants write novels' (Quigly 1958: 86). Despite exotic characters and racy plots, the basic social context of Brooke-Rose's early work was too familiar for it to be deemed truly original.

Yet this is not to say that her contemporaries completely misread her first four novels, nor that they misjudged their merits. With hindsight it is easy to see in an author's uneven early work the later masterpieces struggling to get out, and it is especially tempting to do this with an author such as Christine Brooke-Rose whose fiction underwent such a dramatic change between 1961 and 1964. But it would be an over-simplification to argue that her chosen 'content' simply did not find an adequate 'form' until the mid-1960s. A more likely explanation is that Brooke-Rose was flattered by her own wit and allowed it to determine her style of narration. In 1977 she published an autobiographical sketch entitled 'Self-Confrontation and the Writer' in which she posits her authorial identity as a separate person whom she calls 'John'. She criticizes John for having accepted too readily the standards of the day and for having adapted too easily to the social and literary context in which he found himself:

The rat race. The mousetrap in the House of Fame or Fiction. John is eager to please. John is also easy to please. John is built by the House. Flying reputations can be dangerous . . . John and I, flattered at first by the sweet smell of success, had to get out of it, into another language, forgotten in the House of Fame but happy ever after in the House of Fiction. (1977a: 132)

'Flying planes can be dangerous' is the type-sentence of semantic ambiguity because it can yield both a passive and an active interpretation, and here a variation is used to demonstrate the danger of paying too much attention to public opinion. The writer may seem to be actively creating, whereas in fact he or she is being passively fashioned by the public's desires, 'built by the House' of fame.

There is no ambiguity, however, about the distinction between the 'House of Fame' and the 'House of Fiction'. Brooke-Rose's division of fiction into two classes reflects a tendency prevalent among those writing about the 1950s to group its novelists into two categories. Stephen Spender divides writers into 'contemporaries' and 'moderns' (1962: 555); Malcolm Bradbury distinguishes between the main current of fiction and peripheral but nevertheless important work by people like Samuel Beckett, Malcolm Lowry, William Golding, and Lawrence Durrell (1973); and Iris Murdoch draws a distinction between the 'journalistic' and the 'crystalline' which delineates similar categories. (1961: 27). Each such polarization invariably reflects the values of the writers who impose it, but there is a wide consensus among critics who have written about the literature of the period that the majority of it is unambitious, anti-experimental, and somewhat lacking in originality.[2] Even those such as David Lodge and Malcolm Bradbury who argue against this blanket judgement do not attempt to depict the decade as one of great creative achievement. They readjust the picture to admit a counter-current of more radical authors or point to the less dramatic use of 'experimental' and 'modernist' techniques in the novels of mainstream fiction (Bradbury 1973: 177–7; 1977: 18–20; 1987: 106–11; Lodge 1971: 9–34). Certainly the 1950s were remarkable for the self-assuredness with which writers defended what they saw as a fresh start for English literature, and for the equally unanimous revision this view underwent not ten years later.

There was a strong sense at the time that the novel needed an agenda. The label 'Angry Young Men', a term originally applied to the John Osborne of *Look Back in Anger*, was extended to the new novelists Kingsley Amis, John Wain, and Colin Wilson. Soon it came to include John Braine, David Storey, Alan Sillitoe, William Cooper, Stan Barstow, and even, for some, Iris Murdoch. The experience of these writers was seen as emblematic of the increased

---

[2] See Bergonzi 1979: 11–34; Karl 1962: 4–18; Kermode 1958: 214–18; and Rabinovitz 1967: 166–71.

social mobility that characterized post-war Britain. Their fiction was considered significant because it succeeded in expressing this new experience. While it was generally recognized that the new novelists drew a great deal on their eighteenth- and nineteenth-century predecessors, this was regarded not as a fault but, on the contrary, all the more reason for admitting them as new bearers of the old standard (Hansford Johnson 1949: 235–6; Wilson 1958: viii).

The sense of reaction against pre-war social institutions was strong. In the absence of a moral or social common ground which writers could assume with their audience, the hero as existentialist outsider proved a useful way of taking a critical stand without explicitly defending any given system or ideology. Angus Wilson's *Hemlock and After* (1952), John Wain's *Hurry On Down* (1953), Kingsley Amis's *Lucky Jim* (1954), Iris Murdoch's *Under the Net* (1954), John Braine's *Room at the Top* (1957), Alan Sillitoe's *Saturday Night and Sunday Morning* (1958), and David Storey's *This Sporting Life* (1960) are all first novels in which a lone male protagonist tries to find a means of accommodating himself to a society whose main institutions he views with suspicion. The consequent soul-searching often includes as much self-mockery as it does social criticism, and for this reason it is not subversive. On the one hand, it is evident that the old order is collapsing of its own accord, so any attempt to subvert it would be pointless; and on the other, none of these authors portrays a main character secure enough in his own moral beliefs to propose them as a new global framework. This meant that while criticism was encouraged—often in the form of parody or satire—innovation was kept to a minimum.[3]

The strength of the critical consensus that reigned in the mid-1950s was undoubtedly one of the reasons why Brooke-Rose's first novels took the form they did. The pressure to please must have been especially strong for women writers who, if they wrote novels of ideas, were in danger of either being rejected as over-cerebral or having the intellectual content of their work ignored. Women writers are less likely to identify with the existential plight of the lone male, but even so, a willingness to conform to the narrative conventions of realism is evident in the fiction of a number of writers who are now viewed as innovative. Doris Lessing, for example,

---

[3] See Gindin 1962: 8–11 for a fuller discussion of this phenomenon. See also Bergonzi 1979: 19–20.

began publishing in the 1950s, but did not question the appropriate-
ness of the realist mode to her conceptual concerns until the 1960s.
Other women writers were read in such a way as to assimilate them
to reigning categories. Ivy Compton-Burnett, whose elegantly
minimal and stylized dialogue has similarities with the narrative
technique of Nathalie Sarraute, was appreciated in the 1950s
primarily for her wit in portraying the viciousness of social
interaction rather than for the techniques she employed.

Both these phenomena come into play in Brooke-Rose's case. It is
indicative of the pressure to conform to gender-coded standards that
The Dear Deceit, the most serious and most personal of her first four
novels, has as its protagonist a lone male suffering from an identity
crisis over his patronym. In the other three novels frothy dialogue
and sparkling wit tend to overshadow the deeper philosophical issues
at stake. John Hall describes the early novels as

> competent enough vignettes of the witty, intelligent circles in which one
> might expect to discover Miss Iris Murdoch, and their end result was not far
> removed from the sum of of [*sic*] the parts of Miss Murdoch's own elegant
> connundrums. One could not help feeling that the authoress was an awfully
> clever gel, insofar as she could manipulate quite adequately the basic
> framework of the nineteenth-century novel of manners. (1976: 183)

Iris Murdoch's fiction represents perhaps what Christine Brooke-
Rose was aiming at, not in philosophical or even aesthetic terms, but
as narratives which combine readability and lively story-telling with
intellectual themes. Brooke-Rose used her facility for light, clever
story-telling as a sort of sugar-coating with which to induce readers
to swallow her less palatable conceptual material, but in most cases
the pill was never digested because readers were accustomed to
'serious' novels being concerned with morality.

Unlike many of the writers of the period, Brooke-Rose is not
overly preoccupied by morality in her early fiction. For a period in
the 1950s she flirted with Roman Catholicism, and whether her
Catholic point of view made her see moral issues exclusively within a
religious framework, or whether she simply did not share the same
experience as English-born-and-raised writers who faced the dissolution of their class system is difficult to judge. Nevertheless, this is a
point on which her novels defy easy assimilation to those of Iris
Murdoch or Angus Wilson, with whom she has also been compared.
The lightness and wit of Brooke-Rose's novels do, however, invite

comparison with those of Muriel Spark. Like Brooke-Rose, Spark began writing fiction as a form of therapy after a period of psychological strain (Stanford 1963: 62). Both writers are primarily interested in the ontological and epistemological questions raised by the Catholic view of God, and both found in nervous tension a justification for modest technical experimentation as well as a tool for exploring aspects of reality which would otherwise have been difficult to treat outside the context of philosophical discourse.

Brooke-Rose's first four novels also share with Spark's work an effort to integrate intellectual pursuits with questions of self-definition. Integration proves problematic in Brooke-Rose's novels; there is a growing sense of the impossibility of conveying ideas through a unified realist character without seriously jeopardizing his or her psychological autonomy and integrity. This is indicative of a more general dissatisfaction with the conventions of the realist novel which takes character as its focal point, and Brooke-Rose's disenchantment with realism began to be apparent in other ways as well. *The Dear Deceit* represents a questioning of the causal logic of narrative and the literary heritage which provided both her and her readers with a whole set of ready-made narrative assumptions. *The Middlemen*, for its part, denounces the incestuous and parasitical world of literary journalism in terms that far exceed gentle mockery. The project of integration with which Brooke-Rose began provided sufficient material for 'four average, competent novels' (Brooke-Rose 1977a: 134), but it also led to a frustration with available formal strategies which prepared the way for the radical change in direction her *œuvre* was to take with *Out* in 1964. The following discussion will trace the development of this dissatisfaction. The early novels will be analysed in relation both to Brooke-Rose's conceptual concerns during this period and to the fictional conventions through which she chose to figure them.

The Languages of Love: The Word Made Fresh

The Languages of Love seeks in Catholicism a solution to the problem of linguistic, psychological, and intellectual dividedness. The goal on each of these three planes is unity, and, appropriately, the novel takes as its framework the multi-layered but harmonious structure of medieval allegory. The manipulation and decontextualization of language is presented as a temptation to be overcome but a necessary step on the way to achieving mastery of the 'languages' of intellect and spirit. Thus, despite its ultimate rejection of the playful linguistic transgressions so characteristic of Brooke-Rose's later fiction, her first novel inaugurates the underlying discursive vision of her entire *œuvre*: intellect and psyche are understood in terms of the various conceptual 'languages' that pertain to them, and personal identity is established as a product of their interaction. The conflict between actively fashioning language and allowing oneself to be constructed by conventional systems is provisionally resolved by valorizing submissiveness as Christian humility, but present are the basic elements of a dilemma which is to remain with Brooke-Rose for several decades.

The novel is a tale of apprenticeship about a young woman called Julia who, like her creator, has just completed a Ph.D. in medieval studies and is living in London. Julia is trying to discover who she is and what she is cut out to do. She faces two choices, one personal and the other professional. On the personal front she has to choose between her one-time fiancé Paul, whom she loves but cannot marry because he is Catholic and she is divorced, and Bernard, a fellow philologist who attracts her physically but is selfish, emotionally dishonest, and married. Julia also has to decide between a scholarly career as a university lecturer and that of a 'lady novelist'. In both cases the choice is between the serious but dull (when seeing Paul she had been completing her thesis on religious poetry) and the creative but frivolous (she collaborates with Bernard on a book about adultery in medieval literature). In the end she opts for the serious, renounces carnal love, and decides to become a Catholic. Ironically, by writing the novel Christine Brooke-Rose pursued the opposite route and made her début as a 'lady novelist'. Yet neither her choice nor Julia's is as one-sided as it seems. Brooke-Rose resumed her scholarly work when she finished the novel, and Julia realizes in the end that while the 'frivolous' path precludes the 'serious', the latter can provide a means of channelling her creative energies. Likewise, her divinely inspired love can be extended to both Paul and Bernard. What is initially posed as a choice between two mutually exclusive alternatives becomes that between the exclusion of serious values and the inclusion of the best of both worlds.

This development is framed in the context of discursive initiation: Julia's education in natural languages is paralleled and supplemented by an *éducation sentimentale* in 'languages' of a higher order. The novel closes with a recognition of linguistic competence: 'Julia had learnt the languages of love' (239); and it is significant that these 'languages' are plural. In the penultimate scene Julia and Paul decide that the summer during which the action of the novel has taken place has been like 'an allegorical dream-vision' (212). As in medieval allegory, multiple layers of meaning correspond to the novel's multiple languages. The novel charts an apprenticeship in 'languages' on each of three levels: philological, romantic, and religious. On each level alternatives are transformed into compatible aspects of an all-inclusive Christian discourse which absorbs differences into a higher unity.

When it first appeared, *The Languages of Love* was generally read as a satire of London literary and academic circles, but it was criticized by reviewers for not being satiric enough (Cranston 1957: 90, Allen 1957: 470). Others attacked it for not being sufficiently realistic (*TLS* 1957: 629, Fuller 1957: 62), and one reviewer concluded that 'Miss Brooke-Rose was in two minds about the novel she intended to write' (Allen 1957: 469). As the medieval allegory is not among the categories into which reviewers are accustomed to fitting witty first novels by women, it is not surprising that the multi-level approach should have been attributed to indecisiveness on the part of its author.

At the start of the novel Julia sees philology as a lifeless and uncreative pursuit. When she complains of the drudgery of studying sound-changes, Bernard hints that she does not really have what it takes to be a scholar. Her main problem in both academic and social contexts is that she is not sure enough of herself to be able to assert her point of view in an idiom which is both personal and appropriate. Her position with regard to the discourse of Catholicism is likewise that of an outsider. When she argues with the canon law, Paul explains that: 'Religion isn't something one needs . . . Nor is love. They simply *are*', but he gives up trying to make her understand because they don't 'talk the same language' (43). Both philology and Catholicism are here presented as 'languages' which Julia is unable to master because she wants to question them and change them rather than accept their inherent systematicity.

To overcome her insecurity she resorts to escapist fantasy and linguistically transgressive wit. In her viva her examiner asks her if she does not think that 'dipthongisation in fourteenth century Kentish may have been optional', and her immediate reaction is that: 'The question made no sense at all.' In fact her resistance to the 'sense' of the question is due to the fact that she understands it first in the context of legal discourse: 'She had a brief glimpse of a mediaeval bureaucrat . . . issuing a proclamation: "From 23.59 on the 16th April 1340, dipthongisation will be optional in the County of Kent" ' (5). This opening sequence establishes a paradigm of fictionalization that operates throughout Brooke-Rose's work: a fictional situation is generated out of a semantic slip caused by switching from one discourse to another on the strength of a word or a phrase.[4]

In her later novels Brooke-Rose uses techniques such as these to integrate different discourses, but in *The Languages of Love* linguistic transgression signals a lack of honesty and integrity. Julia uses wit as a means of deflecting the topic of conversation away from serious issues by shifting the referent of a scholarly discussion to the more immediate social situation: ' "Of course," he was saying, "there was no future in the Indo-European period." "And yet," she replied, refusing to be serious, "here we are." ' (31). Punning is the occult logic of language best left aside by those concerned to grasp its evolution. As Jonathan Culler points out, the pun is to the synchronic dimension of language what etymology is to the diachronic dimension (1988: 2), and Julia plays on this parallel by confusing the two. She quips to Bernard: 'I find the change of meaning much more interesting . . . It has changed and not changed: hatred is after all most annoying and cognisance is a very quaint affair' (14).[5] Bernard is fond of punning as well, but whereas Julia uses her verbal skill to compensate for her discursive incompetence in philology, Bernard uses his in order to evade emotional seriousness. Because his refusal to be sincere about his feelings toward her leads her further away from her own values, she begins to resent the way in which he constantly gives her the linguistic slip: 'Concepts which still meant much to her, by which she had once lived, were swerved aside with a smart epigram, a pun, a quotation, a dirty story' (170). Bernard's emotional dishonesty is seen in terms

---

[4] A similar instance of this type of linguistic manipulation occurs when the prospect of studying *hapax legomena* and anacolutha in *Beowulf* generates a reverie about a love affair between 'Anna Coluthon, who was too inconsequential, and Hapax Legomenon, who was too unique' (34–5). The pun on 'anacolutha' is reused in *Amalgamemnon* (43), where it becomes one of the nicknames of a character called Andromeda (or sometimes Anne de Rommède).

[5] 'Annoy' is derived from *odium*, 'quaint' from *cognitum*.

of his ability to split language, which is a product of his psychological duplicity. She asks him:

> 'You can skit over anything, can't you?'
> His eyes flickered as he looked at her, and she knew he was searching his mind for a joke.
> 'Don't worry, I skit ever so phrenic.'
> She winced . . . his own humour was mere flippancy, emphasising the very division within himself which he condemned in others. (146–7)

Puns and similar manœuvres trivialize the serious and instil in Julia a sense of linguistic *mauvaise foi*. She watches her values slowly being eroded, and she describes the process of moral degradation in terms of language: 'You find yourself giving in on little things, twisting words and meanings, always trying to be one-up on whoever you're with, and then suddenly you give in on something else, much bigger' (131–2). In religious terms punning is indicative of sin: the covert substitution of one meaning for another by a linguistic sleight of hand is practised by Milton's Adam and Eve after the Fall, indicating that they have sundered the prelapsarian unity of divine order.

But even in her fallen state, Julia recognizes that there is another, morally superior form of linguistic play which combines creative vitality with genuine understanding: 'The true humour of life, Julia thought, should illuminate, not shut out, its essential melancholy, its macabre elements, and its fleeting moments of unbelievable elation' (147). She experiences this unbelievable elation for the first time during a discussion of phonetic laws with Professor Jarvis-Andersen. Julia admits that she resents linguistic laws just as she resents the canon law of the Church: 'I'm interested in language as a process, not a thing or an essence. Phonetic laws are useful, I know, but they aren't fixed laws, like the laws of nature' (66). The professor replies that in reality language 'is in a constant state of flux, there are no real boundaries or unified communities, and mingling continues through supra-political or social bonds' (67). This view of language brings philology to life for Julia; she suddenly sees its object as the product of individual creativity. The spontaneity of metaphoric innovation in the speech of the professor's children leads her to the revelation that words once thought of as 'the bare bones of language' are actually alive with flesh. She rises to a metaphoric euphoria and discovers her vocation:

Even phonology seemed worth while now, whispering the sounds of time into the very material that poets used, the vowels jealously mutating, angrily fracturing as consonant groups shifted to their conditioned cues in wild adenoidal ecstasies. The flesh and bones of words rose again to the salvation of their etymologies. And the job he was telling her about seemed interesting and desirable. (69)

This experience prefigures Julia's recognition at the end of the novel that the laws of the Church are also a way of describing spiritual harmony. The path to salvation is eventually shown her by the unwitting Messiah figure Hussein, an East African poet who speaks in metaphors and proverbs. He has been forced to leave England and to abandon Georgina, the woman he loves. Hussein tells Julia, 'I have waited for my boat five weeks. And every day of those five weeks has been a knife slowly twisting in a wound. It is not better now' (205). His honest suffering reveals to her the nobility of selfless love and the truth of language which is metaphoric yet direct. Shortly after this episode Julia decides to become a Catholic. She makes peace with Paul, accepts a job as a lecturer in philology, and finally succeeds in establishing genuine communication with Bernard. She realizes that she is as yet too selfish to be truly creative and puts off her artistic endeavours for the time being so that she can first learn the more humble task of interpretation. She recognizes the fact that she loves both Paul and Bernard, but transposes this love on to the plane of the sacred and finds herself released from sexual desire. The pun as a rhetorical motif of both dialogue and narrative gives way to utterances with multiple layers of meaning: ' "I'm sorry, I'm very sorry." She sat up and repeated it, hypnotised by the double meaning' (221); ' "Bless you, Georgina," said Julia, with at least three different levels of meaning in her tone' (232). Harmony reigns over disparity in this new world vision, and a multi-faceted language has been found in which to express it.

In many ways the plot of *The Languages of Love* is similar to that of Iris Murdoch's *The Bell* (1958). In both novels the heroine undertakes a search for her identity that requires her to navigate between the attractions of two men who represent two different attitudes to life. In the end the woman chooses to renounce both men and sets out on her own path.[6] But in terms of technique, *The*

---

[6] By contrast, the male version of the 1950s novel of self-discovery presents women as prizes to be won or tokens of what a man has achieved through his search, as in John Wain's *Hurry On Down* (1953), Kingsley Amis's *Lucky Jim* (1954), and John Braine's *Room at the Top* (1957).

Languages of Love resembles Murdoch's first novel, *Under the Net* (1954), in which learned discourses are interpolated by means of dialogue. Brooke-Rose's attempt to integrate the creative and the scholarly seems, as one reviewer remarks, 'a shade *voulu*' (Wyndham 1957: 491), a problem which haunts Murdoch's work as well. The questions raised by conceptual material are discussed by the main characters and illustrated in their actions, but in neither case do they affect the plot structure itself, which marks a return to formal strategies of the past: *Under the Net* to the picaresque tradition, and *The Languages of Love* to the paradigmatic plot of fall and salvation in which rhetorical devices remain subservient to the basic three-tiered design of Christian allegory.

In Brooke-Rose's later work this relationship is reversed as linguistic felicities are allowed to pierce through the layers of the harmonious hierarchical structure of narrative ontology; rather than replacing pun with metaphor, Brooke-Rose transforms the one into the other. In 'Self-Confrontation and the Writer' she describes her life as a series of 'splits', and the allegorical mapping of language to identity hinted at in *The Languages of Love* is elaborated:

John is a whole language. He has as many selves as he has utterances, virtual or realized, as many selves as there are words in his lexicon, even in the dictionary of his potential language, with each word its aetimology, its phoneyetic fragility and its semiantic sea changes, each word its infinite contiguities and its tall spokes of paradismatic possibilities. (1977a: 129)

The creative vitality that Julia seeks in the 'dry bones of language' is here achieved through textual manipulation of the type she rejects as indicative of a fallen state. Its salvation twenty years later attests to the dramatic shift in Brooke-Rose's values, her style, and her approach to narrative problems, but her propensity to see personal identity and social interaction in terms of language is nevertheless firmly established in her first novel.

The Sycamore Tree: Reality and the Character of Realism

What *The Languages of Love* phrases in terms of language, *The Sycamore Tree* (1958) figures in ontological terms. The problem of split identity is exacerbated, and again the goal of the main characters is to find a way of healing the divisions between intellect and psyche. Catholicism is presented as a potential remedy, but the philosophy of indeterminacy appears for the first time in this novel as a rival discourse. Though Catholicism is championed in the end, it is no longer portrayed as having the power to protect one from the extremes of madness and sin. Doubt as to the efficacy of religion as a solution to fragmentation is implicit in the novel's ambiguous ending. This is paralleled on the technical plane by a sabotage of the verisimilitude on which realism is predicated. The novel launches a covert attack against the ontology of the fictional character which becomes less the representation of an individual in search of his or her 'true' personality than an agent for conveying impulses or ideas beyond conscious control.

The hero, Gael Jackson, is a novelist and philosophy don at Oxford who specializes in theories of perception. He lives in Chelsea with his wife Nina, a fashion columnist and devout mother of three. The story opens with Gael facing a libel suit for his latest novel in which he has unwittingly described the literary hack Howard Cutting. The basic situation of *The Sycamore Tree* is the same as that of *The Languages of Love*. Nina adores her saintly husband but lusts after the sordid Howard. In both novels the solution to the problem the heroine faces is harmony through love, yet the outcome is considerably less satisfying in *The Sycamore Tree* because it entails renunciation of life itself.

While Nina has the same protean tendencies as Julia, they are exaggerated to the point where they become dangerous. Like Julia, Nina is eager to please and dissipates her personality in those around her. When she does finally succumb to Howard's advances, her identity crumbles into its component parts. She is vulgar and crude with Howard, soft and kittenish with Gael: 'She had, in fact, become two persons' (153). Unable to suppress his anger any longer, Gael lectures her on adultery's 'disintegrating splitting effect on the inner personality' (219). Nina eventually has a nervous breakdown, but after a brief stay in hospital she returns to Gael. Marital harmony is provisionally achieved when Nina resolves to behave, and Gael forgives her.

The novel is brought to its dramatic conclusion by the playing out of yet another case of split identity. Howard's wife is having an affair with an exiled Hungarian student called Zoltan Torday, who is writing a book on the adamantly nationalist Hungarian poet Arpad Szendrey. Zoltan meets Gael by 'coincidence', recognizes in him a fellow soul, and seeks Gael out when his problems become too much for him. He reveals that in fact he *is* Szendrey, but that he has had to change his name in order to escape persecution by the Communists. He had given up writing poetry and had been living the duplicitous life of a critic deciphering his own works, but when he fell in love with Howard's wife Elizabeth his former self was reawakened and he ceased to believe in his own existence. Gael sympathizes, for he experiences similar losses of personality, yet he can do little to protect Zoltan. A number of unlikely events orchestrated through telepathy lead to the denouement in which Zoltan shoots and fatally wounds Nina, then kills himself as well. Before Nina dies she and Gael again make peace, she repents her sins, and Gael vows to rewrite his novel.

The critical consensus about *The Sycamore Tree* was that it is good when it is light and witty but that it 'sinks under a mass of elaboration' (Allen 1958: 500), and that Brooke-Rose's effort to add depth to her characters succeeded only in getting them 'thoroughly bogged down' (*TLS* 1958: 557). Brooke-Rose was generally thought to have overdone the serious aspect of her tale to the detriment of its comic potential. The discontent voiced by reviewers appears to focus on the implausibility of the novel's plot and on the incongruity of the unsettling elements in it. This tension may have caused its failure in the eyes of contemporary readers, but it is also the sign of a change which was taking place in Brooke-Rose's attitude toward fiction.

Like the novel we read, Gael's novel of the same name is a 'philosophic fantasy' (9), but it appears to be even less realistic than its real-life double; it is described as a disquisition on the nature of reality with characters that flit in and out of existence. The sycamore tree of the title is a reference to a version of the famous limerick by Ronald Knox which encapsulates George Berkeley's immaterialism.[7] Gael, who is not religious, holds only with the first half of the double

---

[7] The published version of the limerick makes no reference to a sycamore tree, yet the novel specifically mentions the sycamore of the 'famous limerick' (136), which seems to suggest that Brooke-Rose thought that the version she gave was the original. Knox's version goes as follows: 'There once was a young man who said, 'God' | Must think it exceedingly odd | If he finds that this tree | Continues to be | When there's no one about in the Quad." ' Reply: ' "Dear Sir: Your astonishment's odd: | I am always about in the Quad, | And that's why the tree | Will continue to be, | Since observed by Yours faithfully, God." ' The limerick wanders through the minds and dialogue of several characters in the novel with minor variations (Nina makes it into a blues song, Howard quotes it in fragments), but it is possible to reconstruct a common version identical to Knox's poem except that the third line has become 'That the sycamore tree'. See pp. 28–9.

limerick according to which existence depends on being the object of another's perception. For him the tree is therefore a symbol of ontological indeterminacy. Gael's highly 'unrealistic' belief accords with his tenuous grasp on the reality of his own existence. But as both Howard and Nina inform us, the Latin name for the tree is *acer pseudoplatanus*, meaning 'pseudo plane tree'. On her deathbed the Catholic Nina contrasts its illegitimacy with the 'real' sycamore in the Bible.[8] For Nina this is symbolic of the 'pseudo' or illusory nature of life on earth, as compared to the reality of the sacred realm beyond. The intermittent, flickering reality that obsesses Gael is, from the Catholic perspective, itself but a delusion.

Gael is the 'good' character, and Nina the weak, struggling, sinning one. Yet, as in Graham Greene's *Brighton Rock*, the fallen Catholic is in the end somehow right, and the virtuous atheist less so, for if Gael's concept of the soul represents a higher spiritual plane and poetic vision, it also is coupled with neurosis, prescience, and telepathic powers which verge on the absurd. The ability to communicate extra-sensorily can be seen as a sort of literary emblem of that which is fundamentally beyond expression. Gael develops this line of thought; he believes that 'the perceiving self—that basic identity which philosophers have defined as a mere sequence of impressions accumulated by memory—is in fact the human soul, not the mind' (212). Yet when this principle is realized in the literal terms of premonitions and mental telepathy, he baulks and feels that he must be going mad. The graphic illustration of these concepts reveals that in fact they entail a spiritual agency which he refuses to accept, and this is the inner contradiction in his professed theory of reality. Gael believes in a Christian ontology but rejects its necessary corollary, God. Though his theories of perception 'made him slip so easily into a feeling that nothing around him existed, or alternatively that he did not exist in anything around him' (66), he dismisses his own supernatural powers as coincidence until they become too overwhelming to be ignored. In a sense his experience supports his theory, but also mocks it, for the ability to perceive what is happening in London when you are in Oxford is not true spiritual

---

[8] The reference is to the tree that Zacchaeus climbs to see Jesus (Luke 19: 4). Zacchaeus repents his sins, prompting Jesus to declare: 'Today salvation has come to this house because this man, too, is a son of Abraham. For the Son of Man came to seek and to save what was lost' (Luke 19: 9–10). The sycamore tree thus provides a means of seeing the Lord; it is a route to the recovery of souls that have been lost.

knowledge. It is a parodic version of perception through the soul, a form of pseudo-knowledge. True knowledge and true understanding, it is implied, can only come from a divine source.

As in Muriel Spark's *The Comforters* (1957), telepathic experiences are employed in *The Sycamore Tree* to figure a divine presence with a sense of humour, and like Spark, Brooke-Rose breaches the conventions of realism in order to demonstrate a Christian doctrine. Gael has rejected God as a guarantor of reality, but he is being used, despite himself, as an oracular figure through whom the knowledge of other characters may be conveyed. The use of characters as oracles for beliefs they do not themselves espouse in effect divides the character's identity from his or her narrative function. Hussein in *The Languages of Love* is a Muslim, yet it is he who reveals to Julia the beauty of genuine love expressed in honest language which leads her to convert to Catholicism. Gael is even more forcibly spoken through, and he himself does not regain his lapsed faith. Similarly, the narrator's persistent burrowing into the unarticulated zones of her characters' stores of knowledge about themselves indicates a certain disregard for their psychological integrity, a hollowing out of their 'roundness'. They begin to become mouthpieces for an outside force, be it divine will, the necessities of plot, or authorial comment. In this sense they are revealed to have only intermittent existence.

As Nina remarks, this is a condition which afflicts Gael's novel as well, and since it has the same title as the novel we read, comparison is inevitable. Brooke-Rose's novel implicitly presents itself as a 'pseudo' or partial version of the 'reality' beyond. But the mapping of this fictional–real opposition on to the worldly–divine dichotomy raises a number of questions as to the status and role of fictional constructs, given that we have access here and now to this world alone. Only in later novels does Brooke-Rose draw out the implications of this parallel (that is, the 'fictionality' or 'constructedness' of lived experience), but by pushing the possibility of psychological and ontological wholeness into ever-more distant territory in *The Sycamore Tree*, she demonstrates a growing scepticism with regard to the possibility of achieving it. In narrative terms this is reflected as a disregard for verisimilitude and the use of characters as discursive instances through which a number of different discourses can be made to pass rather than as representations of discrete individuals. It is symptomatic of this subtle shift that at the end of *The Sycamore Tree* the Catholic dies, whereas the novelist lives to rewrite his text. The simulacrum within a simulacrum is what survives, though its status as a 'pseudo' reality has been recognized. The same could be said of Brooke-Rose's attitude toward fiction. The pretence of representing lived reality begins its slow death at this point in her *œuvre*. From here on her novels become increasingly aware of their own status as constructs or models through which 'reality' is necessarily mediated.

The Dear Deceit: Truth and Narrative

In *The Dear Deceit* (1960) the dichotomy between truth and fiction hinted at in *The Sycamore Tree* is brought to the fore, and the possibility of reaching a pre-discursive reality is relinquished once and for all. An increased consciousness of conceptual systems as necessary fictions accompanies a growing awareness of the conventions of narrative. By subverting the causal, linear logic of the traditional story, the novel emphasizes the fictionality inherent in any attempt to present the individual as a coherent whole. In many respects *The Dear Deceit* is a summing up of Brooke-Rose's first two novels. It combines the transgression of narrative convention that begins to be manifest in *The Sycamore Tree* with a variation on the technique of recontextualization through linguistic slips employed in *The Languages of Love*.

The main question the novel poses is how we know, remember, or invent the past. Philip Hayley, the main character of the novel, undertakes an excavation of the life of his charlatan father, around whose numerous exploits the plot revolves. Alfred Northbrook Hayley was a self-dramatizing, duplicitous thief who spent his life trying to convince people of his importance by adopting a series of false identities.[9] When Philip tries to unravel truth from fiction, the task proves too much for him. In the end he realizes that the only way truly to understand his father is to become him; he presents the evidence he has collected as a reconstruction of his father's actions, thought processes, and emotions. But in order not to repeat his

[9] The basic plot is in many respects autobiographical. Brooke-Rose's father was called Alfred Northbrook, and like Philip, Brooke-Rose spent her childhood in Brussels with her Swiss mother, only belatedly to discover her father's true character. Other parallels include the fact that Brooke-Rose's mother had recently joined a convent when the novel was written, as had Philip's mother at the start of the narrative. Brooke-Rose explores her relation to her parents in a revealing poem published in 1959, entitled 'To My Mother, Taking the Veil' (see bibliography).

father's duplicity he uses self-consciousness and temporal manipulation to keep the artificiality of this procedure in view. The tale the novel recounts is told backwards: after the first two chapters, each successive episode takes place further in the past.[10]

Philip's project is both a search for the truth and an act of self-distortion, a 'sane insanity, that wilful entering into some reality other than one's own, by way of learning, searching, inventing, dreaming and becoming' (40). Philip claims that this is a domain as yet unexplored by psychoanalysis, and he suggests that possibly this is just as well: 'Some call it truth, some creation, some fiction, history, memory or mere jingling of bells. Perhaps all these are one, beyond analysis' (40). This 'sane insanity' through which one enters into someone's personality—intentionally splitting oneself into both searching, inventing subject and the object of the search—is posed as the very condition of narration.

But narration is seen in *The Dear Deceit* as the original and persistent obstacle to 'truth' because the process of constructing a story inevitably leads to falsification. Philip meditates on the narrative representation of action: 'Strange how the reality of the past comes to our mind most immediately as fiction. Some even say that all our knowledge of the past is fiction' (29). This is both the 'dear deceit' which goes back centuries and the curse peculiar to modern-day society.[11] In an article published in 1959 on what she calls 'signpost language', Christine Brooke-Rose points out that the 'language' of film is composed of clichés which are the product of the technical exigencies of the medium. She gives the following example:

---

[10] This unusual technique was employed by Carlos Fuentes two years later in the story 'Aura', in 1968 in Jean Cayrol's *Je l'entends encore*, and more recently in Martin Amis's *Time's Arrow*. Brooke-Rose may well have borrowed it from Angus Wilson's *Anglo-Saxon Attitudes*, in which it is used to conduct a similar chronological and psychological excavation of the past. But Brooke-Rose takes what in Wilson's novel is a local anomaly employed to dramatize the mental process of self-searching memory, and uses it to promote fictional self-consciousness. In *The Dear Deceit* the chain effect of the narrative can only approximate the chronology of Philip's research. It is highly unlikely that he would have learned first all about his father's later life without coming across any evidence of his youth. The artifice is therefore not motivated by any claim to have representational value either within Philip's mind or in what he recounts; the effect it creates in the mind of the reader is its only justification.

[11] The title of the novel is presumably a reference to Nathanael Cotton's 'Vision of Content' (1810): 'Man is deceiv'd by outward show— | 'Tis a plain homespun truth, I know, | The fraud prevails at ev'ry age, | So says the school-boy and the sage, | Yet still we hug the dear deceit, | And still exclaim against the cheat.' *Visions in Verse*, IV, lines 1–6.

A man is lying on his bed, smoking. Or he can't sleep and lights up nervously. On the bedside table is an ashtray with several cigarettes stubbed out almost unsmoked. After a few quick puffs the man turns and stubs out this cigarette too, three-quarters wasted. Then he gets up and paces the room. (1959a: 45)

Her comment is that this scene demonstrates the underlying dishonesty of the cliché:

the cliché is not necessarily just something banal, in the sense that it occurs frequently, though it is that too: a cliché is a convenient falsification . . . The whole scene is in fact a kind of shorthand, since the film cannot take ten real minutes to show someone smoking a cigarette to the last, which is the more natural behaviour of a worried man trying to think out a problem . . . But of course realism can't be that realistic. The wasteful smoker is part of film terminology, it says 'he is worried—action will follow'. (45)

The danger is that the convenient falsification will begin to manipulate reality:

If something completely or partly false, however innocuous, can be shown as real for so many years, then anything false can be shown as real, and be believed . . . I wouldn't be surprised to learn that many people do now smoke only a quarter of their cigarettes on the bed when worried, simply because they have seen it so often in films. (46)

Brooke-Rose complains that this type of facile cliché has invaded the novel as well, and that though 'younger writers are fed up, and want to "go straight" ', this is no longer possible because 'the currency has been devalued' (48). Through novels, films, and the press, 'signpost language' exerts a determining effect on our minds. It provides paradigms of action and role models through which we interpret 'real life'.

The Dear Deceit explores the consequences of our immersion in this type of fictional convention. Philip becomes aware of the process through which we invent our own identities based on the fictional paradigms at our disposal. Our application of these ready-made stories and stereotypes to our lives may not be particularly apt, but the web of intertextual concepts which forms the substrata of our experience nevertheless plays an inescapable role in our lives.

Though he professes scorn for the outmoded quaintness of things Victorian, Philip's conception of life is modelled largely on the Victorian novel and its Edwardian successors. He says that when he first learned that his father had been in prison he expected the crime to be 'something on a grand scale, something melodramatic, like murder, something novelistic, like ruining in bankruptcy thousands of trusting small investors, as the Town & County Bank had done in *Cranford*, or Mr. Frothingham in *The Whirlpool* or Ponderovo [*sic*] in *Tono-Bungay*' (29). His narrative expectations are, of course, frustrated, but they demonstrate the source of the norms ingrained in his mind. In all three of these novels the 'crimes' are those committed by basically good people who, through no real fault of their own (other than the speculative instinct that is the mainstay of the capitalist system), have been caught up in bank failures for which they valiantly accept responsibility. Hayley's crimes are petty and dishonourable, a contrast which reveals the falsity of the narrative assumptions Philip makes.

Since Philip realizes that it will be impossible to do away with the artifice of narration if he wants to present the results of his search, he decides instead to make the artifice obvious. In this way he forces the reader to go through the same process of retrospective illumination that he himself has undergone. Despite reviewers' complaints to the contrary, the structure of the novel does not preclude suspense entirely; rather it shifts the object of suspense from the result to the cause. We trace Alfred's life back in order to find the origin of his dishonesty, but along the way we come across many peculiar situations before we know what brought them about. There is a curious phenomenon of hermeneutic delay: much of what we read consists either of illumination of the enigmas of a preceding chapter, or new enigmas. The consequence of this is that we are constantly hypothesizing about the possible significance of each event, and often discovering that we are wrong.[12] The novel's early readers were understandably annoyed at having their narrative expectations constantly thwarted. They attacked the regressive structure as 'disconcerting and tiring' (*TLS* 1960: 673), and called it a misuse of the author's talents (Hartley 1961: 74). But in fact Brooke-Rose was

---

[12] There are two narrative paradigms in Western culture which share these peculiarities: the detective story, in which carefully dropped clues followed by retrospective illumination are the norm, and the traditional psychoanalytic encounter, in which the analyst tries to get the patient to reconstruct as a well-made narrative the formative traumatic events of his or her life. But both these models assume that the problem which provides the narrative with its subject has at its source a specific cause. It is this assumption which *The Dear Deceit* sets out to confute.

learning to reuse her talents to new ends, one of which was precisely the readerly frustration that reviewers complained of.

As readers, we too imagine causes and motivations which are based on analogies we draw with other novels and other narratives. It is continually suggested to us, however, that 'reality' is not in fact like novels we have read, that it is mundane and pitiful. We are kept reading by the promise of an original sin or trauma that will justify—either in psychological or moral terms—the very existence of the story; but stripped of the successive identities he has built up over the years, Philip's father is revealed as no more than an insecure, over-imaginative little boy. We then realize that there is no dramatic originary event or 'cause' which would lend significance to all that has preceded it. Our desire to discover one is in the end all that is revealed.

Though our passive acceptance of causal logic and narrative clichés is the novel's main target, it also plays with the related theme of linguistic laziness. Philip implicitly dismisses the value of his own reflections on the ugliness of modern London with offhand self-ironizing comments which imply that he too is a product of the intellectual dissipation he criticizes: 'Life, I said with startling originality as I stepped out of the bus in my mackintosh, is like that' (307). Philip is ironic also about his tendency to think in terms of 'higher' literature, and he discredits the validity of a quotation from Eliot, when it comes into his mind, simply on the grounds that he has been too corrupted by contemporary culture for anything that occurs to him spontaneously to have lasting value:

There was some later affidavit of my mother's, which gave her date of birth, Geneva 1893, the date of her marriage in 1919, the date of his death in 1934. At once I waved away the unjustly famous quotation which sprang with great obviousness to my mind. When lines of poetry spring spontaneously to the mind of a lawyer, I thought, they have surely ceased to be true. Life holds more than birth, copulation and death. (31)[13]

It is doubly ironic that Philip's sense of intellectual and spiritual degradation is in fact very like Eliot's, and his life risks being as impoverished and as meaningless as Sweeney's minimalist 'brass tacks' scenario.

---

[13] The 'unjustly famous quotation' is from 'Sweeney Agonistes, Fragment of an Agon': 'Birth, and copulation, and death. | That's all the facts when you come down to brass tacks: | Birth and copulation, and death. | I've been born, and once is enough' (lines 40–1; Eliot 1936: 127).

Allusions to other texts frequently undergo this same process of depreciation. From the title onward, quotations are abundant in the novel, yet they are often either inappropriate or irrelevant. A superficial similarity, such as the occurrence of an individual word, will trigger a literary reference which has no bearing on the situation at hand. Alfred's lawyer twists allusions in this way: 'It was indeed a sad thing that in these days when the Church had enough enemies outside it should divide itself into hostile forces, because, he added aptly, forgetting the original subject of the quotation, a house divided against itself could not stand' (260). An exchange between two monks includes a similarly ironic misquotation: ' "He ain't got no more vocation in him than a blind sparrow, that's what." "Fear not therefore: better are ye than many sparrows," Brother Cuthbert quoted pointlessly' (245). People's propensity to misjudge the context of a reference is an indication of their willingness to assimilate the situations they encounter to paradigms of thought and action with which they are familiar, however misleading or falsifying this process of assimilation might be. Like the 'language' of narrative, the 'language' of literature serves as a source of stereotypes and models which provide ready-made explanations and prevent people from analysing the specificity of the world around them.

In the 1960s and 1970s Brooke-Rose rediscovered the recycling of our cultural heritage condemned in *The Dear Deceit* as a form of parodic interrogation. Like the pun in *The Languages of Love* and the concept of a variable reality in *The Sycamore Tree*, a discursive practice that is devalued and stigmatized in this novel is later used as a tool for exploring the practices and attitudes it represents. What is, in the early novels, seen as a lower-order truth or a fallen state is saved, or at least salvaged, as the very possibility of any higher-order truth becomes increasingly remote. Though the technique employed in *The Dear Deceit* represents a laying-bare of traditional narrative devices without offering an alternative approach, it sets the stage for the more radical break with the conventions of realism which Brooke-Rose's fiction demonstrated four years later.

The Middlemen: Splits with(in) Convention

The Languages of Love, *The Sycamore Tree*, and *The Dear Deceit* all portray characters who are defined by their roles as interpreters or carriers of information. In each case the fact of being spoken through entails a splitting of identity and a threat to psychological stability. In *The Middlemen* (1961) this mediatory role is magnified so as to become the primary focus of the novel. The individual psyche is irrevocably shattered by being exteriorized in two separate people: the cool, cerebral psychoanalyst Serena, and her passionate, turbulent twin sister Stella. The schema is evident also on a formal level in the breakdown of traditional narrative techniques. Brooke-Rose's evident exasperation with her chosen genre is manifest in the exaggeration of convention to the point of parody. This discursive attack is paralleled by a scathing social critique. Subtitled 'A Satire', the novel is a bitter, pessimistic work in which the ominous subcurrents of Brooke-Rose's earlier novels are seen in their most threatening light, and the gradual disintegration to which she had subjected the traditional realist novel in her three previous works is brought to an explosive climax.

The Middlemen focuses on Serena and the 'sprawling ant-heap of middlemen' (5) that swarms around her. Like Evelyn Waugh's pre-war novels, it collects a large cast of lightly drawn characters, many of whom have appeared in Brooke-Rose's earlier fiction. The novel opens with the combustion of seven housewives who have fallen victim to the latent flammability of the most recent invention of United Volcanic Industries (manufacturers of synthetic fabrics from volcanic ash). The efforts of Rusty Conway, Chief Public Relations Officer at U.V.I., to minimize the publicity caused by this event get him entangled in the competing empires of television and the press. A loosely constructed plot evolves fitfully around the activities of Rusty, Serena, her husband Rupert, and Stella. Serena is torn between her sisterly love and her annoyance with Stella's aggressive insecurity. The two have an argument and vow never to speak to each other again, whereupon Serena leaves for a holiday with Rupert on a volcanic island in the Aegean to which Rusty and his wife have recently been transferred. While visiting the local volcano, Serena is profoundly upset by the sight of hardened lava fields around a bubbling centre, and this causes her to have a nervous breakdown. The next day they are all killed when the volcano erupts unexpectedly. The novel ends with Stella, *en route* to a new job and ignorant of her sister's death, flicking absent-mindedly through a news magazine featuring the tragedy.

The novel was not well received. It was condemned for its 'two-dimensional characters' (Mayne 1961: 316), lack of 'moral passion'

(Bergonzi 1961: 297), lack of profundity (Price 1961: 332), 'misanthropic spleen', and smugness (Hope 1961: 1486). In many respects these are accurate characterizations. *The Middlemen* is uneven and less well-written than Brooke-Rose's earlier novels. Light satire of people's habits contrasts sharply with the severe social criticism with which the text is larded. Narratorial frustration is evident in the disjointed structure of the novel, which focuses briefly on a number of subcultures of professional London without bothering to link them in more than a cursory manner. The realist technique of localizing narratorial comment in the subconscious of a character is also frequently exaggerated. The novel opens with a page-long diatribe about the age of middlemen which appears to be the opinion of a third-person narrator but is subsequently identified as 'disloyal thoughts . . . not precisely verbalised as they turmoiled through the hazily discontented soul of Rusty Conway' (5–6). The obvious artificiality of this device is jarring, and the half-hearted attempt to 'subjectify' a large chunk of sociological analysis soon gives way to more overt narratorial commentary in the same vein. The impression received is that Brooke-Rose had simply given up trying to integrate the conceptual content of her novel with its story.

The didactic message of *The Middlemen* is presented in two long passages which together represent an attack on the phenomenon of 'middlemanship'. The gist of the argument is that, once a relatively restricted and disreputable segment of society, the 'class' of middlemen has grown proportionally larger until now: 'We are all middlemen, selling to others something we do not own, something we have not made' (5). When the principal exemplars of this class are dramatically eliminated the message is clear: middlemanship destroys from within, and the act of passing something on without truly changing or improving it is psychologically nullifying. There is an evident parallel between Brooke-Rose's vitriolic attack on this social system and her disenchantment with the realist novel. The realist novel plays the role of 'middleman' by passing on a world-view which is as 'faithful' as possible to *perceived* reality, but is in fact a clichéd falsification. There appears to be no other solution than either to conform to the system or to destroy it. If *The Middlemen* nominally conforms to the generic conventions of satire, it symbolically destroys the type of world in which these conventions are operative.

The central relationship in the novel between Serena and Stella is emblematic of the contrast between adaptation to convention and rebellion. As her name indicates, Serena prides herself on being under control. She claims to have understood and resolved all her own hidden desires, and she spends her life doing so for others: she is a 'modern middleman between body and soul, a perfect salesman of the unconscious to the conscious' (33). Like the wares of other middlemen, there is something synthetic and not quite genuine about her product, for it enables people to survive within a basically debilitating system. Her patients receive 'fresh personalities, refashioned at least to fit the coming decade, if not perhaps exactly in the style intended by the original designer' (33). The only aspect of Serena's life that is beyond her control is her sister Stella. Stella is a wild card, both in the deepest recesses of Serena's own mind and in the domain of middlemen, for Stella is the only character in the novel who is exempt from this status: 'Stella was in effect her own middleman, alone in the world, selling her personality, and very badly' (30). She represents the turbulence that Serena is unable to eliminate from her life, the residue of chaos that Serena cannot refashion to fit her world. Whereas Serena is concerned to domesticate her problems, Stella consciously strives to exaggerate her own eccentricity, yet her resilience and the regularity of her yo-yo-like existence testify to an underlying solidity. She is the life force of the novel which survives the destruction which the world of middlemen brings upon itself.

But for all their differences, Stella and Serena are the two halves of a basically unsatisfactory character. When Serena reads an article on the plane to Greece about a pair of Siamese twins, one of whom dies, she realizes that she and Stella are like Siamese twins joined at the psyche (40). The same thoughts pass through their minds and they are both aware of their deep ties to each other. When Serena dies, leaving Stella behind, it is as if the dominance of control and stability has come to an end. What is left is not an altogether agreeable person. Stella is self-dramatizing like Alfred Hayley, frivolous and insecure like Nina Jackson, and her company is more distasteful than that of any previously encountered character in Brooke-Rose's fiction. She is the inverted product of a world against which she is continually defining herself, Brooke-Rose's final, desperate attempt to present a 'character' in the traditional realist sense.

With *The Middlemen* Christine Brooke-Rose effectively eradicates the London literary scene from her work. In so doing she destroys the principle of control that had kept her novels within the bounds of the generic traditions of British fiction. When Serena's hidden emotions break through the surface of her calm, it is as if the collective unconscious of an entire society were erupting. The novel's apocalyptic ending takes on a universal dimension by being implicitly compared to a nuclear holocaust. Rusty, who has done some research on the island, assures his companions that the volcano is safe. He explains that the last eruption was a slow, drawn-out affair lasting six years, 'just like the last war' (207). Just like the next war, the new eruption is sudden and its effects immediate. *The Middlemen* can thus be seen as both an acid criticism of British society and a purge of Brooke-Rose's *œuvre*. By killing off the stable element of the fictional character, she abandons a realist notion of individual identity and the narrative norms which subtend it, freeing the way for a concept of subjectivity and a form of writing in which these factors do not come into play.

There are, however, hints in *The Middlemen* of the modes of narration which are to replace what is so brutally disposed of at the end of the tale. Rusty Conway becomes one of Serena's patients because he has had a spell of extreme absent-mindedness which made him incapable of carrying out his work. Shortly before the fateful journey to Greece he begins to be overcome once again by the same sensation. He is unable to concentrate on forms and reports because the words he reads undergo illicit manipulations that, like the pun, involve slippage and linguistic re-synthesis:

For some weeks now, Rusty had been in that peculiarly unreal state when words leap out from pages, voices or one's own thoughts, and rudely rattle their bones about, or shove their meanings under one's nose like exhibitionists until the meanings themselves vanish in a dance of death. Cinderella mutated from rinsedella to rinse-a-leader and denser-liar, nitron became non-try, even trianon, U.V.I. kept changing into I-view-you, and synthetic fibre had long completed its various transitions from fetid cider to fist ethic neighbour and finally to thigh fetish sabre, where it looked like getting stuck for quite some time. (178)

The linguistic acrobatics these words perform in Rusty's mind and the various interpretations which might be attributed to the results are of less consequence in and of themselves than the fact that this performance demonstrates verbal operations of a logic other than that attributed to the rational mind. We see the seeds of alternative patterns of thought also in *The Sycamore Tree* when Nina temporarily loses her mind:

I must get a grip on my mind. I must . . . my mind . . . I dropped it . . . somewhere . . . slipping . . . my mind is a slipped disc, a dropped womb . . . I must . . . get a grip . . . I lost something . . . I dropped it outside . . . in the street . . . walking . . . on the Embankment . . . I dropped it in the river—flowing . . . flowing back . . . under the bridge . . . the Bar . . . daddy . . . he's gone . . . he's in disgrace, debarred. Debarred from the bar . . . no . . . debarred from a barmaid . . . mummy . . . he's gone . . . he lost something . . . (221)

The images that go through Alfred Hayley's mind in the minutes before he dies follow similar patterns, but in all three cases the discursive deviation is localized and explained within the novel as a product of the suspension of reason. While the transgression of narrative conventions manifest in Brooke-Rose's first four novels indicate a frustration with realist fiction, realism demonstrates a remarkable capacity for assimilating such deviations. It is only through the radical reconception of language-use prefigured here that she is able truly to break with the traditional novel.

There is no doubt that the transformation in style and approach which took place with *Out* in 1964 represents a fundamental reconception of the novel on Brooke-Rose's part, but the technical and conceptual development which took place over the course of her early fiction points the way to the change to come. The gradual breakdown of personal identity and the growing dissatisfaction with the conventions of realist fiction which are the most striking features of her first four works laid the ground for a thorough overhaul of fictional technique. What were at the time perceived as the faults of these novels can in retrospect be read as indications of the inadequacy of contemporary narrative models to Brooke-Rose's needs as a writer.

2. *Out*, *Such*, and *Between*: Metaphor and the Languages of Knowledge

> . . . there are moments when I feel I'm on the frontier of something and I must twist language in some way to pass the frontier.
>
> (Brooke-Rose 1990e: 31)

As I suggested in Chapter 1, Christine Brooke-Rose's first four novels constitute a conceptual prologue to her later work, but because they fail to break with the assumptions of the conventional novel, they are unable adequately to articulate the relation of individual identity to language. In the novels which followed, manipulation of language is discovered to be the key to the integration of intellect and psyche which is unsuccessfully sought throughout her early fiction. The main concern of *Out* (1964), *Such* (1966), and *Between* (1968) is the process whereby the subject constructs his or her identity in and through the language of specialized discourses, and the way in which he or she acts on those discourses to make them 'run here and there again'.

Metaphor is the dominant structuring mechanism of the novels, stylized transcription of consciousness their fictional mode. Unlike the straightforward narrative approach of Brooke-Rose's earlier work, this new technique allows the discourses of knowledge to be integrated into the language of the text at the level of syntax and lexis. The focusing device of this chapter will be the role of metaphor in the novels as a strategy for bringing specialized discourses to bear on the consciousness of the fictional character and for 'mobilizing' the discourses themselves. Before undertaking an analysis of the novels, it will therefore be necessary to investigate in more detail what is meant by the term 'metaphor'. I shall examine its status in relation both to Brooke-Rose's own formulation of the 'grammar' of poetic metaphor and to several other current conceptions of the figure.

Brooke-Rose sees in all her novels, starting with *Out*, 'the same principle of interweaving [that] can create metaphors or unexpected meaning' (1988*a*: 137). Though she tries to 'wrap this linguistic experimentation in some sort of narrative situation—a minimal mimetic plot', her real purpose is 'to explode human discourse' (137). She accomplishes this linguistic manipulation or 'explosion' by combining words in such a way as to make them 'activate' one another. In an interview she gave in 1974 she explained that the goal of her fiction was to reactivate the language of conceptual knowledge through metaphor:

> language is capable of far more subtle ways of metaphoric expression than the stock grammatical ways . . . You use the same phrase in a new context and embedded in that new context it acquires a completely different meaning. What I like doing, what interests me particularly, is the fusion of different discourses. (1976*k*: 3)

Metaphor operates in her fiction as a structural principle; it provides the means of bringing two or more disparate fields of knowledge into a relation which organizes thoughts and events.[1]

In her doctoral dissertation and later in *A Grammar of Metaphor*, Brooke-Rose studies the mechanics of metaphoric interaction from a grammatical point of view. She develops a typology according to the different parts of speech, and her analyses reveal a marked preference for the verb metaphor. Of all grammatical types, the verb metaphor displays the greatest amount of interanimation. It 'is more dynamic, not in the sense that it expresses movement (which a noun can also express) but because it creates more activity between the words of the sentence in which it is used' (1955*a*: 75). The verb metaphor is further characterized by the fact that it has no direct link to its proper term, but acts on the noun of which it is the predicate; in the case of the transitive verb it can also act on its direct and indirect objects.[2] She borrows Geoffrey of Vinsauf's example 'the meadows laugh', and comments that while 'laugh' may be interpreted as 'are full of flowers', this interpretation 'is not stated, nor is

---

[1] David Lodge (1977) describes the realist novel as one in which metonymic relations dominate, while in certain more 'poetic' types of novelistic discourse, metaphor is the main ordering principle. The latter half of this assertion is one I would agree with and one which coincides nicely with my own argument, but I do not accept the dichotomy between metaphor and metonymy as a valid tool for characterizing novelistic discourse. See Brooke-Rose 1981: 354–63 for a detailed discussion of Lodge's extension of Jakobson's dichotomy between the metaphoric and the metonymic to fit postmodernist fiction. See also note 6 below.

[2] She takes this observation from Geoffrey of Vinsauf, a 12th–cent. rhetorician.

it necessary to guess it . . . The picture of the meadows laughing is immediate' (1958a: 208). In *A Grammar of Metaphor* she is at pains to show that in English poetry the relation of the verb metaphor to its proper term is weak and less important than its relation to its subject and objects: 'when a verb is metaphoric, its adaptability to the noun is so great that its relationship to it is direct, and much stronger than its relationship to the action it is "replacing" ' (1958a: 209).[3] The consequence of this immediacy is a greater degree of autonomy for the figure:

The verb metaphor is accepted as a complete action in direct relation to the object to which it is applied, while the noun metaphor tends to be divided within itself into proper and figurative terms. It is chiefly the noun metaphor which has caused philosophers and estheticians to worry so greatly about the relationship of these two terms and the basis on which they are compared. (1955a: 77)

As she observes in this passage, her approach contests traditional assumptions about metaphor, assumptions that have often gone unquestioned by more recent theorists of rhetoric. First, it demonstrates that the majority of *types* of metaphor (if not a statistical majority of metaphorical utterances) do not operate on the basis of replacement, but contain both 'proper' and 'metaphoric' terms *in praesentia* (1958a: 23–5). Secondly, it stresses the importance of the immediate context of the poem over the distinction between 'metaphoric' and 'proper', in that it analyses the pre-referential dynamic of the metaphoric process. Finally, it shows that a given term may, as in the case of the verb, engage simultaneously in a number of different metaphoric relations.

Like Brooke-Rose, Jacques Derrida (1972b: 277–8) and Paul Ricoeur (1975: 19–24) trace the bias toward noun-based views of metaphor back to Aristotle's classification, but neither investigates the implications of an alternative view based on a different part of speech. It must be noted, however, that Brooke-Rose's own conception of metaphor is not tied fast to rigorous distinctions between the parts of speech, and that grammatical categories often get blurred in her discussions. She is concerned less with syntactic definitions than with the role a word plays in the metaphoric

---

[3] This syntagmatic view of the verb metaphor questions Jakobson's conception of metaphor as involving a relation of equivalence. See Ricoeur (1975: 99–100) for a related argument.

process.[4] She states in an initial survey of the various theories of metaphor that those of most philosophers are of little interest to her because they treat metaphor from the point of view of its semantic content, ignoring the way it functions linguistically (1955a: 45, 1958a: 15). While this is no longer true today, her grammatical analysis of metaphor is highly original, and its implications have yet to be fully recognized.[5] It is nevertheless worth examining some more recent theories to see if they can suggest ways in which the implications of Brooke-Rose's approach might be applied to novelistic texts.

Recent thinking on metaphor has been greatly influenced by Nietzsche, who recognized that the process of dividing up experience into discrete domains was one of 'coagulation' (1979: 86), the construction of a discursive system on the 'running water' (85) of metaphor. According to this view, conceptualization necessarily involves a dissimulation both of the differences between perceptual stimuli and of the metaphoric nature of knowledge itself. This is then a double process of immobilization which can only be remobilized by art. Rhetoricians ancient and modern have noted that the word 'metaphor' comes from the Greek word *metaphorein*, meaning to transfer or to carry over, and the idea of transport or mobilization inherent in its original meaning has played a significant role in the conceptual evolution of the figure.[6]

[4] In this her analyses can be seen to prefigure theories of metaphor as predication widely held by semanticists. See Ricoeur (1975: 139–41) for a discussion of the similarities between grammatical and predicative theories.

[5] Her method has, however, been influential. Irène Tamba-Mecz develops a grammatical theory of metaphor based partly on Brooke-Rose's work, whose importance lies, for Tamba-Mecz, in the fact that it allows for a concept of figurative language which takes account of the relations between figurative terms (1981: 60–2). In a recent study Jean-Jacques Lecercle uses Brooke-Rose's grammatical approach to develop a Heideggerian theory of metaphor which disputes the commonly held replacement model and sees metaphor as an instance in which 'language speaks' itself (1990: 144–80). See also Briosi 1984: 203–20; Hallyn 1975: 147–8 *et passim*; Henry 1980: 90–4; and Le Guern 1973: 64, 100, 121.

[6] I shall be following Brooke-Rose's loose use of the word 'metaphor', taking it to represent figural relations in general. The common distinction between metaphor and metonymy is difficult to define, as Brooke-Rose herself recognizes (1976k: 6). Attempts to do so tend to lead to schematizations that are logical and psychological rather than linguistic or discursive. It may be noted in defence of this extended use of the term 'metaphor' that in their attempts to apply Jakobson's famous distinction between metonymy and metaphor to novelistic texts, both Lodge (1977) and Genette (1972) end up by concluding that metonymy is in fact an agent of metaphor. Metonymy at the level of the word helps to produce a metaphoric effect in a larger textual unit. In other words, 'metonymy is itself a metaphor' at the deep level of structure (Brooke-Rose 1976k: 7).

As Genette remarks in the title essay of *Figures*, all figural language opens up a topos; it adds a dimension to discourse, turning a line into a space (1966: 210). The work of metaphor then involves the transfer of meaning across that space, from one site to another. Meaning, as the most simple and most common conception has it, is *displaced* from one word on to another. This model has long since been embellished, however, by the Anglo-American followers of I. A. Richards. For Richards, metaphor involves 'a transaction between contexts' (1936: 94) in which meaning is 'smuggled in' (1925: 240) from one semantic domain to another by a 'vehicle' (1936: 96). There is something 'semi-surreptitious' (1925: 240) about this process, as if the boundaries of semantic propriety were somehow being violated. Metaphor is no mere tourist in a foreign land, it is a bootlegger. Paul de Man is even more explicit in his formulation of this notion: 'We have no way of defining, of policing, the boundaries that separate the name of one entity from the name of another; tropes are not just travellers, they tend to be smugglers and probably smugglers of stolen goods at that' (1979: 17). It is no coincidence that, as Barthes reminds us, rhetoric was born of a property dispute (1970*a*: 90). The establishment of proper boundaries is clearly at issue in the use of linguistic structures that have the capacity to found a no-man's land between proper meanings and bounded territories, creating a zone of ambiguity. For Nelson Goodman a single instance of contraband becomes a mass invasion. Goodman describes metaphor as 'no mere distribution of family goods but . . . an expedition abroad. A whole set of alternative labels, a whole apparatus of organization, takes over a new territory' (1969: 73). Here an innocent 'expedition' suddenly becomes a conquest from one sentence to the next.[7] Like the theories Brooke-Rose criticizes in 1958, this view conceives of metaphor in terms of semantic property to be fought over and captured.

Max Black's influential 'interaction' theory builds on Richards's ideas and depicts metaphor as a complex operation in which one semantic field 'organizes' another, acting as a 'screen' or a 'network of lines' (1962: 41) which 'filters and transforms' (42) in order to project on to the proper term an entire 'system of "associated

---

[7] Similarly, Du Marsais's characterization of metaphor as a *demeure empruntée* is described by Derrida as an 'expropriation', an 'être-hors-de-chez-soi, mais encore dans une demeure, hors de chez soi mais dans un chez-soi où l'on se retrouve' (1972*b*: 302).

commonplaces" ' (41). It seems that this dynamic view is closer to what Brooke-Rose has in mind when she describes her use of metaphor in the novels as recontextualization through the fusion of discourses. In his discussion of the metaphor 'man is a wolf', Black describes the work of metaphor in discursive terms: 'Any human traits that can without undue strain be talked about in "wolf-language" will be rendered prominent, and any that cannot will be pushed into the background' (41). He even hints that there may be a reciprocal relationship between the metaphoric and proper components of his schema. Though he does not develop the notion, he admits that if the metaphor 'man is a wolf' restructures the attributes of 'man' to bring out his lupine characteristics, it also 'makes the wolf seem more human than he otherwise would' (44). But while Black's argument for the reciprocity of metaphor is of great interest, it is not clear how seriously we are meant to take it. The primary force at work is clearly the one-way effect of lupinization. The value of Black's theory lies in the fact that it allows for a conception of metaphor as the interaction between two discourses, but like Goodman's concept of imperial appropriation, it has overtones of subjugation.

One might wonder why metaphor so often demands that its work be described in terms of colonization and occupation, and what it is about an initial transportation of meaning that turns it into a conquest or a coercive restructuring. Perhaps the answer lies in the duplicity of metaphor's ancient role as an element in the art of both pleasing and public persuasion. Although largely neglected today, this latter function is unashamedly manipulative. Coercion may well be an inherent part of the metaphoric process, but we may nevertheless ask whether it might not be possible to imagine a different type of metaphor, one that was truly interactive in a positive sense.[8]

The recent trend toward cognitive approaches to metaphor provides a means of formalizing such a conception. The work of Eva Kittay is particularly helpful in this respect. Kittay offers a 'perspectival' theory that expands upon Black's 'interaction' view.

---

[8] Derrida (1972b) has demonstrated by means of theoretical argument, and Lakoff and Johnson (1980) by means of empirical analysis, that it is impossible to conceptualize without recourse to metaphor. As Christopher Butler (1984: 24–5) reminds us, the important thing is to be aware of the metaphorical structures which subtend the concepts we use, and of their ideological implications.

The importance of Kittay's formulation lies in her wide definition of the type of linguistic unit that can be labelled metaphoric. Metaphor has traditionally been taken to be a one-word device, or at most a figure of several words strung together, whereas Brooke-Rose's analyses concentrate instead on metaphor's work at the level of the phrase or sentence. Black too extends its necessary semantic field to the unit of the sentence, claiming that the semantic force of a metaphor can only be measured with regard to its context. Kittay agrees with his argument but questions the validity of stopping with the sentence which, as a semantic unit, is as arbitrary as any other. For her, any unit of discourse can be used as the 'frame' of a metaphor, the only constraint being that the corresponding metaphoric 'focus' must be a unit at a level beneath that of the frame. Thus if the frame is a sentence, the focus can be a single word, if the frame is a larger unit of text, the focus can be a sentence (1987: 64–8). With Brooke-Rose's use of metaphor in mind, we can extend this logic and hypothesize that if the frame were an entire discursive system, the focus could be one discourse within that system. Though this notion of what I shall be calling 'discursive metaphor' may seem itself to be metaphoric, it is, as we shall see, a justified extension of the standard definition, as it accounts for the distinct use of figurality in Brooke-Rose's fiction.[9]

While Kittay's theory has the advantage that it allows metaphor to be seen as operating according to the same basic principles regardless of the size of the discursive unit in question, Brooke-Rose's own examination of the mechanisms of the verb metaphor suggest a view that minimizes dependence on an implicit 'proper' term outside the text and emphasizes the metaphoric interactions between the terms themselves. According to this view the space opened by figural language is not that between metaphoric and proper terms, but that between two or more equally figural terms, which, in Brooke-Rose's case, are two or more discourses. Furthermore, if we take seriously Black's claim that his specimen metaphor 'man is a wolf' serves at

---

[9] This logical extension can be further justified by recourse to Benjamin Hrushovski's concept of frames of reference, which emphasizes their semantic and pragmatic dimension over their formal linguistic structure. For Hrushovski frames of reference 'serve . . . for the transition from the lower, formalized levels of language to the open, individually contextualized, thematic bodies of communication' (1984: 11). In this context 'metaphor is not a linguistic unit but a text-semantic pattern, and semantic patterns in texts cannot be identified with units of syntax' (7).

once to render man wolf-like and to humanize wolves, a reversible metaphor could be imagined at the level of a word, a sentence, or a discourse in which each term was engaged in a metaphoric interaction with one or a number of other terms, organizing them, structuring them, and in turn being structured by them.[10] This is a situation in which multi-directional migration supersedes conquest as the mode in which metaphor is best understood.

The possibilities of employing one discourse as a metaphor for another are first explored in *Out. Out* reveals the coercive aspect of the colonizing use of metaphor and stages subversive counter-strategies which undermine this use. *Such* focuses on a use of discursive metaphor which represents an alternative to the coercive model manifest in *Out.* Finally, in *Between* the multiple, reversible metaphor is put into play.[11] In all three novels the construction of personal identity is intimately associated with metaphor's work at the level of discourse. Each novel presents a main character in a situation in which he or she is in some way alienated. In *Out* and *Such* this alienation is psychological and social, while in *Between* it is the cultural alienation of being in a foreign country. In each case the experience of being wrenched out of the familiar instigates an identity crisis which results in a series of 'rebirths' as the protagonist grapples with the problem of selfhood and strives to construct some form of coherent identity out of the scraps of other people's languages which penetrate his or her consciousness.

In using Brooke-Rose's discussion of poetic metaphor as the basis for an analysis of how this figure works in novels she wrote in the 1960s, I am not suggesting that there is a *necessary* relation, historical or logical, between them. I am simply arguing that Brooke-Rose's analyses point toward her later use of what she herself describes as 'metaphor' at the level of discourse. *A Grammar of Metaphor* does not, by itself, constitute a theory of metaphor, and I have therefore

---

[10] The reversible or reciprocal metaphor is not a recent invention; in fact Aristotle talks of the figure in just such terms (*Rhetoric* III. 4. 1407*a*. 13–17, cited in Ricoeur 1975: 37 n). Likewise, Genette examines the 'métaphore réciproque' (1972: 54) in Proust, and Butor discusses the reversibility of alchemical metaphors in what is clearly an allegory of his own writing (1960: 18). What is original in Brooke-Rose's use of the figure is the way in which she brings together disparate fields of knowledge and their attendant discursive systems.

[11] Discursive metaphor operates within a realist framework in certain of the stories collected in *Go When You See the Green Man Walking.* In 'Medium Loser and Small Winner' for instance, the discourse of mathematics is mapped on to that of personal relations ('prime numbers' and 'isotropes' [*sic*] take on symbolic significance).

had to rely on theories developed by philosophers and literary critics, while indicating where these fail to account for the aspects of Brooke-Rose's writing that seem most interesting. I have tried to show that these are the very points at which her own analyses of the figure prove useful.

Out: Coercion and Subversion

Christine Brooke-Rose describes her use of metaphor as a literalization (1976*k*: 3). This may seem confusing if it is not made clear what she means by 'literal'. She explains in a recent description of her fiction that 'any specialist discourse when transposed into a non-specialist context or, if you prefer, when understood literally, can turn into metaphor' (1988*a*: 129). According to this definition, literalization is a metaphoric mapping of what Barthes calls an 'acratic' or specialized discourse on to an 'encratic' or universal one. Barthes is careful to point out that, though the encratic discourse posits itself as natural, in fact this is an illusion, a necessary camouflage of its own systematicity (1984: 128–9). Only if it is made strange or different do we see it for what it really is. *Out* is a prime example of this technique. In revealing the coercive nature of the discursive mechanisms of a fictitious future society, it illuminates the relationship between a dominant metaphor and the individual language-user. Brooke-Rose here succeeds in solving the problems encountered in her earlier novels with the integration of 'form' and 'content' by demonstrating that metaphor is a powerful cognitive tool with specific social uses.

Out takes place at an unspecified time several decades after the unexplained but presumably cataclysmic event known as the 'displacement'. The anonymous, pronoun-less protagonist is a 'colourless' man who divides his time between the shack where he lives with his wife and the Labour Exchange where he goes in search of employment. During the course of the novel we witness the progressive worsening of his psychological and physical condition. He works for a time as a gardener on the estate of the rich Mrs Mgulu, and later as a construction worker in her house. But because of his deteriorating health, he is unable to keep any of these jobs long, and throughout much of the novel he is confined to his shack where his wife cares for him.

As in Orwell's *1984*, a geopolitical realignment has segmented the earth into previously non-existent countries: Afro-Eurasia, Sino-America, and Chinese Europe. The names of the new countries reflect a reversal in race roles which has taken place since the 'displacement'. The colourless races have a tendency to succumb to 'the malady' which afflicts the protagonist. This is a sickness akin to radiation poisoning which causes a high rate of 'chemical mutation' and makes the colourless an unreliable source of labour. The Melanesian races are immune to 'the malady' and have therefore grown powerful.

The technological innovations which have developed as a result of society's need to adapt to new conditions have been accompanied by a new epistemology. The 'displacement' has been both a demographic and a cognitive recentring, a 'displacement from cause to effect' (117/119, 118/120, 172/174; references are to the first and to the omnibus editions). As part of this cognitive revolution, psychoanalytic machines called 'psychoscopes' have been invented to generate 'biograms', 'the extracted absolute of your unconscious patterns throughout your life . . . telescoped in time into one line that shows your harmonious rhythm, your up and down tendencies' (147/149). The biogram renders human memory obsolete, for it 'telescopes' the old-fashioned diachronic conception of identity into a fixed form accessible in the present. Memory has become restricted and suffers from cultural prohibition. While it is admitted that the past exists, the quest for origins or causes is considered a symptom of disease.

The motto of the new era is 'diagnosis prognosticates aetiology', a phrase which is repeated by members of the ruling races in such varied contexts that it becomes evident that no one really bothers to think about it. It functions as a 'master metaphor', the encapsulation of an ideology which structures all domains of thought:

[*doctor*:] —. . . diagnosis merely prognosticates aetiology . . . The rule is universal in all fields. It is a scientific law.
[*protagonist*:] —An article of faith.
—Until disproved. In the meantime, we are content to know how the thing functions.
—What thing?
—Anything. Society. Life. The universe. God. The unconscious. A land-reclaimer. (167/169)

As described by one character, this catch-all phrase is 'a short way of saying that they don't claim to find either the ultimate cause or the ultimate cure, but they do know exactly how it functions, and can prescribe accordingly' (149/151). The phrase has been taken from the acratic discourse of medicine and literalized, universalized as an encratic discourse or system of belief.

This discourse is, in a very real sense, an instrument of observation, an organizing tool, or as *Out* would have it, a 'conventional weapon' (61/63, 74/76, 128/130, 184/186, 196/198). In 'Dynamic Gradients', Brooke-Rose remarks: 'it has become a truism that, in submicroscopic terms, the object observed is affected by the instrument observing it—part of the famous principle of uncertainty' (1965*a*: 93). Indeed, 'diagnosis prognosticates aetiology' is a rephrasing of this 'truism' in scientific jargon. But what appears to be an admission of radical subjectivity can, as *Out* demonstrates, also lead to subjugation, for if the power of observation to alter its object is harnessed for the benefit of those in possession of the tools of observation, these tools become weapons of cognitive control.

When the protagonist goes for 'psychoscopy', we are given an illustration in concrete terms of how the diagnostic tools of this society condition their object:

I am your doctor, father, God. I build you up. I know everything about you. Your profile is coming up very clearly indeed on the oscillograph, and the profile provokes its own continuation, did you know that, the profile moulds you as it oscillates? Diagnosis provokes its own cause, did you know that? To put it more succinctly, diagnosis prognosticates aetiology. (136–7/138–9)

The discourse of 'diagnosis' represents a coercive use of metaphor in that its aim is to replicate itself faithfully in the conceptual idiolect of all people. But in the minds of the sick it suffers a mutation: the lens becomes a prism, it refracts and splinters the uniform vision of the ideal interracial society. Occupied by its clichés, its principles, and its strategies, the sick mind of the central colourless figure unwittingly deploys subversive discursive counter-strategies that turn these 'conventional weapons' back on themselves and expose them for what they are.

In the Nietzschean view, only art has the power to reawaken dead metaphors and to shake the rigid structures of abstraction, or as Brooke-Rose would have it, to make discourses 'run here and there again'. It is thus appropriate that she should begin her enterprise in *Out* with an investigation of that originary metaphor described by Nietzsche, the act of perception. The opening paragraph of the novel poses the problem of the animate and the inanimate in terms of mobility:

A fly straddles another fly on the faded denim stretched over the knee. Sooner or later, the knee will have to make a move, but now it is immobilised by the two flies, the lower of which is so still that it seems dead. The fly on top is on the contrary quite agitated, jerking tremendously, then convulsively, putting out its left foreleg to whip, or maybe to stroke some sort of reaction out of the fly beneath, which, however, remains so still that it seems dead. (9/11)

This image of copulation serves as a linguistic act of 'insemination' which initiates a period of gestation and provokes a reference to giving birth toward the end of the chapter. In an imagined interview at the Labour Exchange, the protagonist claims that he has only been 'spasmodically in labour', then immediately corrects himself by rephrasing the slip as 'employed intermittently' (19/21). If traditional metaphor brings together two semantic fields by means of a similarity of signifieds, then the pun does the same by virtue of a homonymy or similarity of signifiers. Discursive 'slips' such as this create metaphors which play on the identity of signifiers to highlight the multiplicity of signification and its discourse-dependence. They serve as prisms or refracting lenses which multiply meaning.[12] Semantic mobility of this type is the crime that has caused artists to be banished from the society portrayed in *Out* (149–50/151–2), for the stability of a discourse depends on both its univocality and its universality. The possibility that a word might have a different meaning in another context threatens to relativize the 'master metaphor' on which this society is grounded.

As the novel progresses, the central consciousness is increasingly alienated from the institutions which seek to maintain him under their control, and his own discourse becomes more and more transgressive. Whereas the descriptions of the opening chapter are confined to what can be seen from within his shack, visual perspectives increase in variety and number when he ventures out of doors. This brings into play the logical faculties of discrimination

---

[12] While Brooke-Rose's use of polysemy does not fall within the bounds of conventional definitions of metaphor, its effect is metaphoric in nature: it serves to 'fuse' or bring together two or more semantic fields. As Ricoeur demonstrates, polysemy is the condition of metaphor (1975: 142–70), and in Brooke-Rose's fiction puns, discursive slips, and other technical devices are metaphoric in effect; they establish discursive metaphor as a structural principle.

and selection which assimilate perceptual stimuli to previously encountered images on the basis of structural analogy. Yet contrary to what one might expect, the capacity for assimilation is not accompanied by a discursive restriction. It leads instead to a proliferation of metaphoric links between objects: the bark of a fig tree is described as looking like 'a thigh of creased denim', 'a system of parallel highways' and 'neural cells' (26/28). A double row of plane trees forms a 'network of bare branches [that] functions in depth, a corridor of cobwebs full of traps for flies, woven by a giant spider' (21/23). This image is then used to put in doubt the very existence of its counterpart in the previous chapter: 'Unless perhaps a certain period has already elapsed since that episode, if indeed it occurred. The flies may have been a product of the fine network that functions in depth, in which case they will certainly have got caught in the cobwebs' (21/23). The metaphor of the spider has here replaced that of the flies, engulfed it in its web. The web or network of images spun by the protagonist's discourse has subsumed all past images to its present. The past becomes a projected image created retrospectively at every moment, just as a 'biogram' is 'the abstracted absolute of your conscious patterns throughout your life'. The spider's web is clearly a pernicious weapon; like the network of branches out of which it grows, it frames and structures all that falls within its domain.[13] The status of the metaphoric strategies employed by the character is ambiguous. They are at once a replication of and a threat to the unitary governing structures of the society in which he lives.

This ambiguity is played out in psychological terms as the simultaneous desire and inability to conform to the demands of the master discourse. Mobility is repeatedly linked in *Out* to hypertrophy of the imagination which, like a prism, refracts the 'colourless' light of the protagonist's civic identity into the protean kaleidoscopic images of his fantasy selves by means of the 'coloured' language of metaphor. These fantasy selves are figured as disintegrating reflections (52–5/54–7) or cathartic identifications with objects and people in the world around him (61/63, 100/102, 104–5/106–7). The metaphoric proliferation accompanying psycho-

[13] It will be recalled that one of Black's metaphors for the work of metaphor was projection through a 'network of lines'. Nietzsche too describes the metaphoric processes whereby the mind constructs its systems of ideas in terms of a spider spinning a web (1979: 85).

logical fragmentation is combated by the repeated invocation of analytic apparatuses that would determine the ontological status of objects perceived and events experienced, but the result is a garbled composite of philosophical jargon:

> To live the gesture in immobility is to evoke and therefore to have observed the gesture. But imagination is not an imaged projection of observed phenomena. Sometimes it is sufficient to imagine an episode for the episode to occur, and that is the terrifying thing, though not necessarily in that precise form. The first failure is the beginning of the first lesson. Learning presupposes great holes in knowledge. (173/175)

Immobility is linked to the desire for stable identity, to certain knowledge, to fixed images, and to the various clichés of the discourses of authority. But attempts to fix or stabilize knowledge by means of an array of scientific instruments fail as well, for these instruments generate new metaphors by mixing the concrete with the abstract:

> The white veins in the pink marble tremble and nod, they sway and stretch out to catch the excited atoms. An oscillograph might perhaps reveal whether the hammering which now drives its high-pitched ring of metal on metal into the neural cells also drives into the memory of the conversation, memory being a function, not a place. An electroencephalograph might perhaps separate the components of the conversation into the elements of silence, reality and unreality. (100/102)

If we consider *Out* with respect to the conception of metaphor examined above, the desperate sputterings of the main character can be seen as active or 'verbal' in their metaphoric function: his discourse mobilizes and metaphorizes all others and has only tenuous links with any reality outside its field of operation.

As he falls further and further 'out' of society these links become increasingly strained. Perception gradually yields territory to fantasy and hallucination as the protagonist's faculty for reality-testing breaks down and doubt increases. In his weakened state he is unable to control his own metaphors, to keep the various terminologies he deploys distinct. They act on him and impair his ability to distinguish between thought and perception, between concepts and objects. Again polysemy serves to join the two. Aetiology as the philosophical investigation of causality and aetiology as the study of the origin of diseases provides a link between philosophy and physiology. Symptoms of disease are then 'embodied' as a cancerous proliferation of the cognitive faculty which invents aetiologies for its own condition: 'The imagination increases in size progressively and usually painlessly until it fills most of the abdomen' (64/66). 'At the moment, the fantasies are under control. Sooner or later, however, they will pervade the blood-stream and increase at a striking rate, paralysing the skull with tumorous growths' (66/68).

It inevitably strikes the reader of *Out* that the main character enters periodically into what in many respects resembles schizophrenia.

Freud describes schizophrenia as a narcissistic disorder in which the capacity for reality-testing breaks down and the patient hallucinates frequently. His or her speech is characterized by a tendency to treat words like concrete things and to engage in what Freud calls 'organ-speech' (1915: 204). Gilles Deleuze describes 'organ-speech' as a result of the materialization of language which is then perceived as infiltrating the body. Organ-ization is accompanied by asemia, as language is reduced to sounds and seen as excrement (1969: 107). Jakobson and Lübbe-Grothues note that the speech of schizophrenics is characterized by the tendency to omit the pronoun 'I' as well as a fear of responsibility for independent affirmation or denial which results in ambiguous statements (1980: 135). This corresponds to what Deleuze terms 'schizo-logic' in which contradictory propositions are accepted simultaneously. All these symptoms are displayed by the central consciousness in *Out*: a breakdown of reality-testing, the concretization of words, organ-speech, omission of the first-person pronoun, the proliferation of contradictions, and perception of language as pure sound and as excrement. Nevertheless, it would perhaps be unjustified to label him 'schizophrenic'. The most we can claim is that his social situation and his physical deterioration induces in him a condition that approximates the classical clinical picture of schizophrenia.

Robert Rogers comments on what is commonly held to be the widespread use of metaphor among schizophrenics. While he does not deny that they often speak in a manner that 'normal' people regard as metaphoric, he points out that poets are aware of the metaphoric nature of their linguistic productions, whereas schizophrenics are not; they use what Rogers calls 'unlabelled metaphor' (1978: 42). In *Out* Christine Brooke-Rose makes use of the schizophrenic's unwitting deployment of figurative language as a psychological motivation for her use of it. The significance of this technique is that it allows the novelist to incorporate metaphor at the level of what is narrated, not merely at the level of narration, as is more commonly the case. Brooke-Rose does not impose metaphors on the thematic material she employs in *Out*, rather she chooses to work with material that is already metaphoric. This use of the naturally occurring metaphor in the speech of schizophrenics is a limiting case of the more general phenomenon of metaphor as a thought process. Schizophrenic speech provides a metaphor for metaphor, and it is in this sense that its use in *Out* may be understood, not as a valorization of the psychotic condition but as a literalization of the figure.[14]

In addition to its formal dimension, this use of metaphor also has a political function. The protagonist makes efforts to salvage his crumbling psyche by identifying with the languages of authority. At one point he faints, and as he slowly regains consciousness he imagines that he is being ordered to 'merge' through 'osmosis' (109/111). For those who refuse or are unable to conform to discursive conditioning, the message is unequivocal:

The physical stuff of the universe wraps up the earth with knowledge and communication, and the earth shrinks, and those who do not partake of the great secret growth are eliminated and shrivel away under the physical stuff that is knowledge and communication and wraps the earth with love, for nothing less than symbiosis will do. (178/180)

The colourless are incapable of 'symbiosis' and participation in the communication that 'wraps the earth with love', for they are incapable of 'radiating energy'. Despite the rhetoric of the multiracial society, 'exalting all colours to the detriment of none' (123/125), it would appear that the weak are doomed.

In the closing pages of *A Rhetoric of the Unreal*, Brooke-Rose discusses the mystico-technological dream of Teilhard de Chardin, Marshall McLuhan, and others whom, following Ihab Hassan (1975), she designates as 'new gnostics'. Their vision of 'the planet being as it were wrapped in telepathic or electronic thought of more and more brains working away' seems to her 'dangerously like the

---

[14] This is not to be confused with recent attempts to portray a culture that is somehow itself 'schizophrenic' in the sense in which Deleuze and Guattari (1972) or Jameson (1983: 118–25) use the term, nor with the 'schizophrenic' as a type of literature (Zavarzadeh 1976: 67, Todorov 1978: 85).

pollution that may stifle it' and 'essentially an elitist dream' (1981: 388). She asks why these dreams should 'be given the supreme power of enveloping the planet (conquering the world), when neither those dreams nor man have shown the slightest capacity for solving the world's real problems, only a brilliant capacity for displacing them' (389). In the light of these remarks, *Out* may be read as a dystopic version of a 'global village' in which the technology that 'wraps the earth' has disambiguated and simplified life for the privileged, who then use the founding truth of their colonial system as a weapon against the underprivileged. This weapon is a coercive metaphor or conceptual structuring lens which carves up the world according to its needs, and either conditions or eradicates colourless inhabitants by subjecting them to 'diagnosis' or excluding them from 'symbiosis' in a perpetual present.

Out extends to breaking-point the possibilities of classical empiricist philosophy, and the ultimate failure of this philosophy leads to the full-scale paradigm-shift dramatized in the novel. In a society which has fully internalized the consequences of the Einsteinian revolution and its offshoots, an epistemology based on the postulates of classical scientific models is unable to cope with social structures formed according to this new way of thinking. The single perspective of an individual subject proves inadequate to the task of processing the sensory data that flood his consciousness. In terms of narrative technique, breakdown is manifested through the gradual dissolution of framing devices and ambiguity as to the ontological status of the objects of description. In psychological terms this conforms to the classical description of schizophrenia. In all three respects—philosophical, narrative, and psychological—the novel highlights the failure of traditional conventions and modes of thought by contrasting them with a grotesque parody of the social and discursive consequences of modern scientific theory. This must not be read, however, as a nostalgic plea for a return to the age of classical epistemology. It is a warning that any science which claims to be authoritative has the potential for being used as a discourse of domination.

Metaphor in *Out* is used in two distinct ways: on the one hand, the medical theory 'diagnosis prognosticates aetiology' is extended coercively to other domains of thought; on the other hand, the mind's capacity for variation and mutation leads the main character to produce creative metaphors which distort, subvert, and 'mobilize' the language of authority. In this latter attempt to turn the coercive action of metaphor back on itself lies the seed of the type of metaphor developed in *Such*.

Such: Disrupting Accepted Modes of Thought

Whereas in *Out* a single dominant ideology acts as a structuring device on a wide variety of discourses in the society portrayed, in *Such* two discourses are selected and their interaction is staged within the mind of the protagonist. *Such* thus represents a focusing or narrowing of the type of metaphoric relation developed in *Out*. In *Such* the discourse of astrophysics is used to subvert that of classical psychoanalysis. Astrophysics is concerned with bodies of cosmic proportions, but it is also involved with the smallest of particles, those postulated by quantum mechanics. Specifically, astrophysics studies the origin of the universe through analysis of the characteristics of subatomic particles of light, matter, and energy. Thus, while *Out* dramatizes the consequences of the principle of relativity for the observation of effects, *Such* turns instead to the exploration of the origins of identity in terms of contemporary theories of cosmic birth. The concepts of astrophysics are mapped on to the human psyche in such a way as to contest the assumptions which depth psychology has popularized.

Such begins with a voice in the first-person describing the process of climbing out of his coffin into an unknown world of orbits and ellipses. He meets a character who describes herself as a 'girl-spy'. When he insists that they must have names, she agrees to call him 'Someone' and allows him to call her 'Something'. Something carries on her arm five offspring, variously described as planets, moons, and cylinders. Someone adopts two of these creatures and urges that they too be named. Accordingly, the five bodies are baptized with the names of famous Blues songs: 'Dippermouth', 'Gut Bucket', 'Potato Head', 'Tin Roof', and 'Really'. Upon receiving names they fly off into orbit, and return one by one during the course of the first part of the novel to be given 'rebirth' by Someone.

We eventually learn that Someone is a psychiatrist called Larry who works for a group of astrophysicists at a scientific research laboratory. While undergoing an operation his heart has stopped, but he has come back to life after having been declared dead and deposited in a coffin. The opening of the novel is then the story of his 'death': the time between 'dying' and coming back to full consciousness, a period of uncertain length, but possibly covering two years or more. The adventures of Someone, Something, and their five children are a hallucination experienced by Larry while his body is at a low level of psychic energy. Something is his unconscious, and the planets or children are aspects of his life that return to him as he slowly readjusts to reality.

During his convalescence one of Larry's colleagues, Professor Head, explains to him the basic principles of astrophysics, and it gradually becomes clear that the intra-personal death story is also a metaphoric transposition of the laws of astrophysics on to the dreaming or hallucinating mind. Someone and Something take on the attributes of cosmic bodies. They have 'meridians' instead of arms, as well as 'atmospheric densities' which bend laws, and they emit light. The lost 'geometries of the psyche' that govern their existence are intertwined with the materialized properties of discourse. They take a trip in a 'means of communication' to the limits of language at the ultra-violet end of the verbal spectrum, and Someone is fuelled by the 'internal combustion' of words (22/218, 51/247).

Larry's return to life is recounted most extensively in the second part of the novel. Since his operation he has become emotionally distant from his family and friends. He is not well enough to return to his previous job, and his wife eventually leaves him. A number of journalists try to exploit the novelty of his 'death and amazing recovery'; other people who try to help him find him difficult to relate to. He claims not to remember anything of his 'death', but various events in the death story recur in his second life: he confuses the five moon-children he fathers with his real children, and he speaks of people as though they were cosmic bodies. He also has a new-found ability to 'read' people. His eyes resemble dish-telescopes that seem to look right through his friends, and he sees the psychic energy people emit as an astrophysicist's radio-telescope 'sees' sounds bounced off distant galaxies.

Like the protagonist in *Out*, Larry interprets his own identity through the discourses that organize his experience. Nothing can be taken 'as such' in this novel; it is always read through the screen of metaphoric focus.[15] But the question of the hierarchy between the two discourses involved in the metaphoric relation takes on a new light in *Such*. Domination is not a matter of coercion by a social system, but of the distorting action of one discourse on another in the mind of the protagonist. The discourse of astrophysics dominates as an organizing metaphor in the first part of the novel where it structures Someone's identity. In the second part, Larry internalizes the discursive metaphor and deploys it in order to describe psychological phenomena.

In this second part he discusses his identity in terms of quantum mechanics. After grappling over the course of the novel with his essential nature and that of those around him, he finally renounces his quest for a fixed meaning, a completed story:

—Larry, everyone deserves the attention of definiteness.
—Even if they prefer the uncertainty principle?
—They only pretend to prefer it. While they have to. You used to say that. Someone would come along and find a unified theory that would do away with indeterminate interpretations, you'd say, and revert to causality. I thought perhaps you might.
—I thought so too. In psychic terms at least. But I didn't. In the meantime we do the best we can, some of us preferring to pretend causality exists, and others, others preferring to prefer its absence. (191/387)

Causality is here contrasted with indeterminacy: either one pretends that the origin of psychological peculiarities is known and that it has the force of explanation, as in classical psychoanalysis, or one chooses to relinquish this concept and to see identity as a matter of discontinuity and flux. Cautiously opting for the latter view, Larry bends the laws of astrophysics to construct a theory of subjectivity through the metaphoric lens of the uncertainty principle:

I think I believe that every particle of ourselves, whether combined with those of others in normal electrovalence to make up this or that slice of us, or whether bombarded by those of others until this or that human element mutates into some other, every particle of ourselves returns. So that it has, in that sense, identity. But you can never quite identify it at any given moment. (191–2/387–8)

[15] Brooke-Rose acknowledges that the titles of her novels are 'metaphorical . . . although they're prepositions, or just small link words' (1976*k*: 5). In *A Grammar* she comments on the preposition metaphor, saying that 'its chief idea is one of space. But it also expresses motion, which is always the essence of metaphor' (1958*a*: 258). *Out* is, as we have seen, a portrayal of exclusion, which places the narrator in a position from which he can mobilize, through the work of metaphor, the discourse that excludes him. See pp. 73–4 below on the metaphoric significance of the title *Between*.

According to this theory, people are composed of discrete quanta that exist only in combination with those of others. When the mechanics of causality have been forsaken, identity can never be known or measured, it can only be postulated and experienced. Furthermore, an individual is at each moment only a partial manifestation of an identity revealed over time, what physicists call a 'sum over histories'. As a consequence of this underlying indeterminacy, names change, words are broken, and the laws of social interaction perpetually altered.

As his theory suggests, Larry has lost faith in traditional psychiatry. If the discourse of psychoanalysis is read in the light of the uncertainty principle, it becomes evident that a reconstruction or aetiology of a patient's illness is impossible, for, like the 'biogram' in *Out*, the analytic process itself would alter the unconscious memories and phantasies that constitute traces of the origin of an illness. Furthermore, Larry describes the matter that constitutes the density of his and other people's psyches as 'resistance' (49/245), and in effect the density and opacity of his mind is also a permanent barrier to a clear understanding of his experiences, both past and present. Someone has an 'excrescent scar' (8/204) on his belly which mutates into a camera lens, an 'eye gashed' (25/221), and a 'birthmark' (54/250). In Freudian terms these would be clear symbols of the fear of castration, but the laws of classical psychoanalytic interpretation are bent and broken in *Such*, and if anything it is the concept of the castration complex itself that is mutilated by its subjection to the laws of physics. The scar, trace of an origin, is lost. Professor Head makes this quite clear in the contrast he makes between Larry's former profession and his own:

We tap the silent telephones of outer space, we bounce our questions on the galaxies which answer out of aeons. But they give no names, no explanations, only infinities of calculations. You on the other hand give names to the complex geometries of the soul, you explain perhaps, but do you heal, within spacetime I mean. These maps represent something, certainly, but not the ultimate mystery of the first creation that has gone for ever with its scar inside one huge unstable atom. (75/271)

Analysis will not enable Larry to access the causes of the emotions and fears he 'reads' in the maps of people's minds any more than physicists will be able to 'discover' the origin of the universe.

In his own attempt to 'map' the origins of life on to the individual psyche, Freud came to an unsettling conclusion. *Beyond the Pleasure*

Principle (1920) elaborates a theory of the death drive that very much resembles the concept of entropy used by physicists. All life, he claims, strives in its forward movement to return to the quiescence from which it arose, a state it achieves finally in death. If it is at this point that Freud's theory exceeds itself and is forced beyond the realm of the verifiable into that of speculation, this is also the point at which *Such* picks up the Freudian way of thinking. Larry sees people as things, as emissions of particles and waves which his wife explains as radioactive decay: 'I have come to the conclusion that you see radiation, Larry, and radiation consists after all of decay, degradation so that you see the death that lies inherent in all living existence' (107/303). Larry accepts this explanation and links it with his vague memories of the death world. He cannot reconstruct his death, but its consequences are still felt:

I remember nothing but opaqueness. Or something perhaps . . . moving through space forwards but back at the same time, as if I consisted of anti-matter for ever cancelled out . . . as if in all our words and gestures, acts and attitudes we effected some sort of parallel penetration into whatever had originated them, their primeval atom, with built-in unstableness. (107–108/303–4)

During the death story Tin Roof tells Someone that they don't 'move in time' (133/329), but when he comes back to life, Larry feels as if he 'live[s] backwards' (104/300) and hears conversations 'in waves that run backwards through time' (103/299). He believes that he has 'lost something vital and positive' (146/342) in coming back to life, and wishes to 'die again' (104/300), for he feels like a White Dwarf, or degenerate star that is very dense but not very bright.

Freud's theory of the death wish finds a parallel in the schizophrenic experiences described by R. D. Laing, whose work had a significant impact on a number of novelists of the period (see Chapter 6 below). Laing rejected classical psychoanalysis just as quantum theory rejected classical physics. He believed that clinical descriptions of neuroses do not take into account the inner experiences of the patient, which may be valid and even illuminating. Larry would agree. During his death he takes a series of trips in different vehicles: the airplane-like 'vehicle of communication', a boat, a car, a horse-drawn buggy, and finally the cranial spaceship from which he is ultimately ejected back into life.

In an article originally published in 1964, Laing describes similar voyages into 'inner space' often recounted by people who have been diagnosed as schizophrenics. He characterizes the phenomenon as follows: 'This journey is experienced as going further "in", as going back through one's personal life, in and back and through and beyond into the experience of all mankind, of the primal man, of Adam and perhaps even further into the being of animals, vegetables and minerals' (1967: 104).[16] A sense of loss of identity causes the voyager to project what he or she encounters so as to perceive it as an external phenomenon, and also to introject elements of the familiar world in order to recreate a recognizable context. If Larry's death is understood as an inner voyage of the type described by Laing, a voyage occasioned by the physical trauma of a heart attack, many of the puzzling aspects of the novel begin to make more sense.

The metaphoric transposition of characteristics of outer space on to inner space can be seen as a characteristic attempt to give known form to that which is unfamiliar. The name 'Someone' that the protagonist is given during his death indicates his loss of social identity: he is no one in particular but all people, for his nuclear death family constitutes the 'primeval atom'. This unusual situation provides a motivation for bringing together the extreme poles of our everyday understanding of space and time: the most outer and the most inner, the first and the last. As in *Out*, schizophrenic discourse operates as a metaphoric tool that allows the novel to focus, like its concrete counterpart the radio telescope, on the limits of our spatio-temporal universe. But while in *Out* schizophrenic discourse is an indication of psychological breakdown, in *Such* it represents, in Laing's terms, a breakthrough. Though Larry does not ultimately succeed in reintegrating himself into the world, his efforts to come to terms with the consequences of his experience in the death world of his hallucination indicate a potential mode of interpersonal relation that would provide the basis for a more 'sane' existence.

Psychological alienation provides *Such* with a narrative pretext for bringing the theories of post-Einsteinian science to bear on the way we conceive of ourselves as individuals in relation to other people.

---

[16] This article, 'Politics of Experience', was revised and reprinted in book form in 1967; the page reference is to the latter version. In the introductory chapter of *A Rhetoric of the Unreal* Brooke-Rose cites *Politics of Experience* as one of three books that has altered our understanding of the relationship between reality and insanity (1981: 4).

This is accomplished by metaphorically fitting the discourse of astrophysics on to that of psychology. The 'laws' of the latter are altered as a consequence, and their validity as laws is challenged by their interaction with the uncertainties implicit in astrophysics. The use of metaphor to unsettle a discourse which has widespread authority in our culture demonstrates that metaphor need not necessarily play a coercive role, that it can serve an interrogatory function as well. This extension of the role of metaphor leads the way for the development of multiple, reversible discursive metaphor which is manifest in *Between*.

Between: The Multiple, Reversible Metaphor

In contrast to the main characters of *Out* and *Such*, the anonymous protagonist of *Between* appears to be relatively well adapted to the world in which she lives and travels. This is the world of airplanes, hotels, multinational conferences, and multilingual small-talk, a spinning jumble of infinite variations on the same models. She uses reversible metaphor to perform an integrative operation on this material, bringing it together in a mobile yet highly structured whole that turns around a small number of common patterns. *Between* achieves a balance between the mobility and indeterminacy inherent in the postulates of our post-Einsteinian age and the rigid conventions toward which mass culture tends. It does not provide a resolution of the conflict in either psychological or social terms, but because of the aesthetic coherence of the novel, the problem itself is stated more forcefully than it is in either of the two previous works.

In the traditional realist novel the plot provides a principle of organization, while symbolic structures are fitted in around this frame. But like *Out* and *Such*, *Between* takes as its principle of organization a network of associations formed in the verbal consciousness of the protagonist. This structure is not 'literary' in the sense of being above and beyond the mundane, or at a higher aesthetic level than that achieved by the characters implicated in it. Rather, as in *Out* and *Such*, the structure of the novel reflects the means by which the day-to-day world is apprehended.

The metaphoric juxtaposition of incongruous thematic material is motivated by the exigencies of the main character's job as a simultaneous interpreter. She speaks several languages and partakes of many specialized vocabularies in the context of her daily existence. Although none of the words she utters professionally is her own, fragments of the lectures she translates at conferences constantly invade her thoughts. She is, in her professional capacity, the site of convergence of many discourses but the generator of none. In her private life material from conference lectures is combined with the pop-culture mythology of advertisements, phrase-book dialogues, and other public texts in a number of languages to generate a network of images that is in turn linked to semi-conscious obsessions and childhood memories.

The story-line of *Between* is far from straightforward, but it is logically relatively unambiguous. As in *Out* and *Such*, free direct speech interspersed with actual and remembered dialogue is the primary mode of the novel, but unlike the two previous works, *Between* renders the observations and fantasies of a sane mind in a familiar world. The protagonist has a French mother and a German father. She was brought up in France just before the Second World War, but as an adolescent she was sent to spend a year with relatives in Germany where she was forced to remain when fighting broke out. During the war she worked as a translator, and at the time of the action of the novel she has taken up this trade again recently.

Though punctuated by frequent flashbacks to the period before, during, and just after the war, temporal progression in the present is clearly marked by the development of two narrative lines which weave their ways in and out of the novel. The first is the saga of the protagonist's marriage annulment, involving several hearings, frequent trips to Rome, and a good deal of frustration. The second revolves around a series of love-letters written in medieval French. It is eventually discovered that they are from the ageing Frenchman Bertrand. The protagonist laughs at the letters at first and refuses to answer them, but eventually her curiosity is piqued and she engages in a prolonged correspondence with her admirer. This ends abruptly when the two finally meet and discover that 'fornication by airmail' is more enjoyable than the real thing.

While there is little ambiguity as to what 'happens' in the novel, the temporal perspective from which events are recounted is not well defined. Events do not succeed each other in time; instead reversible metaphor is used to inaugurate shifts between scenes, none of which is more 'proper' or 'metaphoric' than any other. This process is illustrated in the following passage which switches from hotel room to airport on the basis of a structural analogy: ' . . . the black and red patterned blanket folded over with the top sheet to form two parallel white borders from which the planes move slowly off, rise suddenly and vanish or come in out of the low grey cloud . . . ' (10–11/404–5). The novel begins and ends with the description of a commercial airplane interior, to which it often returns. It is possible that the entire text is a combination of description and recollection from the perspective of a single flight, in which case it takes place over the course of a few hours, the time it takes to read it. Equally, the airplane interiors described could all be different, though they look alike, and in fact the novel could span ten years or more. This devaluation of the temporal aspect of the story through temporal ambiguity serves to displace logical emphasis from chronological continuity on to other structural patterns.

The metaphoric networks that bind together thematic sequences are organized by two underlying figures: enclosure and penetration. Enclosure is manifest in many forms; it is at once the womb-like interior of an airplane, the surface of the body, the frame of a window, the border between countries, and the boundary between discourses. In short, enclosure comes to signify insularity and the maintenance of distinct divisions between things. It is associated with the Catholic Church, the institution of marriage, loyalty to the fatherland, and belief in general. The protagonist also feels the need to insulate herself emotionally, a form of protectionism which bears a problematic resemblance to the cultural chauvinism and xenophobia she witnesses during the war. The tendency toward enclosure and fixed meanings is thus political and personal, as well as discursive.

The contrary tendency towards transgression, interpenetration, invasion, and the erosion of emotional walls of defence is manifested most explicitly as polyglossia and the multilingual play of words. This mixing of linguistic and cultural codes is frequently linked to the sexual act: 'As if words fraternised silently beneath the syntax, finding each other funny and delicious in a Misch-Masch of tender fornication' (53/447). Illicit relations with the enemy during wartime echo also in the recurrent phrase 'the languages fraternise behind their own façades' (55/449; variations: 53/447, 123/517, 148/542, 154/548). 'Fraternization' then becomes a catchword for describing the work of the reversible metaphor which plays havoc with entrenched political power relations by transgressing personal, cultural, and national frontiers.

The 'fraternization' of disparate discourses provides a point of transfer between narrative compartments and metaphoric networks that are logically, temporally, or thematically distant.[17] These transition-metaphors operate at several discursive levels. They can hinge on words that have more than one meaning or more than one usage, words that rhyme or sound similar, common thematic elements, or common symbolic associations. The passages that follow illustrate the mechanics of this type of metaphor.

In the first example a transition is accomplished when a single word pivots on its axis of signification during the course of a sentence: 'The words prevent any true EXCHANGE caught in the late afternoon sun' (5/399). The word 'EXCHANGE' transposes the intellectual exchange of ideas into a commercial context while at the same time 'highlighting' the signifier, the letters on the sign of a bureau de change. One definition is exchanged for another, semantic currency is taken from one discursive economy and converted into the currency of another. But this interruption also blocks the passage of ideas by shifting emphasis away from the signified. The polysemic capacity of the signifier is what, in effect, prevents the passage of meaning. Throughout the novel no idea exists in isolation. During the process of 'translation', the signifier inevitably intercepts the signified and draws each word into a network of other concepts. Like the discursive 'slips' discussed with reference to *Out*, the word 'EXCHANGE' partakes simultaneously of two non-commensurate discourses. It thus fulfils the affirmative function of transmission and the negative function of prevention, both of which are designated semantically.

Polysemy again operates as an agent of transition between contexts in the following sentence in which a customs declaration becomes a declaration of love: 'Have you anything to declare such as love desire ambition or a glimpse that in this air-conditioning and other circumstantial emptiness freedom has its sudden attractions as the body floats in willing suspension of responsibility to anyone' (28/422). Even after migration between discursive realms has been effected, the juridical flavour of the customs declaration is not completely relinquished. It haunts the remainder of the passage. The phrase 'circumstantial emptiness' echoes 'circumstantial evidence', and 'freedom' is linked to the 'suspension of respon-

---

[17] This use of metaphor to switch between scenes can be likened to the use of what Jean Ricardou calls 'structural metaphors' in the novels of Alain Robbe-Grillet and Claude Simon. See below, Chapter 6.

sibility' experienced when the body 'floats' inside an airplane, suspended between borders, ideologies, and romantic involvements. The discourse of authority represented by customs is outwitted when the text escapes into the domain of personal relations through a semantic back-door in the word 'declaration'. But the evasion is not completely successful, for the authorities have semantic outposts in other words as well.

In these examples descriptions of exchange and the crossing of frontiers illustrate the move from one discursive domain to another, showing how such actions can be made to function as textual manœuvres and figure the metaphoric strategies of the imagination. It is clear that power relations and territorial rights (personal and otherwise) are implicated in this process. As in *Out*, the invasions operated by metaphor both subvert authority and threaten personal security. But *Between* portrays a successful navigation between the desire to transgress and the need for the stability provided by insularity. Unlike the characters in the two previous novels, the protagonist emerges safe and sound from her semiotic entanglements.

As we have seen, metaphoric reversibility is figured in the text thematically as the condition of being suspended between ideologies, languages, and countries, or as the act of crossing from one to another. This is one's situation in an airplane, for instance, and in linguistic terms it is a state of verbal anarchy, the condition under which languages 'fraternize'. Politically, between-ness 'help[s] to abolish the frontiers of misunderstanding with frequent changes of partners loyalties convictions, free and easily stepping over the old boundaries' (43/437). But sexual and intellectual promiscuity—the frequent substitution of one partner, idea, or belief for another—involves a constant deferral of meaning that leads inevitably to a distrust of language and an uneasiness with regard to self-definition. It is significant that, as Brooke-Rose elsewhere notes (1981: 413), the verb 'to be' is never used in *Between*. This calls into question the concept of 'ontological recognition' which provides, according to one speaker whose paper the protagonist translates, a means for the individual of achieving reintegration and 'totality' (112/506). But the absence is in fact only a dissimulation, for etymologically the word 'between' is a fusion of 'be' and 'two'. The condition of 'between-ness' is then one of doubling which is at the origin of 'fraternization' and transgression. The body is repeatedly described as floating between two states and harbouring contradictory feelings simultaneously. Nothing *is* simply or singly, to be is to be between ideas, beliefs, cultures, and discourses.

The images and symbols that are used in *Between* to demonstrate the mechanics of the imagination do not pretend to be original; they are self-consciously mined in the cultural history of the West. Brooke-Rose attempts rather to use old material in new ways. By means of juxtaposition and carefully wrought connections, she fuses the cognitive processes of metaphoric structuration and epistemological organization. What 'happens' is linked in the protagonist's mind to the networks of her imagination. The latter become the *mensonge vital* of fantasy and fiction that provides her with a means of coping in a hostile world. *Between* demonstrates how a multiplicity of different discursive systems intertwine to form the substrata of an individual mind which plays them off against each other, combines them, and uses them to generate the repertory of stories that determine how she 'reads' the world in which she lives.

By focusing the conception of metaphor Brooke-Rose developed in the 1950s on *Out*, *Such*, and *Between*, I have demonstrated how these novels elaborate the implications of what she herself recognized then as metaphor's chief virtue: its ability to animate and to mobilize the structures on which it works. Her use of metaphor is based on the 'poetic' technique of repetition and variation of the same elements in an ever-expanding cosmos of contexts. In *Out* the proliferation of various permutations of the same material is a reaction against the coercive use of metaphor, but it eventually leads to psycho-discursive disintegration as the central consciousness loses control over his own faculties of thought and reason. In *Such* an alternative world is proposed, a world of indeterminacy which allows for variation and flux, with a theory of identity to match it. But though this world informs the real world, it does not have the power to change it, for Larry is unsuccessful in convincing others of the validity of his theory. Finally, in *Between* a balance is struck between the proliferation of metaphor on the one hand, and fixed semantic boundaries on the other, and it is in the more formally controlled context of this novel that discursive metaphor achieves the full realization of its potential as an agent of linguistic and conceptual refraction.

Out, Such, and *Between* represent the first steps in Christine Brooke-Rose's ongoing exploration of the complex relations between subjectivity and the discursive matrix in which it is embedded. This has led her beyond the sciences, but the philosophical and literary implications of her involvement with the theories of Heisenberg and others have left a lasting mark on her work. In seeking to develop a technique that would be compatible with the findings of modern physics, she demonstrates the relevance of even the most abstract of concepts to our understanding of ourselves and our relation to others through language. She also succeeds in integrating conceptual and psychological material in such a way as to portray individual experience without turning the fictional character into a mere conduit for information. The technique of discursive metaphor allows the individual to be depicted as both passively spoken through by language and actively involved in the discursive process of identity-construction. This conception of subjectivity paves the way for the contestation in Brooke-Rose's later fiction of the hierarchical relations implicit in the conceptions of discursive identity by which we live.

3. *Between, Thru,* and *Amalgamemnon*: Gender and the Discourses of the Human Sciences

Plus vaut encore de ne parler que par équivoques, allusions, sous-entendus.

(Irigaray 1974: 178)

Christine Brooke-Rose's growing interest in structuralist linguistics is evident in her novels of the 1960s in the use of creative juxtaposition and other devices which depend for their effect on the relations between elements rather than on the elements 'as such'. In *Out* and *Such* one discourse is brought to bear on another through metaphor; in *Between, Thru,* and *Amalgamemnon* the same type of metaphor is used to bring a number of discourses together in an increasingly interrogative conjunction. In these novels Brooke-Rose exploits the rhetorical force of the metaphoric technique by employing it to explore, among other things, gender stereotypes as they are manifest in specialized discourses.

The three novels exhibit a growing confidence in a central female persona's attitude toward her use of language. In *Between* the protagonist confronts the jargons of a number of fields from a female perspective. Though the result is often parodic, she is a conveyer, not an active producer, of these jargons. In *Thru* the discourses of literary theory are manipulated in part by a female voice, but active questioning of their status and function is accomplished on the level of the novel's overall orchestration and its symbolic structure. In *Amalgamemnon* the central female character takes an overtly subversive approach. She both appropriates and adulterates the discourses of history, challenging their claim to tell the truth and their implicit exclusion of women from positions of discursive authority. In each novel there is an effect of double-voicing: the female voice speaks through the discourses in question in such a way as to shift their emphasis. She uses them selectively and strategically to reveal the assumptions behind them and their hidden agendas.

Brooke-Rose's use of double-voicing is a natural extension of the metaphoric combination of discourses in her first two experimental novels. But it is also a technique that is 'parodic' in the Bakhtinian sense, or 'subversively mimetic' in the sense that Luce Irigaray uses this concept. Both theorists valorize polyphonic discourse because it implicitly questions the notion of the unitary subject and the binary logic which subtends this notion. Bakhtin's theory of dialogism had a significant influence on French theorists of the late 1960s, and many of their conceptions of the disruptive power of certain kinds of language follow a similar logic. Julia Kristeva and Gilles Deleuze both reject the Aristotelian logic of the excluded middle which they see as being based on the subject–predicate structure of the sentence. Kristeva posits a poetic 0–2 logic that is 'transfini' or 'dialogique' (1969: 92, 141–4). It is the logic that transgresses the unitary 1 of 'Dieu, la loi, la définition' (90); it is the logic of ambivalence and of the 'polyphonic' novel, for fiction, as she defines it, is 'cette réunion non-synthétique entre "est" et "n'est pas" ' (1974: 353). Deleuze elaborates a 'logique du sens' valorizing paradox and 'synthèse disjonctive' (1969: 84), while Derrida's 'logique du supplément' (1967) and his quaternary chiasmatic logic (1972a) provide a means of integrating indeterminacy or 'play' into the heart of binary structures.

The attempt to subvert binary logic threatens to invalidate the structuralist enterprise, and it is not without reason that in the early seventies Kristeva, Irigaray, and other women theorists began to map structuralism's binary logic on to the social and discursive oppression of women by men. Lévi-Strauss had already described the fundamental structure of society and language in terms of the exchange of women, which he saw as the basis of all exchange: 'les règles de la parenté et du mariage servent à assurer la communication des femmes entre les groupes, comme les règles économiques servent à assurer la communication des biens et des services, et les règles linguistiques, la communication des messages' (1958: 95). Citing Lévi-Strauss's analogy between the object of exchange in each of these systems and Jakobson's zero-phoneme, Jacques Lacan draws out the consequences of this paradigm for (male) discourse:

la Dette inviolable est la garantie que le voyage où sont poussés femmes et biens ramène en un cycle sans manquement à leur point de départ d'autres femmes et d'autres biens, porteurs d'une entité identique: symbole zéro, dit Lévi-Strauss, réduisant à la forme d'un signe algébrique le pouvoir de la Parole. (1966: 279)

He goes on to link Lévi-Strauss's idea of exchange as the mastery of women to Freud's interpretation of his grandson's game of *fort/da* as a representation of the alternation of presence and absence. Lacan reasons that the accession to subjectivity is accomplished through the accession to language, which involves the substitution of linguistic presence and absence for the presence and absence of the desired object (284–5, 318–19). The child becomes a discursive subject when it succeeds in controlling the departure and return of its mother through symbolic mastery. Language-use is thus dependent on the suppression of the mother 'beneath the bar' of signification, because 'le symbole se manifeste d'abord comme le meurtre de la chose' (319).

Women obviously have an interest in contesting this understanding of language as the exchange and symbolic annihilation of their sex. Since it is based on Lévi-Strauss's binary conception in which women figure as absent (0) and men as present (1), the unitary male discursive subject is the first target of the feminist deconstructive enterprise. The logic of 0–2, or disjunctive inclusion, rejects the principle of the excluded middle; like the Freudian unconscious, it is thus able to accept contradiction. The unconscious as 'process', the 'imaginary', and the zone of the pre-symbolic are privileged in the feminized logical structures of Cixous (1975), Kristeva (1974), and others because they mark the areas in which male domination and discursive control are incomplete or ineffective. The gendering of logical structures leads Kristeva in 1974 to posit a distinction between the 'semiotic' (Lacan's 'Imaginary') and the 'symbolic'. The semiotic is closely associated with the mother in that it is pre-discursive (pre-Oedipal). It can therefore not be articulated on its own; it must be spoken through the language of the symbolic, just as in Bakhtin's 'dialogic' conception of parody one voice speaks through another which it seeks to undermine. The semiotic surfaces as rhythmic pulses, disturbances in logic, and other 'poetic' mechanisms that mark it as the source of the 'poetic' in writing (1974: 22–30; see also Brooke-Rose 1981: 342).

Luce Irigaray sees a similar process at work in the language of the hysteric which is never able to assert itself as definitive or complete (1966: 29–30). In her analyses of Freud's conception of female sexuality, she demonstrates that Freud's view of women as lack or as absence forces them into the discursive position of the hysteric because it denies them autonomous identity and obliges them to mimic the voice of the dominant male if they wish to be heard at all (1974: 66–71). Their voice is stigmatized by men as a 'foisonnement de phantasmes, de fantômes, d'ombres' (70), in other words, as the voice of non-truth. It can only ever be a mimicry, for, as Irigaray argues, women can never accede to the condition of subjectivity: 'Toute théorie du "sujet" aura toujours été appropriée au "masculin" ' (165). They are forced to operate in the pre-subjective domain of the specular imaginary, using a tactic of *mimétisme* (subversive mimesis) that Irigaray both describes and illustrates in her writing. Women's discourse may only be a flawed copy of its male counterpart, but, as Irigaray shows, women can use this apparent deficiency to their advantage by allowing the 'bad copy' to become a subversive caricature in which the difference between the double and the 'original' reveals the gender bias underlying male discourse and (male) subjectivity (1977: 73–4).

What Irigaray describes as *mimétisme* can also be thought of as parody. According to Bakhtin, parody is a 'dialogic' form which frees consciousness from the coercive force of 'monologic' language by registering the distance between language and reality (1981: 60). In an article first published in 1985, Brooke-Rose discusses the theories of parody developed by both Bakhtin and Genette (1985c; revised in 1991a: 191–203). She compares Bakhtin's definition of parody as divergent bifocal discourse based on the degree of presence and orientation of 'voices' with Genette's more restricted definition of the term. Genette distinguishes parody from other forms of 'hypertextuality' as that ludic mode which effects punctual and systematic transformations of specific texts while retaining the noble style of the original (1982: 33–5). According to both these definitions, *Between*, *Thru*, and *Amalgamemnon* exhibit parodic elements.[1] They contain punctual alterations of specific texts, and they stage the confrontation between two or more voices. But all three novels also exhibit significant variations on parody as it has been practised in the past. The internal relations of the multiple 'voices' in Brooke-Rose's parodies are considerably more complex

---

[1] Definitions of parody vary widely, from William Empson's conservative view of it as 'appreciative criticism' (1953: 249) to Pierre Macherey's claim that all literature is characterized by its parodic function which is by definition subversive (1965: 75). Margaret Rose (1979: 33) and Linda Hutcheon (1985: ch. 2) acknowledge the inherent ambivalence of the term, and because of the ambiguity surrounding it, I have chosen to use the definitions Brooke-Rose herself cites to guide my discussion.

than in the examples Bakhtin analyses; though their 'orientations' are not always directly opposed, they nevertheless succeed in deflecting the text away from its nominal object and making the reader aware of the devices they use. With reference to Genette's definition they are exceptional in that their object texts are not only other 'noble' works of literature but quotations from scholars, product labels, radio broadcasts, advertisements, propaganda slogans, and various other 'public texts' or textual *objets trouvés*.

The radical 'para' found in both 'paradox' and 'parody' provides a spatial model for a variety of techniques displayed in the novels. Meaning both 'against' and 'beside', 'para' suggests a tactic of confrontation through juxtaposition.[2] *Between, Thru,* and *Amalgamemnon* manifest structures of adjacency or alterity in which exemplary texts of both past and present are invoked and implicitly questioned by being brought together and made to interact; their semantic orientation is refracted by the context in which they are placed and their referential function remotivated. This form of parodic engagement with the discursive edifices erected by a male-dominated society is depicted in the novels as a distinctly feminine linguistic strategy. It is suggested that only by acting on the systems which constrain them can women hope to free themselves, and each of the three novels explores different possible forms this discursive action can take.

Nevertheless, Christine Brooke-Rose does not classify herself as a feminist. Though *Between* and *Thru* exhibit striking parallels with the emergent thinking in the late 1960s and early 1970s about the relation of women to language, it was not until nearly fifteen years later that she began to make use of gender-specific arguments in her critical writings. In the mid-1980s she became increasingly conscious of the links between gender and reception. Since that time she has published four articles in which she discusses the problems women experimental writers face (1986*d*, 1988*a*, 1989*a*, 1989*c*; see also 1989*e*). In each case she argues that female creativity has been constructed by men as a contradiction in terms. In the article

---

[2] 'Paradox', from *para* and *doxa*, denotes the transgression of binary logic which is a characteristic strategy in the novels, but its etymological connotation is that of opposition to received opinion (Barthes 1973: 31). 'Parody', from *para* and *odes* suggests a similar relation between a parodic text and a sanctified 'song' or masterpiece of the past (Hutcheon 1985: 32, though this etymology is disputed: see Rose 1979: 18–19).

'Illiterations' (1989*a*; revised in 1991*a*: 250–64) she demonstrates that the development of the Western conception of creativity in women and men is based on metaphors of reproduction which figure woman's role as the material 'work' of child-bearing, and the experience of men as spontaneous spurts of genius. But she points out that men have also appropriated the female role (which is more active) as a painless metaphor for their own artistic endeavours:

For men have always had it both ways: the begetting *and* the travail (the travail which, as 'work' belongs to culture, but which as bearing and 'labour' belongs to nature); the genius *and* the work (the genius which is itself both passive possession and authoritative production), the penis *and* the womb. Man has in fact appropriated, to represent his relation to truth or God, both aspects of woman's role in relation to man: the being made fecund and the travail. (1991*a*: 256–7; italics in the original)

In *Between, Thru*, and *Amalgamemnon* Brooke-Rose reappropriates for women the role of one whose relation to language is both active and passive, that of the producer as well as the means of production. This paradoxical role is represented in *Between* and *Amalgamemnon* by the symbol of Jonah inside the whale, waiting to be 'reborn'. It is the provisional position of the female subject who is still dependent on discourses developed by men and saturated with their prejudices. While she awaits her birth into her own voice, she can only speak through the voices of others, but this 'speaking through' also constitutes her struggle to get out.

The refraction and fusion of discourses accomplished by discursive metaphor provided Brooke-Rose with the technical means for the strategy of *mimétisme* with which she began to experiment in *Between*. Soon after, she recognized in a certain strain of feminist theory an approach to language which had much in common with the approach she herself had been developing over a number of years. The feminist arguments in favour of dialogic forms of language-use helped her to clarify her own reasons for employing discursive metaphor and parody, and the gendering by feminists of the notion of the 'bad copy' enabled her to incorporate her own techniques of misrepresentation into a readily recognizable social context. Brooke-Rose's engagement with feminist theory is typical of her encounter with literary theory in general. In a recent essay she claims to have had a strong sense of *déjà-vu* upon first reading theories of post-structuralism and postmodernism, for though she had never been able to articulate them clearly in conceptual form, she had discovered many of the concepts these theories present through writing fiction (1991*a*: 165).[3] The double-voicedness of the novels examined in this chapter is thus itself double: not only are they illustrations of how the voice of an individual interacts with the anonymous collective voice of a discursive system, they also stage the confrontation between the language of fiction and that of the human sciences which have the same object but different methods. By articulating the fictional through the 'scientific', the novels question the authority of the latter and reassert the specificity of the former as a discourse which has as its function to mimic and to question.

Between: The Semiotics of Culture and Gender

It will by now have become apparent that Brooke-Rose shifts her attention increasingly toward language over the course of her *œuvre*. This is particularly noticeable in *Between*; indeed she herself says 'it's really with *Between* that I discovered what I could do with language' (1989*e*: 83). In *Out* phrases of government jargon reverberate within the protagonist's mind and the multiple meanings of words generate associations which guide his train of thought. In *Such* the dissection of conventional locutions is contrasted with the 'transparent' day-to-day use of language. But it is in *Between* that the function of language to convey meaning is most actively questioned. As we saw in Chapter 2, the number and variety of messages with which the main character is bombarded causes her to reflect on the role they play in her daily life. I shall examine in this section the means by which different discourses and public texts are ground together to reveal the common structures that underlie them and the common strategies they employ.

With *Between* the relationship between language and gender becomes significant both thematically and structurally for the first time in Brooke-Rose's fiction. Brooke-Rose started writing the novel in 1964, but she became blocked and eventually put it aside in order to write *Such*. When she again took up *Between* in 1967 she decided to change the gender of the main character from male to female and

---

[3] See Chap. 6 below for a fuller treatment of the relation in Brooke-Rose's *œuvre* between the theory and practice of writing.

'it suddenly worked' (1990c: 32). She suggests that this was perhaps because women have traditionally been seen as having a passive relation to language which is similar to that of a simultaneous interpreter who translates the ideas of others but does not produce any of her own (32). Brooke-Rose acknowledges that this is a 'cliché', but claims that it was 'true enough generally . . . for the purpose of creating the language of the novel' (1991a: 7). The language of the novel makes use of this cliché to demonstrate first that there is a profound ambiguity in the social construction of femininity according to which women are passive but at the same time subversive of the binary distinction which so construes them; and secondly that all people, male and female, are condemned to being at least partially the product of the language of others.

According to the gender stereotypes that permeate the novel, the mixing and crossing of multiple codes is a characteristically feminine approach to language.[4] By contrast, the (masculine) discourses of knowledge weaken symbolic systems by treating them as 'true': 'our masculine-dominated civilisation . . . has turned vital lies into fragile truths' (175/569). The female version of knowledge is characteristically an inversion: 'our masculine-dominated myth turned upside down, in, out, around' (118/512). A mock-textbook example drawn from a conference paper symbolizes the figure of ambiguity and multiplicity associated with femininity: 'Comment on the gender of amour' (163/557). Masculine in the singular and feminine in the plural, the word *amour* encapsulates a structure which serves as a model for the respective conceptions of unitary masculine logic and multiple, reversible feminine logic.

Linguistic and sexual terminology come together most often in the context of the Saussurian theorization of binary opposition, illustrated by an excerpt from a paper given at a conference on linguistics:

Et comme l'a si bien dit Saussure, la langue peut se contenter de l'opposition de quelque chose avec rien. The marked term on the one hand, say, the feminine, grand*e*, the unmarked on the other, say the masculine, grand. Mais notez bien que le non-marqué peut dériver du marqué par retranchement, by subtraction, par une absence qui signifie. (32/426)[5]

---

[4] See Chap. 6 below for a discussion of similar linguistic gendering in the novels of other contemporary woman writers.

[5] The phrase 'la langue peut se contenter de l'opposition de quelque chose avec rien' is a direct quotation from Saussure (1915: 124).

Derivation of the masculine from the feminine 'by subtraction' sets up a logical opposition between positive, present feminine and negative, absent masculine. This corresponds to the main character's own personal situation of being without a man. But paradoxically, the phrase 'une absence qui signifie' is also used to designate her conception of herself as being without identity (which corresponds to Freud's characterization of femininity as a 'lack' or symbolic castration). An analysis of feminine and masculine symbolism delivered at a conference on 'archetypology' characterizes 'inversion by double negation' as 'typical of the imaginative function in its descending aspect of depth, night, femininity, container which becomes contained, swallower which becomes swallowed' as opposed to the 'upward masculine aspect' (109/503). Later the masculine myth is restated as a phallic 'spiral . . . like a ziggurat or seven-terraced Tower of Babel' (139/533).[6] The inauguration of linguistic difference, associated with the Tower of Babel, is then typically masculine, whereas mythic 'femininity' subverts distinctions through inversion. According to this scenario, the maintenance of oppositional structures is constantly being protected by the masculine aspect, while its feminine counterpart strives to undermine them, and even to undermine this constitutive definition itself by the use of reversible structures echoed in the novel's metaphoric construction.

The liminal position of the female voice with regard to the texts she translates provides an illustration of this 'female' tendency to undermine distinctions. Like the Saussurian sign, she defines herself by and through her relations with others. She feels she has no intrinsic self but only the provisional identity of the texts she translates. Her role as a simultaneous interpreter is a hyperbolic figuration of the Barthesian character who is no more than the point of intersection of a number of different public codes (Barthes 1970b: 74). The absence from the novel of the verb 'to be' corresponds to this differential definition of the self that *is* no one thing but can *say* anything, and the 'loss of identity through language', which Brooke-Rose regards as one of the most important themes of the novel (1989e: 84), is evident in the character's consciousness of living 'between ideas' (19/413). Though her job is to translate as faithfully

---

[6] Maria Del Sapio (1988) traces the mythico-anthropological symbolism employed in *Between* back to E. Neumann's book *Ursprungsgeschichte des Bewußtseins* (1949).

as possible, this process is replicated in her mind by 'bad copies' in which analogous discursive systems are conjoined in such a way as to emphasize disparities between them or unexpected parallels.

Very often her ludic manipulation of language takes the form of intentional 'errors'. Multilingual puns are a favourite plaything of both her and her friend Siegfried. When accused of using words 'most imprecisely', Siegfried replies 'I use them simultanément' (36/430). The subtle flaws inherent in any equation of equivalent terms becomes a generative device. I demonstrated in the previous chapter that the use of discursive metaphor causes simultaneity and association to replace causality and linear chronology as the compositional principles of the novel, allowing changes of scene in mid-sentence and the coexistence of a number of often-incompatible signifieds in a given signifier. This process is described as 'telescoping time with an error' (13/417,110/504), but it can also be understood as a creative transformation.

In *The Dear Deceit* misquotation generates an ironic effect of mis-contextualization. The device of misquotation is used in a similarly ironic fashion in *Between* when an American character mangles a passage from *Macbeth*: 'lirrechur, eh? Tomorrow and tomorrow and tomorrow, creeps in this petty place from day to day . . . ' (35/429). The act of quotation is a demonstration of supposed knowledge, an exhibition of what Pierre Bourdieu terms 'cultural capital'; but here it misfires and the quoted text becomes the agent of parody. Several pages later the central voice sabotages this transaction of symbolic worth by crossing the American man's substitution of 'place' for 'pace' with a creative mis-translation: 'I luoghi: Slowly now. The places: La Francia, la Germania, e sopratutto la Britannia, la dolce Inghilterra . . . Tomorrow and tomorrow creeps in this petty luogo dove esplose il divorzio tra uomo e Dio . . . ' (41/435). The 'explosion' in and of the sentence recalls the protagonist's lapsed faith. In her mind she associates the act of translation with transubstantiation through a chain of associations (see 13/407, 20/414, 112/506, 139/533, 164/558), and the lapse in her relations with God corresponds to similar 'flaws' in her use of language. The same metaphor is employed in *The Languages of Love*, but rather than representing tragic alienation as it does there, here it acts as a principle of formal and thematic patterning.

The 'bad copies' the main character produces are made possible by the fact that a number of comparable codes are juxtaposed simultaneously in her mind. In an interview Christine Brooke-Rose illustrates the capacity for this type of juxtaposition to generate parody:

> when the Nixon pardon was announced on television . . . it said CBS special, you know, complete and free pardon, etc. and then, on the local station, 'this program is presented to you by X, the deodorant that kills domestic odors.' I just collapsed with laughter . . . Maybe the announcer thought it was funny, but these things happen, the coincidences in life. So that rather than doing what language is supposed to do, that bit of publicity, it does exactly the opposite. You know, one whiff and it's clean, and of course with the Nixon pardon this is exactly what happened. (1976*k*: 15)

The semantic remotivation characteristic of parody is accomplished in this instance not by exaggeration, but by the repetition of an 'equivalent' message in two different contexts. This technique is evident in *Between*, published six years earlier:

> the men in the café sit transfixed by the flickering local variation in the presentation of opposite viewpoints on every aspect of an instant world through faceless men who have no doubt acquired faces for them as their arch-priests of actualità that zooms flashcuts explodes to OMO! Da oggi con Perboral! Lava ancora più bianco! Gut-gut. Più bianco than what? We live in an age of transition, perpetually between white and whiter than white. (24–5/418–19; cf. 38/432, 125/519)

For Bakhtin, parody and stylization objectify their target by introducing 'a new semantic intention into a discourse which already has, and which retains, an intention of its own' (1984: 189). In the case of parody, this intention is 'directly opposed to the original one', and the result is 'an arena of battle between voices' (193). The 'battle between voices' in the above passage is not so much a semantic opposition as a fight for rhetorical supremacy. Conforming to Genette's definition, the target is a specific pre-existent text incorporated literally into the parody (though in this case the original is 'vulgar' not 'noble'). Semantic inflation devalues the referential relevance of the advertisement's claim. The comparative 'più' has no object; the difference between 'white' and 'whiter than white' is neither quantitative nor qualitative, it is a difference between determinate meaning and its abolition. As with the misquotation cited above, the function of the advertisement is deflected: the text is made to refer to its own rhetorical device of washing meaning out of language. It is also used as an agent of ironic comment whose target is the 'actualità' of the news broadcast from which all distinguishing features have been purged. The discourse of rhetoric (advertising) and the discourse of truth (the news) are implicitly equated through their juxtaposition, and the purgative action described by the one is operated on the other.

In *Mythologies* Barthes discusses advertisements for *Omo* and *Persil* in terms of the connotations they invoke. He argues that the products are portrayed as chasing away dirt without harming the fabric:

> on met en mouvement la vanité, le paraître social, en donnant à comparer deux objets dont l'un est *plus* blanc que l'autre. La publicité *Omo* . . . engage ainsi le consommateur dans une sorte de mode vécu de la substance, le rend complice d'une délivrance et non plus seulement bénéficiaire d'un résultat . . . L'important c'est d'avoir su masquer la fonction abrasive du détergent sous l'image délicieuse d'une substance à la fois profonde et aérienne. (1957: 39–40; italics in the original)

Indeed, the advertisement cited in *Between* engages the central figure in a 'mode vécu de la substance'. She thinks of herself as a discursive fabric in which beliefs get lodged and are subsequently removed. In an ironic vulgarization of Christian symbolism she is 'delivered' from her marriage, her country, and even her religion through the purgative action of language. In order to get a job at the end of the war, she and Siegfried need to obtain what she calls a 'Persil-Schein certificate denazifying us whiter than white' (79/473). But the language she uses to describe this process demonstrates her parodic attitude toward it. Like the implicit analogy between the Nixon pardon and a cleaning product, the comparison between denazification and the action of washing powder points to the arbitrary nature of the performative act and questions the authority on which it is based. By tacitly demonstrating that the claim of denazification is no more legitimate than the commercial propaganda of television publicity, it levels them semantically and reveals the similarity of the linguistic techniques they use.

There is a fundamental ambiguity, however, in the protagonist's relation to language: the levelling of meaning and the abolition of distinction is at once the device used by parody and the effect it attacks. The surfeit of codes and jargons in which she is immersed brings about a loss of faith in the power of the word, but her attitude toward the 'instant world' that is 'whiter than white' because it has no memory and no values makes her uneasy. Because of the inherently paradoxical nature of her existence, she is a representative figure of the 'age of transition'. As Susan Suleiman observes, she is an 'emblem of our ambiguous present' (1989: 127), 'on the one hand, close to being submerged by the detritus of civilization whose broken-up quality she both registers and exemplifies . . . on the other hand, *playing* with that very sense of loss, that same detritus, and producing (sometimes) an exhilarating laughter' (126; italics in the original).

The object of parody in *Between* is not so much theories and belief systems themselves as the linguistic manœuvres by which they attempt to convince. All efforts to communicate, whether in the context of a scholarly debate or a love-letter, are reduced to propaganda and rhetorical gimmicks designed to co-opt the truth in the name of patriotism, love, or science. But in none of the above cases do the manœuvres by which the main character resists her passive relation to language engage her in active polemic with other texts. By making language do other than what it is designed to do in its original context, parodic manipulation undermines its illocutionary force rather than its explicit semantic content.

Though local assaults using pre-existent texts are not uncommon in the novel, they constitute a subset of a more generalized strategy described by Genette as pastiche and by Bakhtin as discourse with a 'sideward glance at someone else's word' (1984: 199).[7] *Between* is a hotch-potch of different 'voices' with degrees of autonomy ranging from direct quotation to the barely noticeable trace of the influence of a specialized discourse evident in a single word or the syntax of a sentence. Most of the novel falls between these two poles: pastiches of learned vocabularies are interwoven with the 'vulgar' language of travel, and the effects this produces vary widely. What joins the various devices under a common heading is the fact that in all cases the discourses invoked are spoken *through* by a voice which has little or no inherent identity of its own but is defined as a principle of interrogative conjunction. This tactic of disarming a discourse by inverting it and tacitly denying its claim to tell the truth is implicitly linked to the feminine mythology that the novel elaborates thematically. Linguistic posturing of this sort is the extreme reaction of a

---

[7] This is among the types in the 'active subgroup' of dialogic discourse which Brooke-Rose identifies as one of 'the really revolutionary aspects of [Bakhtin's] work' (1991a: 202).

character in an extreme situation, but it dramatizes rhetorical manœuvres available to both men and women who are forced into a position of discursive subservience.

Thru: Theories of Fiction and Fictions of Femininity

With *Thru* Brooke-Rose turns from the discourses of culture in the wide sense of the term to the discourse of 'high' culture. While *Between* explores the discursive role of women from a semiotic perspective and isolates characteristically female forms of language-use which hold the potential for critical examination of our contemporary cultural 'mythologies', the object-discourses on which *Thru* works are those of which it is itself an object. The same parodic tactics used in *Between* are evident in this novel, but transposed on to the self-reflexive plane of metafiction they become magnified, hence more overt. *Thru* subverts the literary theory which has as its premiss that every narrative contains a meaning and that this meaning can be accounted for in terms of a universal 'elementary structure of signification' which posits woman as an object of exchange between men. The novel does to structuralist theories of meaning what Irigaray does to Freud's theory of feminine sexuality: it mimics them, draws out their implications, and ultimately demonstrates their limitations, using the structures they propose as metaphors for personal relations.

In the early 1970s Brooke-Rose described the different 'houses of theory' she encountered when she moved to Paris in 1968:

Living in France . . . is rather like walking round a national exhibition, entering one fantastic and beautiful structure after another, the Lévi-Strauss Palace, the Derrida Daedalus, the Lacan Labyrinth, the Kristeva Construct, the Barthes Pavilion, the Planetarium showing the Sollers System. (1973*b*: 614)

She comments also on the ambiguous fascination these theorists exhibit with regard to their own practice: 'it is all a beautiful, theoretical game, that they themselves don't perhaps really believe in, but indulge in it as one indulges in a passion, overwhelming at the time then looked at with mild amusement, a passion for beautiful systems' (614). The characteristic stylistic tic 'tout se passe comme si' puts their discourse technically into the mode of the hypothetical or the fictional, reflecting 'this curious paradox, the ardent desire for a system and the basic scepticism about all systems' (614). The same ambivalence is evident in the prevailing attitude toward language. Brooke-Rose follows structuralists and post-structuralists in their belief that language is the only tool we have at our disposal for apprehending reality, and that linguistic structures have a formative effect on the mind. She concludes that an individual 'can only protect his own patterning from the invasion of others by a kind of wild jay-walking among the traffic, trying not to get run over' (614).

Thru enacts this strategy of 'wild jay-walking' between theories by side-stepping their systematicity and making them into stories. It shares with Brooke-Rose's 1960s novels the same basic technique of literalizing specialized discourses by means of a metaphoric mapping of one discourse on to another. As in *Between*, the binary definitions on which structuralist theory is founded receive parodic treatment which voids them of their original function and uses them for the purpose of telling the tale(s) of the novel. That this project is based on a 'feminist' logic is significantly more obvious in *Thru*, however, than it is in *Between*. *Thru* models many of its narrative strategies directly on the writings of Julia Kristeva and Luce Irigaray, and more indirectly on those of Jacques Lacan and Jacques Derrida.[8] The status in the novel of the different types of theoretical discourse varies according to the degree of 'internal dialogization' these writings possess. The novel does not question the concept of 'theory' so much as those theories which refuse to acknowledge the fact that they are 'fantastic structures' in the mode of the hypothetical, and that their status as autonomous systems will always be compromised by their relation to their object. In the case of narratology, systems which fail to recognize the fictionality inherent in their constructs

[8] Though *Thru* was not published until 1976 it was completed in 1973 and the theoretical works to which it alludes were, for the most part, published between 1966 and 1972. (Because of its typographical complexities the novel took a long time to set; nearly two years passed between the time Brooke-Rose submitted it to her publisher and its appearance.) A complete list of proper names mentioned or referred to in the text is given at the end, but a more limited selection of names indicates the major theoretical forces in the novel: the linguistics of Saussure, Chomsky, and Greimas, the narratological and textual theories of Todorov, Genette, Barthes (of the *S/Z* period), Derrida, and Kristeva, and psychoanalytic theory as interpreted by Lacan and Irigaray. Hanjo Berressem analyses the role in *Thru* of the theories of Lacan and Derrida which he sees as forming the 'basic tension' in the novel (1989:129), and Emma Kafalenos (1980) traces some of the most significant literary references, many of which are to texts which have been the object of well-known critical analyses by literary theorists.

and strive to maintain a rigorous distinction between 'houses of fiction' and 'houses of theory' are subjected to subversive mimesis. In what follows I shall analyse how one such theory—the narrative semantics of A. J. Greimas and the Lacanian theory of subjectivity with which it is associated—is 'played with' in this way.[9]

The gender stereotypes inherent in binary definitions of 'male' and 'female' are explored in *Between*, but structuralist theory as such does not come under attack. By contrast, a keen awareness of the sexist bias of many structuralist theorists is evident in *Thru*. In 1985 Brooke-Rose published an article entitled 'Woman as a Semiotic Object' in which she analyses the 'deep, ancient, phallocratic' (1991*a*: 249) structures for which thinkers such as Greimas, Lévi-Strauss, and others have an unconscious nostalgia. Chief among these is the logical rectangle which Greimas sees as the 'structure élémentaire de la signification' (Greimas 1970: 160). This 'rectangle' is composed of four arrows pointing diagonally outward from a central 'O' to four corners which represent the four terms in a homology: A : B : : A' : B'. The deixes relate each term to both its contrary and its contradictory. As a narrative paradigm, this diagram represents the exchange of an object 'O' between two 'actants' and two topographical sites. Greimas maps on to his diagram Propp's basic narrative chiasmus: traitor ravishes king's daughter and transfers her elsewhere to hide her, hero finds somewhere king's daughter and gives her back to her parents. Brooke-Rose's main objection to this model is that Greimas follows Lévi-Strauss in making of woman a silenced object of exchange whose signified has been repressed (ravished) into the unconscious (elsewhere). This reflects, she claims, man's attitude toward woman in general, split between the 'Pygmalion urge' to form her to suit his own desire and the 'demolition enterprise' (1991*a*: 247). She points out, however, that man's power over woman, like his power over language, is illusory, for 'man thinks he shapes and masters and exchanges words and women, while all the time language is shaping and mastering him (and women), so that his exchanges and controls and double standards must be as mutable as language itself' (246). The process

---

[9] Greimas acknowledges his debt to the psychoanalyst, whose concept of subjectivity helped Greimas to formulate his actantial model of narrative semiotics (1966: 100, 190). His famous 'X' diagram, if not taken directly from Lacan's 'Séminaire', bears an obvious likeness. See Greimas and Rastier 1968: 137 for a discussion of the diagram's multiple sources.

of exchange, the underlying grammar of narrative so cherished by Greimas as a fixed structure, 'must' in fact be 'mutable'. Moreover, its mutations must follow those of language: when the functioning of language changes, so must narrative functions. This hypothesis, although difficult to prove or demonstrate in the context of theoretical commentary, is dramatized in *Thru*, published some ten years earlier in 1975.

As in Propp's folk-tales, characters in *Thru* are variables while their functions are constants. The principal characters, Larissa Toren and Armel Santores, teach literature and literary theory at two equally radical universities. Similarly, the thematic structure of the novel vaguely follows Propp's paradigm: Armel takes Larissa into matrimony only to betray her; Stavro, a gallant but naïve young man, 'saves' Larissa, begging her to marry him and go with him to Peru, or: 'The anti-hero anti-rescuing her from an anti-monster in an anti-romanzo' (149/727). Yet as a tool for 'de-coding' literature, structural analysis is labelled 'already out of date' (52/630). Larissa talks of going beyond structuralism and goes so far as to disown it: 'of course I am not a structuralist I never have been I merely played with it' (84/662). Likewise, the novel plays with normative paradigms such as those proposed by Greimas which seek to standardize narrative by defining it according to a canonic conception of what a story is.

In the late 1960s and the early 1970s Greimas, Todorov, Genette, and Barthes all argued for the autonomy of narrative theory with respect to its object.[10] According to this position, the aim of narrative poetics is to produce a typology which includes all possible narrative forms, not only those that have been realized in the past. But Paul Ricoeur points out that most such theories are simulations of our internalized grammar of narrative, which is based perforce on narrative structures that have been made common in the past (1986: 139–40). It follows that narrative poetics is in fact a form of historiography, a highly abstract story of stories. *Thru* reveals that many structuralist theories of narrative are simulacra of the story we have all internalized of the constitution of subjectivity through the reification of women. It also confutes their claim to completeness by staging narrative structures for which they cannot account. This

---

[10] Greimas 1966: 15, Todorov 1971: 10–12; Genette 1972: 10–11; Barthes 1964: 79–80.

points to gaps in their typologies which indicate their dependence on a historically determined narrative competence. The result is a ludic collapsing of autonomous theoretical systems on the basis of structural similarities or 'slips' from one to another which point to the common 'story' underlying them.

Brooke-Rose distinguishes her novel from the plethora of 'fiction about the writing of fiction' in that its purpose is to play with 'the reader's habit of trusting the reliable narrator' (1976k: 4–5). The reader's expectations are elicited only to be thwarted. She explains that *Thru* is 'a text that is really constructing itself and then destroying itself as it goes along . . . whenever I slide into a realistic scene . . . something happens later to destroy it, to show that these are just words on a page' (4). In this sense *Thru* marks a break with *Out*, *Such*, and *Between*, which are all, in one way or another, attempts to create a textual equivalent of the experience of a single consciousness. Brooke-Rose's encounter with Lacanian theories of subjectivity made it possible for her to relinquish her last link with realism by breaking with the notion of character as discrete individual. The Lacanian split subject is from the start a discursive subject traversed by the other. This splitting of the subject is literalized in the novel as a shattering of the narrative voice into a multitude of surrogate 'bearers of the tale'.[11]

Thru opens and closes with the central figure of the driving mirror or 'retrovizor'. The driving mirror is first and foremost an image: a self-reflexive representation or, in psychoanalytic terms, a narcissistic identification. But the mirror has two characteristics that indicate those ways in which *Thru* goes beyond the self-reflexive novel. First, the person who looks into it sees not only his or her own reflection but also the other cars on the 'thruway': the viewer looks ahead in order to see behind. The self-reflexive text is thus also an intertext: it looks into itself and sees all the other texts of the past. If this notion of looking ahead in order to see behind is understood temporally, it can be recognized as the constitutive structure of narrative itself,

---

[11] Brooke-Rose realized when she was writing the novel that she was starting in a new direction, and she decided to indicate this shift by a break with the prepositional titles of her three previous works. The original title of *Thru* was 'Textermination' which, like the neologisms 'Amalgamemnon' and 'Xorandor' is cryptic in its agglutinative word-play. In the end her publisher asked her to change the title because he mistakenly thought that William Burroughs's recently published *Exterminator!* was entitled *Texterminator!* (1976k: 5). She reserved the title 'Textermination' for a later novel which also plays with reading habits (see Chap. 4 below).

which Genette describes as a series of 'déterminations rétrogrades' in that the action of a story is a function of its outcome (1969: 94).[12]

This same structure is conflated in the novel with Lacan's model of the constitution of subjectivity. In 'Subversion du sujet et dialectique du désir dans l'inconscient freudien', Lacan notes that the 'fonction diachronique dans la phrase' is an 'effet rétroactif' (1966: 805). He then uses this analogy with the sentence to describe the trajectory by which the subject constitutes itself through the other. This is figured as a retroactive effect specifically linked to the mirror: 'tout ce dont le sujet peut s'assurer, dans cette rétrovisée, c'est venant à sa rencontre l'image, elle anticipée, qu'il prit de lui-même en son miroir' (808). The condition of anticipated completion in which the subject experiences itself 'au futur antérieur' (808) corresponds to the movement of semantic retroactivity, just as the visual term 'rétrovisée' corresponds to the spatial image of the mirror—the two moments of this process being one temporal and the other spatial (806). But the description passes through the curious term '[e]ffet de rétroversion' (808) which seems strangely out of place. The word 'rétroversion' can be understood etymologically as 'turning back', yet in modern usage it is reserved exclusively for the turning or tipping of organs, especially of the uterus. One wonders why Lacan's narrative of the genesis of the subject has to pass 'through' this flaw in the female anatomy—a flaw in the 'proper' functioning of the female body.

This leads to the second main characteristic of the retrovizor in *Thru*: unlike the Lacanian mirror, it is flawed, causing it to reflect not two but four eyes, two in their correct position and two further up the brow (1–3/579–81). The rectangular figure which this creates provides a frame for the Greimassian narrative chiasmus in which the four eyes become four 'I's or 'actants'. It fuses this schema also with the Lacanian version of the diagram which *Thru* lifts from Lacan's 'Séminaire sur "La Lettre volée" '. Here the two 'other eyes' (72/650, 146/724) are the locus of the 'other scene' or 'elsewhere'. The Greimassian chiasmus functions in a literal sense as the 'elementary structure of meaning' in the novel, organizing

---

[12] Armel devotes a class to this article, 'Vraisemblance et motivation' (49–51/627–9). *Thru*'s playful manipulation of this concept can be seen as a development of the reversal of temporal order first enacted in *The Dear Deceit*.

circuits of exchange on narrative, interpersonal, and pedagogic levels. In each case the text has to 'pass through' this figure.[13]

Being a discursive subject and speaking are a matter of having access to a mirror, and it is not insignificant that a male subject is initially in control of the retrovizor. When one of Armel's string of mistresses is riding in the car with him, she notices the effect of the flaw in the glass and tries to appropriate this phenomenon of double retro-vision for herself:

> She shifts the mirror to her rearward glance. It doesn't work for her the mistress of the moment of sudden isolation at not seeing back to the black magician who fantastically juggles luminous hoops in the recto-rectangular hey put my mirror back.
>
> So it needs adjusting. (4/582)

The phrase 'so it needs adjusting' is an a-posteriori justification for a failed narrative coup. The narrative process the mirror represents 'doesn't work for her', she fails to see behind to the 'luminous hoops' of other subjects, which is a necessary condition for her accession to the position of subject of discourse. She experiences a 'moment of sudden isolation' before her male companion demands that his specular image be restored to him. 'Put my mirror back' can be read as the cry of all men who have the narcissistic relation they enjoy with the image of their own desire threatened by a woman. Nevertheless the flaw in the mirror suggests that all specular images are from the start marked by their passage through an 'imperfect' female discourse.

The reiterated question in the novel is precisely one of mastery of language: 'Who speaks?' (1/579, 22/600, 42/620, 59/637, 110/688, 116/694). This is largely a matter of narrative voice, but it is also a question of accounting for subjectivity. It is Lacan's question in 'Subversion du sujet': 'Qui parle? quand il s'agit du sujet de l'inconscient' (1966: 800). The unconscious *ça* speaks, to be sure, but the role of the Lacanian unconscious in subjectivity is complex. The unconscious is 'la place de l'inter-dit', and the voice of the Other can only be spoken *through* the subject. When this happens—and it happens constantly—the classical subject is eclipsed, it undergoes

---

[13] In subjecting the diagram to playful manipulation, *Thru* also demonstrates the propensity of the signifier to 'slip'. The crossed arrows are manifest in the text as a variety of different structures that figure inversion, exchange, intersubjectivity, and subversion (the 'X' as chiasmus, circuit, crossing, and crossing out respectively).

the effects of 'fading', and what is spoken is in fact 'l'intra-dit d'un entre-deux-sujets' (800), a discontinuous, intersubjective voice (801).

In *S/Z* Barthes interprets Lacan's concept of the intersubjective voice in terms of narrative instance. He argues that in the 'modern text' it is language alone that speaks: 'Dans le texte moderne, les voix sont traitées jusqu'au déni de tout repère: le discours, ou mieux encore, le langage parle, c'est tout' (1970*b*: 48). But in a modern text such as *Thru* which mimics the classical narrator in order to counter classical conceptions of subjectivity and narrative voice, the narrator undergoes the effects of 'fading' peculiar to the traditional novel as well. In the 'texte classique', Barthes argues,

il arrive que . . . la voix se perd, comme si elle disparaissait dans le trou du discours. La meilleure façon d'imaginer le pluriel classique est alors d'écouter le texte comme un échange chatoyant de voix multiples, posées sur des ondes différentes et saisies par moments d'un *fading* brusque, dont la trouée permet à l'énonciation de migrer d'un point de vue à l'autre, sans prévenir. (48–9)

The multiple voices in *Thru* do often suffer the effects of 'fading', they fall into the 'hole' that Lacan and Barthes refer to, the 'blue lacuna' in the 'delirious discourse' (14/592, 26/604, 54/632, 59/637), of the novel.

For Emile Benveniste the peculiarity of 'histoire' as opposed to 'discours' is that it tells itself, no one 'speaks' (1966: 241). *Thru* literalizes this defining characteristic of narrative by constantly thwarting the reader's attempts to assign the text to a given 'voice'. Because of the ontological indeterminacy inherent in the narrative, it is often impossible to tell who an interlocutor is, or whether a scene is being remembered or merely imagined by one of the characters involved. It is even possible that either Armel or Larissa might be a figment of the other's imagination (8/586, 26/604, 53/631, 91/669). Matters get more complicated still when it becomes evident that a group of students may well be inventing them both as an assignment for a creative-writing course, until the students admit that they too are 'a pack of lies dreamt up by the unreliable narrator in love with the zeroist author in love with himself but absent in the nature of things, an etherised unauthorised other' (155/733). The narrating instance is an object of exchange in *Thru*, indeed it figures in Greimas's diagram as an 'O' (117/695). It is a role passed from character to character, each of whom makes different use of it.

Though we often think we know 'who speaks', we invariably find out that we are mistaken when a slip in narrative level catches us unawares.

But none of the above-mentioned theorists works this logic through in terms of the male–female relationship and the respective relation to language of men and women; this is accomplished by Irigaray and Kristeva, whose writings are interpolated into the novel, like the quotation from Shakespeare in *Between*, as the agent of parody rather than as its object. While there can be no doubt that the polyvalent image of the retrovizor has its source in Lacan's article,[14] a closer examination of the structure of the mirror image will reveal that it also resembles Irigaray's version of the constitution of the subject. Larissa is described in her narratorial capacity as 'some teller or Other' (27/605). Her narrative corresponds to the 'other eyes' which have 'psychic invisibility' (5/583, 14/592, 25/602, 26/603, 27/605, 32/610, 107/685, 120/69) and 'reflect nothing' (5/583, 72/650, 120/698). She writes to Armel that what matters in their narrative are 'the innumerable and ever-escaping levels of Utterance by the I who is not the I who says I' and she advises him to 'read Irigaray' on this concept (53/631).

In the article 'Communications linguistique et spéculaire: modèles génétiques et modèles pathologiques', Irigaray traces the constitution of the subject not to the symbolic mastery of the mother by the child, as do Freud and Lacan, but to a recognition of the positionality of subject and object in language use. This is only possible after the child has been forced to recognize itself as 'il', as an object of exchange between its parents. This objectification temporarily reduces it to zero, to the 'forme vide qui répond de la structure . . . Impliqué dans la communication comme sa possibilité de fonctionnement, ce troisième nombre . . . est un blanc, un vide, le lieu d'une exclusion, la négation qui permet à une structure d'exister en tant que tel' (1966: 17). When the subject emerges from its temporary death into the position of the 'je' it can then assume a name. The proper name thus figures 'ce paradoxe de l'engendrement du "un" à partir du "zéro" ' (18). But this 'one' of subjectivity is in

---

[14] The two best known quotations from this article: 'Qui parle?' and 'Che vuoi?' make multiple appearances in *Thru* (107/685, 145/723; 76/654, 97/675), and there are also numerous references to the 'dialectic of desire' (17/595, 22/600, 74/652, 81/659), as well as more oblique allusions to and paraphrases of the material the article includes. See esp. 17/595, 25/603, 44/622, 64–5/642–3, 72/650, 82/660, 103/681, 144/722.

fact double, for the subject experiences 'la disjonction du "je" lui-même en (je), sujet de l'énonciation, et "je", sujet de l'énoncé' (20), the first of which is invisible. The utterance is therefore always an enigma, a 'rébus, où le sujet s'occulte' (20). The specular experience recalls this passage through the zero by which the subject is engendered:

Face à son image le sujet s'éprouve comme situé au lieu de cette exclusion, non spécularisable . . . Ainsi, l'expérience spéculaire est-elle réminiscence de ce passage par le néant que suppose l'introduction du sujet dans l'ordre du signifiant, figuré au mieux par l'imposition du nom propre. (24)

Irigaray's version of the specular (imaginary) experience corresponds to the flawed retrovizor where the 'other eyes' represent the non-specularizable 'I' behind the discourse, the 'other author' who is never present in the text. This absence also figures the male definition of woman as lack, as an inverted image of man, as a hole in the male economy of signification (Irigaray 1974: 57), or 'O' (object and zero) as opposed to 'I' (singular subject and penis).

This might appear exorbitant, and indeed as a symbolic castration of the Oedipus complex it represents a partial subversion of Lacanian theory. But there is ample evidence in the novel, in addition to the flawed mirror, to suggest that it is Irigaray's version, not Lacan's, that functions as *Thru*'s theoretical 'deep structure'. The Master (borrowed from Diderot's *Jacques le fataliste*) tells a somnolent Jacques about Kristeva's use of Irigaray's pronominal framework to describe the role of the narrator:

out of the zero where the author is situated, both excluded and included, the third person is generated, pure signifier of the subject's experience. Later this third person acquires a proper name, figure of this paradox, one out of zero, name out of anonymity, visualisation of the fantasy into a signifier that can be looked at, seen. You should read Kristeva that's what she says. (69/647)[15]

Jacques's Master follows Kristeva in her argument that, just as the subject is eclipsed or subverted in the process of its creation, so the author must pass through the same 'zero' in order for the reader to be able to participate as receptor in the economy of communication established by the novel:

[15] This paraphrase is actually a combination of Kristeva's and Irigaray's texts; cf. Kristeva 1969: 95 and Irigaray 1966: 17–18.

the construction of a character has to pass through a death, necessary to the structuring of the subject as subject of utterance, and for his insertion into the circuit of signifiers, I mean the narration. It is therefore the recipient, you Jacques, or anyone, the other, who transforms the subject into author, making him pass through this zero-stage, this negation, this exclusion which is the author. (69/647)[16]

It is at this point that the Master realizes that Armel Santores and Larissa Toren are near anagrams, except that 'I' is missing from his name and 'me' from hers (69/647). The characters and their conjugal disjunction have indeed been generated out of a play of pronouns, out of 'words on a page', for it is due to the lack they experience in each other that they are not able to constitute themselves through each other as subjects.

Irigaray's analyses of the use of pronouns by hysterics and obsessives (1966: 29–31; 1967: 55–68) reveal that whereas obsessives are unable to say 'me' because they are caught in a specular image of themselves in which there is no object, only an undifferentiated self (Irigaray's 'on'), hysterics are unable to say 'I' because they are unable to complete the trajectory through the other that would allow them access to full subjectivity. It thus becomes clear that the play of pronouns in the chiasmus of the narrative circuit through which the subject plays out its split existence does indeed function as an 'elementary structure of signification' in *Thru*, though not in the way Greimas intended.

For a female story-teller such as Larissa, the act of narration is therefore a risky proposition, for her story is always in danger of being labelled a 'hystery'.[17] The 'crossword' on page 6/584 weaves together voices from a number of other texts in a 'hysterical' imitation of male story-telling. The uppermost portion of this page suggests the link between female discourse and fiction:

---

[16] cf. Kristeva 1969: 96–7 and Irigaray 1966: 19. The reader is the radical other through which the text must eventually speak. As the paraphrase of Kristeva's concept of narrative voice suggests, the reader ultimately assumes the place of the 'I'. Shlomith Rimmon-Kenan describes *Thru* as a novel that 'employs the reader's metalanguage as its own object-language. The reader thereby becomes an element of the very text he is reading, losing his secure external position' (1982: 28).

[17] In 'Woman as a Semiotic Object' Brooke-Rose comments on the etymological link that ties 'hysteria' to 'uterus' and hence to women, making it, like retroversion of the uterus, a distinctly female disorder (1991a: 241).

```
never        the          lesS
this is                    noT
                           nO
             (My)
the       h  Y  s  T  e  R  y        of        The
             S           Y                                   Eye
             T
             E
             R
             Y
                                                             . . .
```

The message is enigmatic: 'nevertheless this is not no the my/hystery of the eye'. The 'hystery of the eye' is presumably a reference to Bataille's story 'L'Histoire de l'oeil', a story of enucleation, which is, of course in Freudian terms equivalent to castration.[18] The 'Histoire' of Bataille's title has been appropriated by the female voice which turns it into 'hystery'—a 'bad copy' of the original, and an enigmatic, repressed female story, a mystery.[19] The passage could be read as 'this is not *my* "Histoire de l'oeil", but a male story that I have been subjected to', or as 'this is not "L'Histoire de l'oeil" but my story of the eye which is not a his-story but a hystery, i.e. a female story'. The play of negatives: 'never', 'not', 'no', causes an additional ambiguity. Is 'no' added to 'not' for emphasis, or do the two negatives cancel each other out? What precisely is being disclaimed or denied, the story or its possession? Given the fact that insistent negation in dreams and speech is interpreted by psychoanalysis as resistance to a truth which the conscious mind would sooner deny, are the negatives not perhaps to be disregarded altogether? And given the identification in the text of 'eye' with 'I',[20] the passage could also be read as 'this is not the hystery of the I', in other words: 'this is (not) the (hi)story of a hysterical subject'. Not suprisingly, this indeterminacy is itself the main characteristic of 'hysterical' discourse, which is never willing to assert anything definitively (Irigaray 1966: 29–30; 1967: 67–8).

---

[18] References to stories with the same theme are threaded through the lower portion of the page.

[19] The play on mystery–hysteria is also an oblique tribute to Hélène Cixous, who often brings together the two concepts in her writing. For further discussion of the relation between the two authors, see Chap. 6 below.

[20] The four eyes in the driving mirror become four 'I's united by a pair of crossed arrows' on page 7/585. Cf. 'I-contact' (620), 'gouge out the I' (17/595).

But if the move from history to hystery were simply a matter of role reversal it would be relatively unproblematic. In fact, as the Lacanian schema indicates, the self and the other are caught in a more complicated relationship. The relationship between Jacques and his Master is founded on a tacit agreement that the roles they occupy are the reverse of what they appear to be, but when Jacques tries to articulate this he risks losing his power which depends on its going unacknowledged. Transferred to the realm of gender relations, this would describe the state of affairs in which a woman has influence over a man and manipulates his discourses, but is allowed this power only as long as she agrees not to flaunt it and remains in the position of silent partner with no autonomous voice. She is then reduced to the unconscious side of man, his Other who speaks through him. In *Thru* this condition is posed as a choice between two masters: 'couldn't she be happy with y o u in the orbit of an eye and no referent without? Or with the Other with he passed into hystery within?' (12/590). Woman's inability to be content with either living in the orbit of the male 'I' or repressing her desire into 'hystery' is a result of the fact that male desire is an essentially narcissistic 'Pygmalion urge' to invent woman in its own image, while permitting the male subject the freedom to enjoy multiple reflections. 'If the woman objects she is being hysterical and making a scene' (58/636), an accusation that is demonstrated when Larissa and Armel quarrel about his extra-marital sex life and he tells her to 'stop this hysterical rewriting of history' (76/654). It is precisely this rewriting of 'history' as 'hystery' that is forbidden to woman. She is not allowed her own story, her version is by definition a retroversion, an imperfect, displaced version that appears in the wrong place in the mirror.

In a recent article on her fiction, Christine Brooke-Rose describes *Thru* as 'the only truly deconstructionist novel' she knows of (1988a: 133). By 'deconstructionist' Brooke-Rose does not simply refer to the fact that her novel 'deconstructs' itself. This it manifestly does, but it is aware that it is not unique in doing so (whence the many references to *Tristam Shandy* and *Jacques le fataliste*, archetypes of the novel that undermines its own stated project of telling a story). *Thru* is 'deconstructionist' in the additional sense that it places itself in multiple positions within the field of literary discourse. Not only does it constitute the object of its own criticism, it also contains a number of theories of this criticism, and in a recursive move that can truly be termed deconstructive, it presents criticism of these theories and it narrativizes this criticism. Just as it collapses the hierarchy of narrative levels, so the novel un-builds the hierarchy of metatextual discourses that has come lately to encrust itself around 'metafictional' novels. It does this by folding the entire structure back into the narrative. What Derrida describes as the 'double jeu' (1972c: 14) of deconstruction is thus accomplished: the hierarchical relation between narrative theory and its object is reversed, and at the same time the subject–object relation is itself challenged, illustrating Lacan's widely disseminated dictum 'il n'y a pas de métalanguage' (1966: 813).

But if many of the theories with which the novel grapples have their roots in or near the work of Lacan, Lacan's text does not escape the double move of appropriation and subversion which characterizes the feminist enterprise. Irigaray's strategy of *mimétisme* makes use of Lacanian conceptual tools simultaneously to appropriate and to undermine discursive authority (including that of Lacan himself). It is for this reason that this approach proved so helpful to Brooke-Rose when she chose to turn her creative attention to narratology. She too exhibits both a fascination and a scepticism with regard to structuralist theories of the text, manifest in *Thru* as a healthy mistrust of theory whenever it becomes over-systematic. The subversive tactics deployed in the novel are a direct consequence of the male construction of gender roles within the discourse of narrative theory. Both as social models and as models of narrative functioning, structuralist theories have gained wide currency within the institutional framework that determines how literature is read and the role it plays in society. *Thru* demonstrates by means of a parodic conflation and manipulation of selected literary theories the problems inherent in such an approach to literature, and it uncovers the value-laden stories which subtend it.

Amalgamemnon: Women and Myth

In *Amalgamemnon* the technique of *mimétisme* is generalized as the awareness of gender bias becomes more prominent. If *Thru* may be read as a deconstruction of the androcentric preconceptions in the theories of certain structuralists, *Amalgamemnon* can be seen as a burlesque exposition of the procedures of exclusion operative in dominant versions of truth about the world, from the texts of antiquity to modern-day news broadcasts on the radio. As Foucault and others have demonstrated, the interpretation of information in contemporary society follows a set of discursive criteria which determine what is classified as objectively true and what is seen as subjective opinion or fiction.[21] *Amalgamemnon* suggests that this split between fact and fiction corresponds to spheres of action and influence appropriate for men and for women. Woman's domain is that of private relations and psychological matters, while men deal with the public concerns of politics and economic affairs. Herodotus's *Histories* and Aeschylus's *Agamemnon* serve as touchstones for Brooke-Rose's novel, for in going back to the classical period, it is able to return to the point at which these distinctions began to be associated with different ways of talking and writing attributed to fact and to fiction.

The 'hysterical rewriting of history' of which Armel accuses Larissa in *Thru* is literalized in *Amalgamemnon* where the founding text of history is literally rewritten. By selective citation the novel foregrounds the link between Herodotus's epistemological ambiguities and his ambivalent attitude toward the role of women in society. Aeschylus's tragedy represents a loss of faith in the prophetic voice of women and the consequence of that loss for the Western discursive tradition. The mythical story of Cassandra functions as an allegory for the fate of alternative forms of language use; truthful but 'unheeded and unhinged' (12,144), the figure of Cassandra is an example of the extreme to which women's frustration at not being heard can push them.

The principal voice of *Amalgamemnon* is Mira Enketei, a university lecturer in the humanities who is on the verge of being made redundant due to the seeming irrelevence of her field in present-day society. Her conjectures as to her possible future occupation lead to a number of wild escapades involving kidnapping and terrorism, as well as to more humble pursuits such as pig-farming. These are intercalated with long nights of insomnia which she spends on the sofa with the radio and Herodotus, having fled her snoring lover Willy (later Wally).

In relation to both Willy and Herodotus, Mira sees herself falling into the role of Cassandra who was cursed by Apollo to have her prophecies ignored because she had refused to yield to his desire. Cassandra's rage finds its outlet in the distortion of male discourse to the point at which communication falters. She is described by the Argive elders as speaking in riddles because they fail to understand

[21] See esp. Foucault 1971 and Bourdieu 1982.

her predictions. Clytemnestra thinks her mad because her exasperation at not being understood or believed drives Cassandra to a
hysterical frenzy of gestures and grimaces (*Agamemnon*, ll. 1061–5).
Amalgamemnon takes Cassandra's voice as representative of the way
in which the discourse of women is seen by society at large.
'Cassandra Castratrix' (119) is both the breaker of men (Cass-andra)
and the powerless captive. Not only do her efforts to assert her
freedom from male domination lead her into the hands of another
man, but she is also punished for her resistance by having her words
deemed valueless, just as today 'pseudo-escaperoutes will so lightly
turn sado-escape, and . . . women's very freedom will so easily be
used against them by even moderately clever men' (12). Though
women are typically characterized as prophets of doom, Mira's
modest demand in relation to both personal and political situations is
'let us recognize one another before annihilating one another' (15,
136; variations: 20, 74, 136). But it is suggested that even this is not
possible, for in refusing to recognize their autonomy, men often
effectively annihilate women from the start.

Mira's only possible recourse is to a parodic ventriloquy of male
modes of communication which subtly undermines them by using
word play to expose the 'fictions' that underpin supposedly objective
information and 'expert' analyses from Herodotus's time to the
present. From one point of view this is a defiant retreat into the
'utterly other discourse' (5, 15, 143) of Cassandra who yields to her
penchant for lexical distortion because she has been forced into an
impossible position. But it is also a vindication of the creative
manipulation of language and a revalorization of the traditional
relation between women and fiction.

The distinction between public and private spheres of existence
has been used for centuries to exclude women from the activities
through which larger social processes are effected; it has made of
them goods to be protected, the stakes for which wars are fought by
men. This segmentation of spheres of action and influence along the
lines of gender difference is reflected in the radio programming in
the novel. There is a sharp distinction between news broadcasts in
which men tell the facts about the world and phone-in programmes
run by women in which people discuss their personal problems.
When one caller transgresses this line of demarcation, asking the
presenter Dolores what she thinks of a terrorists' kidnapping, she
replies: 'That would be a little outside the scope of this programme

Charlie, there'll be experts commenting again in the morning to tell you what to think of it, why don't you talk to me about yourself . . . ' (80). The realm of public discourse is that of events, expert diagnoses, and scientific prognoses, whereas the private sphere is that of opinion and anecdote, subjective reaction, and cultural mythology which is devalorized by its implicit feminization.

In order to challenge this complex of interlocking polarities, *Amalgamemnon* goes back to a time when the two domains, though distinct, were not yet differentiated by separate modes of narrative, back to Herodotus, the first prose artist and 'the father of fibstory' (22, 113). Out of Herodotus's attempt to distinguish truth from myth arose our own codification of discursive types, but in his text this structure is still in a state of flux. Herodotus has long been regarded as a mythographer as much as a historian, for he records not just the bare facts, but the multiple versions of events he has gathered from a variety of sources. Where these are lacking he readily substitutes rumours, conjecture, and legend, as well as his own hypotheses. The *Histories* is particularly relevant today because it represents the common discursive origin of historiography, sociology, anthropology, ethnography, and prose fiction.

Herodotus opens the *Histories* with a brief statement of intent: 'Herodotus of Halicarnassus, his *Researches* are here set down to preserve the memory of the past by putting on record the astonishing achievements both of our own and of other peoples; and more particularly, to show how they came into conflict' (41). His aims are thus established from the outset, both to record the evidence he has gathered and to evaluate it for the purposes of determining the truth. But rather than starting straight away with 'the facts', he begins with the traditional account of the cause of the wars which he rejects because he has no way of substantiating it. This is the story of a quarrel over women involving a series of abductions and retributions which culminate in Paris's kidnapping of Helen. Herodotus cannot bring himself to believe in a story which gives as the cause of centuries of rivalry 'nothing worse than woman-stealing on both sides' (42), for he does not think the Greeks could possibly have gone to war over anything so trivial, and indeed he appears to concur with the Persian view that 'no young woman allows herself to be abducted if she does not wish to be' (42).[22] But this pre-history he rejects

[22] cf. *Amalgamemnon* 16.

serves as a symbolic equivalent of the narrative of multiple usurpations and misappropriations of territory that occupies the following 600 pages. This is possible because in the cultural tradition of the West, as described and exemplified by Lévi-Strauss, the exchange of women is figured as the source of all exchange. Herodotus's account of the 'true' history of the Medic wars can be read as an elaborate repetition or working out of the 'truth' about misappropriation encapsulated in 'fictional' form in the first two pages.

It is not fortuitous, then, that *Amalgamemnon* should begin its reading of Herodotus with a citation of the tales of abduction he himself rejects as fanciful: 'Herodotus, the Phoenicians kidnapping Io and the Greeks plagiarizing the king of Tyre's daughter Europe' (5). Like the quotation of Greimas in *Thru*, *Amalgamemnon*'s abduction of Herodotus's text is clearly an act of retribution. The word 'plagiarize' (meaning originally 'to kidnap') makes this explicit: Mira denounces the sexist bias of the *Histories* by quoting the text selectively, cross-examining it, altering it to suit her purpose, and interweaving it with bits of the radio news.

Unlike many of his successors, Herodotus was a firm believer in the explanatory power of oracles, and he frequently cites their predictions in lieu of causal arguments.[23] But *Amalgamemnon* traces in the *Histories* a pattern of male appropriation of the oracle's discourse. Either she is relegated to the status of mere spokesperson, transmitter of the divine *logos* of Apollo: 'I'll know it'll be he who'll end up cassandring me, precisely in nomansland where the male gods will ever take over the pythian oracles, turning them into twittering spokespersons' (136; variation: 14); or she is in some way masculinized: 'Pedasus will get warning of impending disaster through the priestess of Athene growing a long beard, I'll read to him to make him laugh and he will, and talk with his sidetrack mind . . .' (14).[24]

This juxtaposition of the myth of Athena growing a beard with the strategies Mira employs to bolster Willy's ego points to the fact that in each case a female voice transforms itself into a voice men will trust. Woman's ability to assimilate the language of men and man's inability to fathom that of women is craftily demonstrated by a

---

[23] Carolyn Dewald counts forty-five occasions on which the Pythian oracle alone is consulted in the *Histories* (1981: 111).

[24] cf. Herodotus I 12.

selective summary of Herodotus's account of the oracles of Dodona and his description of the Amazons:

> And yet the story which the people of Dodona will tell about the black dove from Egypt becoming their oracle would surely arise because the foreign woman's language would sound to them like the twittering of birds. And later the dove will speak with a human voice because of course the woman will stop twittering and learn to talk intelligibly. Similarly the young Scythians will be unable to learn the language of the Amazons but the women will succeed in picking up theirs, and therefore disappear. (11)[25]

As Brooke-Rose observes elsewhere, the ancient oracle is the only instance of an institutional valorization of women's voice as truthful (1991a: 241). But by forcing it to conform to 'male' discursive norms, society succeeds in bringing oracular speech within the realm of 'male' criteria of veracity. The novel challenges this 'amalgamation' by turning 'male' discursive strategies against themselves.

Amalgamemnon is parodic in Genette's sense in that it makes punctual and systematic alterations on a pre-existent 'noble' text of the past, and in Bakhtin's sense because with regard to sex roles its 'orientation' is directly opposed to that of Herodotus. As in *Between* and *Thru*, the works invoked are divided into agent and object of parody. The voice of 'Cassandra Castratrix' is adopted strategically to perform an operation of creative mut(il)ation on the text of Herodotus. This procedure involves two basic linguistic techniques: the anteriorization of discourse with respect to the events it describes, and lexical distortion.

First, the 'true' discourse of male authority is defamiliarized by being removed from the present and preterite forms of the indicative and transposed into the future, the conditional, the imperative, and the subjunctive.[26] In the interview quoted above, Brooke-Rose discusses her use of the negative in *Between* as a means of asserting and not asserting something. A statement that something does not happen both creates an event and abolishes it in the same act (1976k: 21–2). *Thru* makes use of similar techniques at the level of narrative.

---

[25] cf. Herodotus 152 and 308.

[26] Brooke-Rose describes *Amalgamemnon* as a novel 'written in the future and conditional tenses, the subjunctive or imperative moods' (1991a: 8; cf. 1988a: 136). In fact, in modern English the subjunctive is expressed either by the bare infinitive (present subjunctive) or by the preterite (past subjunctive), verb-forms that are not used in the novel. By 'subjunctive', Brooke-Rose evidently refers to the modal auxiliary verbs (can, could, shall, should, will, would, may, might, must) that abound in the text. These are often used when a subjunctive would be used in, for example, French.

But the problem with this type of creation-as-destruction is that the negative aspect is easily equated with nihilism. Moreover, the positive–negative opposition is inescapably binary, and any text structured on this polarity will be, like *Thru*, a constant oscillation between the two poles. In *Amalgamemnon* Brooke-Rose gets round this problem by using non-realized tenses and moods. The result is a text that operates in the mode of potentiality. This is what Irigaray calls the hysterical 'comme si' (1974: 70), a caricature of the discourse of the (male) subject which is complete or 'finalized'.[27] All 'events' in the novel are virtual; it is irrelevant to debate whether Mira imagines buying a pig farm with her severance pay or whether it 'really' happens, because nothing is ever 'really' accomplished.

In *A Rhetoric of the Unreal* Brooke-Rose cites Genette's claim that anterior time is a rarity in narrative, a mode reserved for subordinate accounts of dreams and prophecies (1981: 329).[28] She says the reason for this is 'the need to believe that the event recounted actually took place, or is taking place: no one believes a prophet, and even a prediction needs to be realised within the narrative for sense and interest' (329). But she gives Maurice Roche's novel *Compact* (1966) as an example of a narrative which uses the future tense effectively for purposes other than prophecy. In *Compact* the future entails 'a fundamental undermining of the reader's need to believe in fictional events . . . the detail and intensity are such that we do believe that what is predicted not only will occur but is occurring/has occurred, while at the same time not occurring, abolished, a mere fiction of words' (329). Though she points out that *Compact* is not consistent in its use of the future, this description anticipates the development of the tense in Brooke-Rose's own novel. Just as the constant circulation of narrative voice in *Thru* makes the reader at all times aware of the fact that the characters are just 'words on a page', so the use of the future in *Amalgamemnon* operates to maintain the reader's awareness of the fictional status of the events described.[29]

[27] Though presumably not a conscious reference to Irigaray, the phrase 'we'll go on as if' is a frequent refrain in *Amalgamemnon* (7, 12, 15, 17, 18, 21, 61, 80, 135, 136).

[28] See Genette 1972: 231–2. In a recent discussion of her novels, Brooke-Rose implies that one of the reasons she uses the future throughout *Amalgamemnon* is to prove Genette wrong in his generalizations (1991a: 8).

[29] The effect of 'de-realization' in *Amalgamemnon* is not to be confused with Lacan's structure of retrovision which has as its temporal correlative the *futur antérieur*. The future perfect is not used in *Amalgamemnon* for the reason that it foresees completion, it is oracular, and Brooke-Rose is trying in this novel to 'avoid the oracular' (1991a: 8).

The second discursive strategy used in the novel is the portman-teau technique exemplified by the title. The combination of the words 'Agamemnon' and 'amalgam' mimes on the linguistic plane the process by which Mira's Agamemnon, her amalga-mate, assimilates her to himself and denies her autonomous identity.[30] In an interview contemporary with the novel, Brooke-Rose explains that '*Amalgamemnon* is in fact about the violence which we all commit when we're always trying to amalgamate people and put them in a category' (1984*b*), but the novel also turns this strategy back on itself and uses 'amalgamation' to shatter categories.

The specificity of the lexical amalgam and its variation, the pun, is that they partake simultaneously of two different contexts which they join on grounds that are quite obviously a function of the free play of the signifier. For Jonathan Culler, the pun provides a demonstration of language's inherent instability, mutability, and susceptibility to spurious motivation based on chance phonemic associations. This last procedure, 'the exploitation of formal resemblance to establish connections of meaning', Culler characterizes as 'the basic activity of literature' (1988: 4), and it is in this sense that the pun can be seen as a cognitive model which accounts for the 'literariness' of even the most rigorous forms of language use. Whereas in *The Languages of Love* the pun is indicative of the tragic breach between the human and the divine, in *Thru* it is described as 'free, anarchic, a powerful instrument to explode the civilization of the sign and all its stable, reassuring definitions' (29/607). The pun challenges models of cognition based on analytic reasoning and proposes instead a conception of language as a force capable of altering its object.

The fact that language can be used in this way as a political tool is a key to understanding the link between politics in the public sphere and personal politics. In *Amalgamemnon* the pun and the lexical amalgam or portmanteau word work in the same way as discursive slips work in *Out* and mistranslation works in *Between* to create metaphors by revealing structural parallels between disparate discourses. As in *Between*, this technique serves to map the terminology of geopolitical conflict on to personal relations:

And since even a polygonal story should have at least two sides in all intergnashional farewell orgies, how about packing it in and having a bash at

---

[30] Amalgamemnon can also be read as Agamemnon + mal, amalgam + no men, amalga + Memnon, am + megaloman, etc.

normal behaviour eh, so as to get bashed again as whipping boy despite my morseled-out attempts to break free or go shiating on, turning the other cheek to sheer cheek as sitting target for the unclear missiles of affreux dizzy acts or as wailing wall of blame beyond the demarcation line or bowstring frontier that will boomerang back and much joy may it give me. (102)

Amalgamemnon's conflation of these two domains through the transformation of language prefigures a possible transformation of the discursive systems which maintain distinctions between public and private, fact and fiction.

But on another level the linguistic acrobatics which the novel displays provide Mira with verbal strategies that enable her to cope with her fear for the future and her personal situation in the present. In her relations with Willy she has constantly to choose between her 'postface' and her 'preface': 'I shall put on my postface and mimagree, unless I put on my preface and go through the routine' (16,138). The 'postface' is both a po-faced stoicism when confronted with male egotism, and the face of 'mimagreement' (14) whereby Mira pretends to allow herself to be amalgamated to Willy. It is a 'post' face because it mimes the finality of male discourse, the self-assured certainty of the preterite. The 'preface', on the other hand, is the language of the novel in which a statement is always a preface to that which it purports to describe, since only the language itself is ever realized.

If the 'postface' is the attitude of feigned female acquiescence to male views, the 'preface' is that which objects, that which goes through the tiresome 'routine' of explaining exactly why these views are objectionable. The first attitude involves a conscious repression of her own identity on Mira's part, whereas the second attitude, though supposedly more contentious, often leads Willy forcibly to repress her 'disagreeable' qualities: 'All my objections, which I'll put as genuine unacceptabilities of my cassandring person, which no man'll take, will be swept under his magic carpet with the ho-ho joke if no man will and I will, what am I?' (136). Willy sees himself as the beneficent saviour who will 'irrigate' her 'emotional desert' (17,138), and any attempt by her to suggest that she might be happier without him is 'blackmarked against me as pretentiousness' (136). Like the Trojans, Willy simply laughs away Mira's 'cassandring' voice. The only viable alternative is to 'mimagree' otherwise, to mime agreement in such a way as to contest subtly the authority of the language used rather than launching a direct challenge to male discursive authority.

The fictional is a role Mira is forced into; she has no option but to tell a story about herself. Yet if she plays at telling the truth, she also plays with the telling of the truth. Willy's synthetic abstractions which generalize and falsify are countered by her analytic and critical rewriting of Herodotus. By exposing the story of the silencing of women which underlies Herodotus's project, the novel demonstrates that 'originary myths' are at the heart of factual descriptions about the world, and that in this sense women, by virtue of their historical ties with the discourses of fiction, have a privileged relation to the voice of knowledge.

Luce Irigaray maintains that for her 'l'enjeu n'est pas d'élaborer une nouvelle théorie dont la femme serait le *sujet* ou l'*objet*, mais d'enrayer la machinerie théorique elle-même, de suspendre sa prétention à la production d'une vérité et d'un sens par trop univoques' (1977: 75). One of the means she advocates for 'jamming the machinery' is the disruption of syntax (73). This is because the 'syntax' of theory, the logic on which it is based, is at the root of structures which have historically been used to trivialize, marginalize, and devalue the discourse of women, to pass it off at best as a mere fiction, and at worst as an illicit form of language-use or one in poor taste, like the pun. If they are to avoid falling into the theoretical machinery that perpetuates such stereotypes, women are obliged constantly to dodge the conceptual apparatuses that seek to mould their language. But this 'jay-walking' or 'side-stepping' can result in unforeseen discoveries as the logic of juxtaposition, simultaneity, and other 'lateral' processes are explored.

Rather than rejecting objectionable discourses past and present, this approach entails an unstable coexistence with that which it contests, and it manifests this textually as the parodic adulteration, manipulation, or 'doctoring' of another's language. *Between, Thru,* and *Amalgamemnon* exhibit an increasing awareness of the gendering of discourse—both the implicit gendering in Western culture of different modes of speaking and writing, and the explicit efforts by certain women to appropriate for 'the feminine' modes of language use that are inherently interrogative. That there is a necessary link between this form of discourse and 'fiction' is grounded both in the historical links between them and in their contemporary utility as means of contesting the legitimacy of the language of authority. The three novels chart an attempt to develop linguistic techniques which represent the current state of affairs and at the same time challenge it by enlisting subversive laughter as a tool to destabilize fixed systems and tear away their protective layers of discursive convention. The concern manifest in these novels with the status of fictional discourse and its relation to the discourses of 'truth' lays the ground for the examination of the place of the novel in contemporary society which Brooke-Rose undertakes in the Intercom Quartet.

4. *Amalgamemnon, Xorandor, Verbivore*, and *Textermination*: Technology and the Novel

> I can imagine, I suppose, the binary languages of the computers making love to each other.
>
> (Brooke-Rose 1976*k*: 18)

Amalgamemnon, Xorandor, Verbivore, and *Textermination* form what Christine Brooke-Rose has tentatively called the 'Intercom Quartet'. The Quartet picks up the novel where *Thru* leaves it, dissected and decentred *in vitro*, and returns it to the social and historical context out of which it arose. The four novels deal with the status of the genre relative to the public discourses of the media and the discourses of specialized expertise in the domain of communications technology, both of which have become contemporary discourses of authority. Each warns of the consequences of failing to recognize the merits of the novel and the fictionality of many of the non-literary forms of representation which threaten to supplant it.

With the Quartet Brooke-Rose moves away from abstract theories and scientific models as a source of new concepts and toward the consequences of the technological innovations which advances in pure science have made possible. Her closer engagement with concrete social change has been accompanied by a *rapprochement* with the conventions of science fiction. The Quartet is distinct from most examples of this genre, however, in that its focus is firmly fixed on its own status within a world which is increasingly under the control of non-verbal forms of communication. But as the social role of technology changes, so must the genre whose task has traditionally been to keep one step ahead of science as we know it.[1] In an article on science fiction, Jean Baudrillard maintains that the traditional mode of the genre depended on a simulation of expansion

---

[1] See Chap. 6 below for a brief survey of certain science-fiction novels which share the Quartet's concerns and methods.

that is no longer feasible in the contemporary world. This is because all possible fictions of scientific progress are virtual in present-day technology, which has taken over the function of 'productive' simulation. The only recourse for science fiction is to turn to 'simulacres de simulation, fondées sur l'information, le modèle, le jeu cybernétique' (1981: 179). The Quartet can be read as a 'simulacrum of simulation' in this sense: it reveals the simulated nature of the projections, speculations, and reconstructions fed us by the oral media and the role of story-telling in all so-called 'objective' compilations of factual information.

Though the novels of the Quartet are linked by common characters and motifs, they cannot be said to have a continuous story-line. Their common concern is rather the effect of technological innovation on our thought processes and our ability to communicate. Each in its own way, the four works examine the role of the novel in an age in which electronic networks have begun to overtake the printed codex as the archetypical manifestation of the word. Though the novel is not the sole domain of either narrative or fiction, in contemporary Western culture it exemplifies both. By foregrounding the historical specificity of novelistic discourse, Brooke-Rose is able to explore both narrative and fiction in what are, from the point of view of contemporary discursive categories, their most characteristic guises.

The distinctive features of the novel as a genre are threefold: it is written, it is fictional, and its principle device is that of narrative. According to this definition we are living in a particularly 'novelistic' age. First, undecidability and paradox are the basis of the 'new sciences' which have made possible the technological innovations we currently enjoy, and written narrative is uniquely suited to accommodating logically impossible situations and mixing heterogeneous ontological postulates. Secondly, even physics, the most rigorous of sciences, has recognized the fact that it is an elaborate fiction or secondary modelling system, not a re-creation of its object. Finally, it is becoming increasingly evident that scientific enquiry is an ongoing narrative through which generations of thinkers have sought to understand the world around them, and also that narrative as a mode of knowledge can be used as a means of accommodating the logical paradoxes of contemporary sciences. But despite the widespread awareness of these three characteristics among those who analyse the practice of science, the institutions through which technological advances are implemented and disseminated tend to present the results of scientific research as facts or codified knowledge, ignoring their inherent paradoxes, their fictional status, and the cognitive evolution which made them possible.

In Brooke-Rose's view, the role of the novel as a self-consciously written, fictional, narrative genre is to remind other discourses that they too possess the same attributes of logical paradox, fictionality, and narrativity. Furthermore, if we recognize that the discourses of codified knowledge are not fundamentally dissimilar to novelistic discourse, it becomes evident that the novel has validity as a cognitive tool which fosters individual creativity and interpersonal communication. The 'intercom' of the Quartet's title refers not only to technological developments in information-processing systems, but also to how these developments have affected intercourse between individuals in everyday situations, and how this has in turn made possible a new role in society for narrative fiction.

In *The Act of Reading*, Wolfgang Iser argues that the literary work should be understood as a means of communication rather than as a representation of the world: 'It is a vital feature of literary texts that they do not lose their ability to communicate; indeed, many of them can still speak even when their message has long since passed into history and their meaning no longer seems to be of importance' (1978: 13). But Brooke-Rose is careful to point out that a novel is not an act of oral exchange, and that most communication models are thus inappropriate to it (1991*a*: 70–1). The novel needs to be understood in the context of the modes of textual communication which have been made possible by the digital revolution. With the advent of word-processing and other cybernetic-based means of producing and distributing text, the possibility for interaction between writer and reader increases, while the distinction between them becomes ever more blurred. The text itself is transformed into a protean tool for unfolding ideas and responding to those of others. Only a conception of the novel as an evolving genre will be able to take the potential of this development into account, and it is such a conception which the Quartet adumbrates.

Yet the Quartet also hints at the threat technology poses to the novel. We tend to describe our lives using images from the conceptual languages with which we are most familiar, and the metaphor of life as a novel or the world as a book has yielded in contemporary culture to cybernetic models.[2] A fear that 'techne . . . will soon be silenced by the high technology' (*Amalgamemnon* 5) lurks behind the futuristic tales of these novels which echo the suspicions first hinted at in *Out* of the intentions of those who implement technological innovation. In the pessimistic scenario, the writing of fiction is a last-ditch effort to salvage humanist discursive forms. The contemporary relevance of narrative fiction is one of the things that is at stake in the technological 'revolution', and Brooke-Rose addresses the issue from a perspective that is both sceptical and hopeful, ludic and apocalyptic.

In what follows, the three main attributes of the novel—its written, narrative, and fictional status—will be treated in turn in relation to the four novels which comprise the Quartet. *Amalgamemnon* inaugurates the theme of fiction versus fact. As we saw in Chapter 3, it takes a historical approach to the origin of factual narrative (Herodotus) and the origin of fiction as discredited language (Aeschylus), comparing these to their modern-day equivalents in the oral media. *Xorandor* examines the narrative aspect of the novel by exploring the theoretical problems of story-telling from the point of view of children whose minds have been formed by their exposure to computers; here, techniques specific to narrative are shown to be central to even the most logical of sciences. *Verbivore* focuses on writing as a form of communication: it posits a society in which writing has become outmoded and is then rediscovered, prompting a renewal of discursive modes peculiar to the novel. *Textermination* examines the fictionality of the novel from the point of view of the reading process.

In all four novels the link between technology and narrative technique is characterized in terms of innovations in both areas which challenge the commonsensical conception of what is possible. All four employ the variable narrative voice found in *Thru*, and *Amalgamemnon*, *Verbivore*, and *Textermination* contain metalepses. This return to the pre-nineteenth-century use of anti-realist techniques is accompanied by a recognition of the wealth of discursive forms which the more narrowly conceived realist novel has left untapped. Changes in technology have made it possible to imagine means of communication that would have been unthinkable two hundred years ago: radio broadcasts, instant word-processing, telephone conversations, and so on. Brooke-Rose incorporates these

---

[2] For an analysis of the social and intellectual effects of this transition, see Paulson 1989.

into her novels but refuses to subordinate them to the narrative conventions of realism. In so doing she demonstrates that the potential scope of the novel is enriched, not exhausted, by technological development, and that, conceived as an 'open' and heterogeneous genre, the novel still has a significant role to play in contemporary society, both as a mode of knowledge and as a means of communication.

Amalgamemnon: Fiction and the Media

The genre of the novel long competed with 'the news' as a primary means of circulating information about the world, but its advantage as a source of entertainment as well as information failed to maintain its edge over the less demanding oral media of radio and television. The novel then began to stake its claim as a genre which could give insight into the human psyche that no news broadcast or film ever could. This led, however, to a drastic reduction in the scope of its subject-matter and fostered the gender-coded distinction discussed in Chapter 3 between the public sphere of events and discoveries presented as factual statements on the one hand, and on the other hand the inner world of psycho-social dramas presented as narrative fiction. The consequence of this division is one of the problems Brooke-Rose set out to examine in *Amalgamemnon*: 'the crisis today is that we have fictions which no one admits to be fictions, whereas before people had myths, people had religions, and so on, and a lot of it was believed in as a matter of faith, whereas now everything is presented as real, and it is no more real than the myths of before' (1987*d*). As demonstrated in Chapter 3, the future and conditional tenses of *Amalgamemnon* put all 'facts' about the world under the sign of 'fiction'. If we follow Bakhtin in tracing the origin of the novel back to Menippean satire, this unusual use of tense can be understood as a typical novelistic device in that it brings the 'completed' past into the present and 'contemporizes' it.[3] *Amalgamemnon* foregrounds the 'novelistic' aspect of contemporary society by using the future tense and other conspicuously fictional devices to reveal the speculative and constructed nature of the supposedly factual information conveyed through the media.

[3] Bakhtin sees Menippean satire as a 'confrontation of times' (1981: 26), and he stresses its orientation toward the future: 'The inconclusive present begins to feel closer to the future than to the past' (26).

Yet *Amalgamemnon* is steeped in anxiety about the fate of the novel and other forms of individual creativity in a world of secondary orality where humanist pursuits are fast becoming obsolete.[4] It is not so much the production of the novel in the literal sense as its production in the social sense that is at issue. There is a tangible risk involved in introducing a novel, and a difficult novel at that, into a world of instant accessibility in which fiction is discursively 'redundant'. *Amalgamemnon* takes the pejorative term 'redundancy' and uses it to fight the very exclusion it designates.

Redundancy is figured as an existential situation which is used to exemplify the condition of the humanist academic in an increasingly technocratic world. The novel opens with the sentence: 'I shall soon be quite redundant at last despite of all, as redundant as you after queue and as totally predictable, information-content zero' (5). We soon begin to see the double-voiced nature of this supposedly 'useless' discourse. The sentence is itself 'redundant' with respect to the opening sentence of Beckett's *Malone Dies* which it self-consciously imitates,[5] and the implication is that all discourse is but a rehashing of another's words. In reiterating its own superfluity, however, Mira's 'redundant' language spells out the hidden resources of the novel's position.

Richard Martin shows that redundancy in *Amalgamemnon* functions as a catalyst for creative generation through variation and elaboration (1989*b*: 180 *et passim*). There is also another sense in which redundancy is employed strategically. In reducing the flow of daily life to 'information content', the mass media present as primary data a series of facts which have been culled through a complex process of information-processing. Mira takes these facts and reinserts them in narrative—not the original narrative representations from which they were drawn, for these are inaccessible to her,—but playful conjectures as to what might have been. Logically Mira's version precedes the 'events' it details, for a narrative is always implied in a list of facts. This discursive pre-emption is reflected in her use of the future tense which pre-dicts the story it relates. She subtly contests the assumption that narrative fiction is

---

[4] The concept of 'secondary orality', i.e. the return to oral culture brought about by the rise of the oral media, is discussed by Walter Ong in *Orality and Literacy* (1982).

[5] 'I shall soon be quite dead at last in spite of all' (1958: 7).

'redundant' with respect to 'reality' by grammatically inverting the relation of her stories to those she hears on the radio.

The discursive mode of *Amalgamemnon* is also plausible realistically in as much as the future and other unreal verb forms are commonly used in news broadcasts to describe scheduled events, to make meteorological and economic forecasts, and to speculate as to the possible consequences of events that have already taken place. The voice of the future mimes the supposed experts who presume to know what lies in wait: 'Soon the ecopolitical system will crumble, and sado-experts will fly in from all over the world and poke into its smoking entrails and utter smooching agnostications' (15), or: 'The ecozoologists will then fly in from all over the world and poke its entrails and fraudcast a stooging diregnosis' (18). But, as here, this mimicry often has the effect of comparing such experts with soothsayers, challenging the contemporary distinction between rational knowledge generated out of numbers and graphs and the irrational predictions of those who 'fraudcast' on evidence from stars or the entrails of animals. De-realization is used to suggest that economic and other 'scientific' models are no more real (nor even more accurate) than the fictions and oracular pronouncements from which they seek to distinguish themselves.

Like the discourse of the realist novel, the discourse of the news media operates according to a specific set of technical conventions (reliance on the word of 'experts', abundant statistical and other quantitative information, scrupulous use of qualification, and so on) which guarantee that it appears truthful. The stories Mira tells to divert her attention from her personal situation and to exercise her imaginative powers reveal the link between the conventionality of the supposedly transparent discourse of realist fiction and the conventionality of news stories. She constructs out of bits of stories heard on the radio elaborate dramatic scenarios which parody genres such as the thriller, the spy novel, and the popular romance. Imaginative story-telling thus represents an alternative to information, but also to the realist novel which shares the media's obsession with factual precision. Her stories are a playful mimicry of the techniques of realist writers who use devices such as genealogical trees as 'semiological compensation' to help the reader assimilate the complex world they have invented.[6] Far from clarifying the world

---

[6] See Brooke-Rose 1981: 87, 100.

envisaged, these devices serve in *Amalgamemnon* to generate the fiction itself. Mira starts by drawing a genealogical tree and then proceeds to invent stories to account for it. She is eventually drawn into the stories she tells, and she is obliged to redraw the tree with herself in it. Other metalepses include letters written to Mira by the characters she invents, and arguments with terrorists of her own creation. By fusing news broadcasts with traditional novelistic tropes, she foregrounds the conventionality of both discursive genres and points to the fact that they both rely on an assumption of verisimilitude which her flagrant transgressions of narrative ontology undermine.

The voice of the media portrayed in *Amalgamemnon* is that of 'afterthought' (21) which operates by 'rearranging history past and present in the light of national self-esteem for political ends' (21). Mira's dream is to get away from both this approach to the past and the alternative approach of realist fiction, to found a school of history in which: 'The highest marks will be given, not to the most correct which will be unverifiable but to the most ingenious' (21). There she 'could speak to an issue with a tissue of lies' (140). This is an imaginary world where fiction would be indistinguishable from fact because, like the novel, it would be under the sign of potentiality.[7] In *Amalgamemnon* story-telling in the future tense is at once a reassertion of individual creativity and a counter-attack on the discourses of the media which ignore the fictionality of the material they present and the conventions which are at its source.

Xorandor: Narrative and Cybernetics

The sceptical attitude toward information technology that surfaces in *Amalgamemnon* is tackled directly in *Xorandor*, but from a very different perspective. The first thing someone familiar with Christine Brooke-Rose's fiction notices about the novel is that it reads almost like conventional science fiction. The characteristic verbal acrobatics of Brooke-Rose's earlier work are kept to a minimum, and when they are employed they are always motivated in a naturalistic way. There are two child narrators who work in tandem, but distinguishing between them poses no problem, and their identities

---

[7] This school is realized in what Brooke-Rose calls 'palimpsest history', of which *Textermination* is an example. See below.

are never overtly threatened. As the novel progresses, however, it becomes apparent that *Xorandor* does in fact address many of the same concerns as Brooke-Rose's earlier novels, and that her assumption of the narrative idiom of the popular novel and her mimicry of a childish language are carefully calculated. The seemingly ingenuous children discover that as a model of reality, narrative can have explanatory force to rival even the most powerful scientific theories, and indeed that narrative has many of the same characteristics as the concepts on which modern science is founded. Furthermore, it becomes evident over the course of the novel that the story of this founding is itself illuminating in the context of contemporary scientific practices.

Xorandor is a tale set in the near future of two 12-year-old fraternal twins called Jip and Zab who find a talking stone at an old cairn in their native Cornwall. They discover that although the stone is capable of communicating on 'vocal', its more natural medium is 'softalk', or direct interface with their pocket computer. They call the stone Xorandor but, still half believing it is the ghost of Merlin, they amuse themselves by teaching it to speak their own peculiar cybernetic slang. Their secret is soon discovered, however, when the local nuclear-waste storage facility where their father works as a physicist records mysterious disappearances of radioactive materials. Xorandor explains that he lives on radioactivity, that he has come from Mars in search of food, and that he has been stealing the waste to feed himself. His consumption of nuclear waste would seem at first to be an ideal solution to the problems of both Martians and humans, but of course there is a hitch. Xorandor has inadvertently eaten a dangerous isotope which has caused a 'syntax error' to occur in one of his offspring, Xor 7. This mutant stone takes over a nuclear reactor and threatens to blow the reactor up if he and his race are not permanently supplied with 'high quality food'. Only the twins are able to convince the terrorist stone to renounce his plan, yet once the crisis has been averted they are sent off to school in Germany. When they are finally allowed to return a year-and-a-half later, they discover that Xorandor and seventeen of his children are under close surveillance in different parts of the world, but that he has 'programmed' them to escape and neutralize nuclear missiles. The governments of nuclear-armed countries rightly perceive this as a threat to their defence strategies and decide to send all the stones back to Mars.

Though Xorandor resigns himself to his fate, he tells the children a secret: he has not in fact come from Mars at all but is a member of a race that has been living on Earth for millions of years, communicating over vast distances through radio pulses in binary code. He has broken his age-long silence in order to warn humankind that he has committed a dangerous 'syntax error'. Or perhaps he has intentionally made the 'syntax error' in order to alert people to the danger of their nuclear inventions. The question is never resolved, but neither is it a new question. Did Christ come to save man from his original sin, or did man commit his *felix culpa* in order to be redeemed by and in Christ? Though the 'facts' of his existence are ultimately undecidable, as a 'story' the information Xorandor conveys makes sense. Jip and Zab criticize the scientists who analyse Xorandor for their obsessive concern with his 'synchronic' functioning to the exclusion of his 'genealogy' (60, 191).[8] They, who know his 'true' history, are the only ones to grasp the significance of origins and myths of origins.

Like narratology, cybernetics takes linguistics as its model discourse, and the analogy between narrative and programming provides the underlying conceit of the novel.[9] As computer whizzes, the twins' main expertise is the logic of programming languages, so it is natural for them to discuss story-telling in terms of program-writing. They discover, however, that the logic of narrative is far less rigorous and relies far more on individual taste: 'it seems harder to tell a story, even our own, than to make up the most complex program. Or at least to choose how to tell it' (8). They complain that 'even with hindsight we can't decide what's really relevant and in what order' (35), which causes problems with 'sequence-control' (23, 28) because of 'spaghetti stacks' (poorly ordered sequences of instructions, 12). They also criticize each other for including 'waste instruction[s]' (8).[10] The narrative method they eventually choose is 'dialogic' in the most literal sense, for together they dictate the story directly into their computer.

---

[8] The pagination of the 1986 paperback edition is identical with that of the original.

[9] The terminology of programming distinguishes between the syntactic and semantic aspects of a language, between symbols and pointers (deixes), between deep structure (assembly language) and surface structure (programming language), though these need not necessarily be distinct (Pratt 1975: 19).

[10] The reader of a popular science-fiction novel is more likely to be computer literate than versed in narratology, so from this perspective the analogy is doubly effective. It both naturalizes the metaphoric mapping of programming on to story-telling and makes this mapping do work as a heuristic device.

The twins' ignorance of narrative technique stems from a change in education which has been brought about as a result of the increasing dominance of science over the humanities. In the society they inhabit they will have to choose at the university level between physics and hi-tech; philosophy and literature may be pursued only as hobbies. Zab wants to study both physics and philosophy 'as it used to be' (187) in Aristotle's day. The novel represents an attempt to bring these two domains back together through the common discursive mode of narrative. Far from being a romantic reaction against science, this represents an effort to make people recognize that the scientific concepts which permeate our society have implications far beyond the immediate domain of their technical application, and that they are rooted in seemingly more primitive modes of thought such as story-telling.

Xorandor's principal strategy for communication, which the children term 'play-acting', is, like theirs, an *ad hoc* narrative technique: 'As mothers with children, and sometimes women with their men. Xorandor doesn't laugh at people, he goes along with them at their level, telling them what he knows they want to hear. After all, we all play language-games . . . And what started as a language-game had to go on as a lie, or a myth' (190). He simulates the picaresque ingenuousness of the alien, pretending to learn English from the children in order to gain their confidence, and gradually modifying the historical account he gives of himself to meet peoples' changing conception of him. Near the end of the novel Jip and Zab discuss the status of what Xorandor has told them, whether or not it is the truth, and how they can be sure. But as they analyse what he has said to different people, they begin to see that the question is not really pertinent. They realize that in every case he has answered people's questions according to their particular logic. Thus, when the postmistress asks him if he has come from Mars, he answers 'yes' because she has just told him the story of Merlin that is a local myth. His 'myth' has the same status as hers, though later when scientists attempt to verify this he has to alter the chemical composition of his exterior in order to substantiate his claim. He has 'told a story and altered his reality to fit' (186).[11] As in *Amalgamemnon*,

---

[11] In a formulation which fits nicely with my own argument, Susan Hawkins declares that 'to cast these various language gems as myth or story reduces neither their explanatory power nor their efficacy; it ironically dramatizes the contemporary assumption that discursive systems are more or less fictional ones' (1989: 141).

there is a blurring of the distinction between 'originary myth' and 'truth'.

As Peter Brooks argues in *Reading for the Plot* (1984), narrative is a mode of explanation used when other forms of logic break down, in the case of insurmountable contradictions, undecidability, or other seemingly irrational states of affairs. Because narrative is able to cope with these problems, it is often enlisted by the human mind to work through logically impossible situations. It is also the communicative technique Xorandor uses to smooth over the paradoxes inherent in his make-up. One of the first things the children notice about the stone is his odd logic. Because he 'fails' to grasp the concept of pronouns as shifters (the understanding of which is, in Irigaray's terms, the necessary condition for entry into the discourse of the symbolic), they term him 'slow' (16). But when he does eventually 'learn' the concept, they concede that: 'Even now it still seems as if his sense of identity is quite different from ours' (17). They name him Xorandor because they notice that: 'His logic could be both absolutely rigorous and absolutely contradictory at crucial points, some arguments could be both XOR and AND, or XOR and OR' (18). These are terms used in digital electronics to designate the basic logical operations on which digital systems are founded. The terms, derived from the concepts of Boolean algebra, correspond to specific types of logical operators, or gates, in an integrated circuit. In an OR gate (also known as inclusive or) an initial input of two binary terms will yield one if either or both of the terms is one. In an XOR gate (exclusive or) the output will be one if either but not both of the initial terms is one. An AND gate will yield one if and only if both initial terms are one. In all other cases the output is, of course, zero. Xorandor's logic transgresses that of binary systems because he combines mutually exclusive operations. When the children ask him why he has contacted them, he replies: 'for security and insecurity xor insecurity andor communication' (81). His paradoxical logic is in many respects similar to the non-binary logical structures developed in France in the late 1960s to account for the peculiarities of literature and of narrative in particular (see Chapter 3 above).

But there is also another sense in which narrative is pertinent to the concept of undecidability, for the narrative of cybernetics as a field of study has this concept at its source. Jip tells of something he has seen written on a wall: 'If the human brain was simple enough for us to understand we'd be so simple we couldn't' (88). Zab pipes in with the comment: 'Why, it's a popular version of the Gödel theorem' (88). She goes on to link Gödel's theorem to Alan Turing's proof that 'no machine could . . . completely understand itself, I mean, tackle all its own problems' (88).[12] In 1936 Turing succeeded in demonstrating that there are undecidable problems which no algorithm can solve. He did this by means of a conceptual prototype of the modern computer which was in effect a definition of the algorithm (Stewart 1987: 214–18). The concept on which computing is based thus contains an element of the indeterminate: the history and origin of computers is inextricably linked to the discovery of 'originary' undecidability.

But this history is easily overlooked, as is the modern computer's capacity to accommodate 'semantic' undecidables, in scientists' eagerness to construct a myth of the internal consistency and autonomy of their discipline. Jip and Zab's father claims that computer logic, unlike human logic, 'can't cope with a word used in a figurative sense, or with humour, which depends on word-play, which is like assigning two values to a character' (87). The twins point out that this conception of polysemy has only limited applicability, for it does not explain ambiguity caused by contextual factors. Xorandor is capable of word-play, he even puns on Shakespeare: 'softwarily we are observed' (179), and he gives a reply to one of the twins' questions that they later discover to have been 'syntactically clear but contextually ambiguous' (183–4). They then realize that not only is this type of undecidability possible in Xorandor's logic, but that it is also the founding condition of their binary systems. Even in their own computer 'in a context-free grammar no general procedure exists for determining whether the grammar can be ambiguous in any one of every single case, however long one ran the program. The question is then said to be undecidable' (182). Xorandor is not in fact an alien creature from another planet; likewise, his seemingly irrational logic is implied by their own.

In their encounter with Xorandor, Jip and Zab discover a race that is radically 'other' to their own conception of life, a race that, though voiceless, and apparently powerless, nevertheless surpasses

---

[12] Gödel's theorem is summarized by Ian Stewart as follows: '1) If formal set theory is consistent then there exist theorems that can neither be proved nor disproved and 2) There is no procedure which will prove set theory consistent' (1987: 218), which is another way of saying that no system can demonstrate its own infallibility.

humankind in cognitive capacity: 'their life-purpose, their survival kit, seems to have depended on silence—not to each other but towards us, though they learnt from us and went beyond us' (192). They recognize that even the most basic logical processes involve an element of indeterminacy; they also base their techniques of communication on the strategies of narrative fiction rather than the endless flow of information. Inventing the past to suit our needs, telling stories to account for paradox, and acting out roles are the forms of narrative which make possible all our cognitive endeavours and all communication. Modern science ignores this at its peril, and *Xorandor* may be read as a fable for scientists and would-be scientists, written in their own idiom, warning them of the consequences of cutting their project off from its conceptual genealogy, its own founding story.

Verbivore: Writing and Communication

Like *Xorandor*, its sequel *Verbivore* examines the social and discursive implications of present-day technology by postulating the consequences of a radical variation on communication as we know it. In *Verbivore* the focus is switched from the principles on which high technology is based to the media through which it is transmitted. Recalling Marshall McLuhan's dictum that 'the medium is the message', the novel posits the possibility of an obligatory shift in the primary medium of communication from oral and cybernetic forms to a 'secondary literacy' in which the world is required once again to rely on the written word. The consequences of this shift for people's habits and thought processes provide both the subject-matter and the technique of the novel which is composed entirely of people's written accounts of their experience of the crisis. As in the first modern novels of the eighteenth century, technical experimentation in *Verbivore* is closely linked to generic conventions specific to the written text. It is the interaction of high technology with traditional novelistic modes which is the focus of the work.

Of the four volumes which comprise the Quartet, only *Xorandor* and *Verbivore* have directly related story-lines (though characters from *Amalgamemnon* surface in both *Verbivore* and *Textermination*, most notably perhaps, Mira in the role of narrator). *Verbivore* takes place twenty-three years after the action of the previous novel. The twins have gone their separate ways and become estranged: Jip is a nuclear physicist at NASA and Zab is a Euro-MP in Aachen, which has become the new seat of the European Parliament. Since the adventure of their adolescence they have had no contact with their mineral friends whom they have all but forgotten. But strange occurrences prompt them each to wonder whether Xorandor's progeny may not again be interfering with human activities. The story starts with various accounts of what journalists have dubbed 'Verbivore', an unexplained phenomenon in which the modulations of electromagnetic waves are being mysteriously 'flattened' by some unknown agent. At first the cuts are only occasional, but they become increasingly common until finally all signals have disappeared from the airwaves. Radio, television, and the radar-dependent navigational devices of planes and other vehicles are affected, as are computer networks and satellites. The economy comes to a virtual standstill as the population is forced to turn to print and writing for communication purposes.

Sensing that the stones may be at the root of the problem, Zab contacts one of Xorandor's offspring, and she learns that 'Verbivore' is a reaction by the mineral race to information overload. Because it cannot cope with so many messages, its only recourse is to sabotage the airwaves themselves. Aided by Jip and their old friend Tim, who is now head of the BBC, Zab acts as an emissary between humans and stones and strikes a deal: people will voluntarily agree to curb the amount of material transmitted if the stones will agree to stop their interference. Yet, as with many agreements on environmental pollution, voluntary abstention is unsuccessful. After an initial period of relative restraint, people return to their former prolixity and the novel ends with 'Verbivore' being resumed for good.

Verbivore starts and ends with Mira as narrator. Like several other story-tellers active in the novel, she includes in her narrative bits and pieces of what she reads and hears around her. In the opening pages she interpolates a radio play called 'A Round of Silence' by Perry Hupsos—a character she invented as a radio presenter in *Amalgamemnon* (74) out of the title *Peri Hypsos* (the Greek title of Longinus's *On the Sublime*). The play functions as a *mise en abyme* of the novel as a whole. Two of the main characters are Julian, who is writing a thesis on 'neopostdeconstructionism', and Decibel, a voice he hears inside his head when he is recovering in hospital from an accident.[13] Julian cannot tolerate noise, while Decibel cannot live without it. This much is established in the play, but, unable to think of a suitable ending, Perry anticipates the events to come by aborting the drama prematurely with a radio cut written into the script. The two characters continue to appear throughout the novel, however. It becomes evident that Julian is a representative figure of the writer when he decides to write a novel (82), and Decibel that of the oral media when she declares writing to be her natural enemy (186). Though they are opposing principles, Julian and Decibel need each other. Julian is aware of his status as a character in a radio play, and he laments the paradox whereby he hates noise but relies on being broadcast in order to exist (113). Decibel is an oral character in the sense that she is part of a play, but she has nevertheless been conceived of and *written* by Perry. This opening parable may be read as an allegorical figuration of the main idea behind the novel: written and oral means of communication are interdependent in the modern world.

Certainly *Verbivore* is characteristic of its cybernetic times in that it is more 'user-friendly' than much of Brooke-Rose's previous work. Linguistically it is even more straightforward than *Xorandor*; the twins have largely abandoned their cybernetic slang (though they fall back into it when excited), and while frequent, multilingual puns are always motivated realistically. The novel can plausibly be labelled science fiction by virtue of the fact that it takes place in the future and involves 'alien' life forms, but the use of science and other specialized discourses is kept to a minimum. From this perspective *Verbivore* is the most accessible of Brooke-Rose's novels since *The Middlemen*. It nevertheless refuses to conform to the narrative conventions of nineteenth-century realism. Instead, it takes as its model the typically eighteenth-century genres of direct discourse: the epistolary novel, the journal novel, and the fictional autobiography. By developing these devices in the light of modern technology, Brooke-Rose is able to circumvent the conventions of realism while still remaining within the bounds of what is accepted as novelistic.

The intimate relation of the novel as a genre to the written word is evident in its historic evolution out of letters, diaries, and autobiographical accounts. In the eighteenth century the first modern novelists recognized that these genres could be used to tell a

---

[13] There are obvious parallels between this scenario and the thematic situation in *Such*: Julian's wife leaves him during his convalescence because he hallucinates a romantic liaison with an 'unreal' character belonging to an embedded story.

story. The conceit of the 'found document', discovered, preserved, and presented to the public by an 'editor', was a justification no longer necessary in the nineteenth century when the novel was firmly established as a genre. It is at this point that the historical link between the novel and the written text began to be lost sight of; the highly unrealistic convention of the omniscient third-person narrator then became a realist norm. But because the novel is still a written genre, it is threatened by the rise of 'secondary orality'. The onus is on writing as a medium to demonstrate that it is capable of forms of communication which are impossible in the oral media, and that it therefore still has a place in contemporary society.

The specific effects of the written text have been the preoccupation of literary theory from Derrida and Barthes onward, and the writerly nature of the novel has often manifested itself in the form of typographical devices which defy oral utterance or those specific to the codex. This is the approach taken in *Thru*, where 'concrete prose' is used to exploit the possibilities of the printed word, creating a text that is 'unspeakable' by virtue of the fact that it relies on visual as well as auditory performance. But concrete prose is borrowed from concrete poetry as practised by Carroll, Mallarmé, Apollinaire, and others; though it is a form possible only in written texts, it is not one specific to the novel. In *Verbivore* Brooke-Rose makes use of techniques that are possible only in prose narrative: the mixing of documentary-like realism with 'events' which are unthinkable from a visual or aural point of view, and the circular embedding of narrative fragments.

Verbivore combines the fantastic ontological postulates of *Amalgamemnon* with the basically realistic postulates of *Xorandor*, creating a hybrid form which can be likened to magic realism as practised by many Spanish-American writers, and more recently by a number of British authors. The characters from the two novels carry their ontological status with them and pass it on to those they engender. Thus Perry, Julian, and Decibel are 'unrealistic' characters. Julian is aware, for instance, that he is a character in Perry's play; Decibel is the personification of an abstract quality. When at one point Decibel meets Zab, Zab wonders if she must not be dreaming. She relates her 'dream' to Jip and he confirms her interpretation of the episode, for in their realist world, 'only dreams mix real and fantasy items' (139). This is a classic case of dramatic irony which alerts the reader to the fact that novels too are capable of mixing fantastic and realistic elements, that indeed the capacity to do so is one of their defining characteristics.

The imagining of what someone else is writing is the mechanism by which the novel switches from one first-person narrator to another. Mira imagines what Zab must be typing into her word-processor; soon we are reading Zab's text in which she imagines what her brother Jip is typing, and so forth, through their mother Paula, the playwright Perry Hupsos, his characters Decibel and Julian, and finally back to Mira. While the effect is a variation of point of view, the structure is that of a 'strange loop'—by definition a transgression of conventional ontology—which works itself through several narrative levels.[14] Just as the 'Verbivore' phenom-enon is caused through a flattening or levelling of the modulations of air-waves, so the hierarchy of narrative levels is 'flattened' such that it becomes impossible in any given instance to determine whose account we are reading or whose mind we are supposedly 'inside'.

As in much self-conscious fiction, we are constantly being reminded of the fictionality of the novel, but *Verbivore* makes it clear that this fictionality also applies to the 'simulations' of the media which its 'fictions' purportedly replace. Far from enabling true communication, 'communications' networks process informa-tion which is immediately outdated, and can therefore never claim a response. In *Verbivore* people's dependence on the endless flow of facts and interpretation has reached the proportions of an addiction to 'that best narcotic, vox humana' (31). As Mira sees it, this form of language use has had an indelible effect on human conscious-ness:

our minds and psyches, our entire nervous system and networks of expectations have been transformed by the media . . . We depend on the media for our life-blood, the stream of information, the adventures, the violence, the romance . . . the eternal commentary that lines our lives like a loving companion, a double, making sense of it for us. (30–1)

The 'eternal commentary' or 'double' is absorbed in a one-way continuous-feed process which has replaced dialogue. This is a sinister view of the world of simulacra and simulation described by Jean Baudrillard, the world in which people have the illusion of being actively hooked into vast information networks, whereas in

---

[14] For a discussion of the phenomenon of the 'strange loop' with reference to its similar use in *Thru*, see McHale 1987: 119–21.

fact they are only the passive recipients of processed data, more and more isolated in front of their televisions and their computer screens (1970: 186–91; 1981: 121–31). It can also be likened to the world envisaged by Hassan's 'new gnostics', who see the future as a vast network of information systems produced, as Brooke-Rose points out, by the few for the many (see Chapter 2 above).

At one point Zab asks: 'What have we lost . . . since the disappearance of books?' (38), and as if in reply, Tim describes cybernetic abstractions as the cause of mental and physiological degeneration: 'We've become stunted human beings. Loss of senses and muscle through the media, loss of memory and logical capacity through computers' (92). Indeed, Jip and Zab have lost their almost telepathic ability to communicate, and, as witnessed by the outcome of the novel, the world is unable to communicate well enough to reach a full consensus or enforce a communal decision. Simulation has also begun to supplant individual creativity. Being an inveterate story-teller, Mira is quick to remark on the degenerative effect the dominance of the media has on personal development: 'Gradually all our secret treasures have been removed and we've all been made to share the same abstracted and alienating public knowledge' (111). According to Tim, this has resulted in a return to an élitist society in which: 'The population has learnt to live on abstractions and interpretations of the world as presented by a few' (92).

With the advent of Verbivore, however, people are forced once again to rely on their own cognitive and creative resources. It is not long before their imaginative faculties are reactivated and word-processing becomes a universal withdrawal symptom. For lack of information about what is happening elsewhere in the world, people record 'screen-diaries' or 'mimic minimemoirs' (7) on their 'chatterscreen[s]' (127). Not only do they write of their personal experiences, speculations, and fears, they also begin to imagine what people they know are thinking, saying, and most of all, what they are typing into *their* word-processors.

This spontaneous surge of 'substitute fictions' (169) is commented upon by many of those who take to keeping computerized journals. Zab finds herself using the now obsolete narrative conventions of the memoir. She notes that 'clearly I am deriving pleasure, just as fiction-writers used to, from the mere fact of noting facts' (37). When it comes to her imagined transcriptions of Jip's diary, she goes

on in the same descriptive vein for a paragraph, then stops herself
with an abrupt exclamation of: 'No, he wouldn't say all that' (54),
whereupon she starts again in more concise fashion. Jip, for his part,
imagines his mother Paula writing, and then he catches himself and
reflects on his motives: 'why am I writing all this out as if I were
trying to assimilate myself to her? Are these increasing breaks in our
daily fictions turning us all into d.i.y. fiction producers? Which, Zab
would cut in, we've all been all along anyway, but in our heads, not
on paper' (75). Paula (who writes in longhand) reflects in turn on the
genre of the journal *per se*: 'Why am I scribbling all this to myself? . . .
Perhaps I'll send these pages to Zab for comment. I've certainly
never kept a journal before, it's not the age of journals . . . Perhaps
everyone will now, it's catching' (79).

As these passages demonstrate, the passive consumption of information and oral commentary is contrasted with characteristically
written forms of language-use which encourage intersubjective
communication by forcing people to imagine, in the case of the
journal, what others are doing or, in the case of the letter, how they
will react to what is being written to them. This active projection of
consciousness outside the self is the condition of true communication, and also the condition of the creation of narrative fiction. But
just as the invention of print prepared the way for the traditional
novel (Watt 1957: 196–200; Couturier 1991: 93–144), so the fictions
characters produce in *Verbivore* are conditioned by the technological
advances which have made them possible.

Taking a broader perspective, Mira remarks on the situation at
large. She notes that there is a difference between the stories people
have been producing and traditional fiction. The facility with which
a fiction in the mind or on the word-processor can be altered means
that the effect is nearly as 'evanescent' (169) as the fictions provided
by the media. Already in *Out* the narrator was obsessed with the
mind's capacity for erasing one version of a story and substituting
another: 'We can make our errors in a thought and reject them in
another thought, leaving no trace of error in us' (51/53). Likewise,
Mira in *Amalgamemnon* describes the stories she tells herself as
writing 'on sand' (140). The oral media have accustomed people to
continual and infinitely practicable mutability. With a text on a
word-processor no one version is final, any version can be altered
without a trace. As if to demonstrate the facility with which word-
processed text can be subject to systematic manipulation, Perry

repeats an entire paragraph of his text in which he lists the commands that effect this repetition (167).

It is in the nature of longhand and typescript that corrections and annotations are visible, as in *Out*, whereas in *Verbivore* there is very little of Brooke-Rose's characteristic variation on the same phrases. This technique is grounded in a form of composition that is outmoded: the age of the word-processor has made possible *in practice* a perpetual variation and continual performance which can only be indicated obliquely in print.[15] In the society portrayed in the novel the printed codex is obsolete; books are distributed on diskette which can be altered at will, heralding the end of the definitive text.

Marshall McLuhan and Walter Ong see the print revolution as an enabling condition for the establishment of fixed point of view which led to the rise of the novel (McLuhan 1962: 126–7, 135–6; Ong 1982: 133, 148–9). Maurice Couturier disputes the necessary relation between print and perspectival unity in narrative, arguing instead that 'print has allowed the novelist to multiply the points of view without making his book unreadable' (1991: 142). But here he confuses the issue, for while print may well have initially encouraged authors to focus on an individual's perception and cognition of the world, this does not mean that this technique is necessarily bound to be dominant in printed texts, for as the novel evolved, so did the concept of point of view. Moreover, the examples Couturier gives are of multiple discrete points of view carefully distinguished within the novels in question (*The Sound and the Fury*, *Pale Fire*), whereas the mutable point of view employed in *Verbivore* is a technique developed out of the possibilities inherent in print, but moving toward the mutability of cybernetic text.

Couturier is more convincing in his demonstration of how the increase in available textual material brought about by the invention of print led to new strategies for incorporating one text into another without overt plagiarism (48). The even greater increase in the availability of textuality made possible by the digital revolution, combined with the facilities it allows for altering, merging, and adding to already written texts, presents a related but different set of problems to the novelist. In his analysis of the relationship between literary study and advances in cybernetic technology, Richard

---

[15] Obviously it is not the manner in which this or any other novel is actually produced which is of primary importance, but rather the ideas that the new technology brings to light.

Lanham argues that the computerization of knowledge—including fiction—will change our conception of the nature of textuality. Not only will we be obliged to recognize the 'perpetual immanent metamorphosis' (1989: 273) characteristic of contemporary multi-media texts, but our understanding of the 'great works' of the past will be modified as well. Lanham predicts the emergence of a new 'rhetoric of the arts' which will focus not on a set of 'Great Ideas' but on 'how knowledge is held' (286), both on the medium and on the message, and of course, on their interaction. What Lanham describes as 'perpetual immanent metamorphosis' comes in *Verbivore* to infect the coherence of both point of view and plot structure. That the mutability of a text should be based on a cybernetic paradigm as opposed to a print paradigm in no way threatens to affect the characteristics specific to its status as a *written* text. Rather, certain elements of the written narrative—its ability to mix different modes of discourse and to create logically impossible situations—will be foregrounded to the detriment of elements such as unity of point of view which came to narrative with the invention of print.

In *Verbivore* as a whole, as in its fantastic sub-plot, the oral and the written dimensions of language are opposed but also intimately related. Jip and Zab succeed in contacting Xorandor's offspring orally, and of course it is orally that they themselves finally work out their differences. Furthermore, the written narratives which con-stitute the novel are shot through with the vestiges of oral culture: incomplete sentences, a tendency toward verbosity and digression, as well as an abundance of transcriptions of actual dialogue. It is clear that Brooke-Rose does not propose a return to the hegemony of the printed word, and that her tale of the sabotage of communication technology is not merely the vengeful fantasy of a frustrated novelist. We have, as the novel suggests, been immersed for too long in a predominantly oral culture for it not to have permanently altered our minds. If there is to be a 'secondary literacy' of the kind imagined and enacted in *Verbivore*, it will necessarily have a reciprocal relationship with contemporary technological inventions and institu-tions. It will be one which relies on its oral counterpart for its survival (through television and radio adaptations, interviews with authors, and so on). But the dependence is mutual: Decibel needs an imaginative creator to invent her, and without the creative impetus represented by written genres, it is hinted that the powers of the imagination will slowly die.

Textermination: Creative Reading and the Ontology of Fiction

Just as there is a break in the four volumes which constitute the *Omnibus*, *Thru* being in many respects a new departure, so the final volume of the Quartet breaks with the technological preoccupations of the first three novels. *Textermination* is not directly concerned with technology; rather it elaborates the issues raised by the current place of the novel in our technological society. Many of the questions of communication and individual creativity which are explored through media and cybernetic models in the earlier novels are treated in *Textermination* with relation to the communication between a fictional text and its readers. Similarly, science-fiction motifs give way in this novel to fantasy elements which maintain it at one remove from realism but prevent it from falling into a generic category.

Like its three predecessors, *Textermination* is a cautionary novel, for it deals with the gradual (ex)termination of novelistic worlds. But it is neither an elegy of the novel nor a grim prediction of its imminent demise. Instead it plays with the 'death of reading', for novels have always relied on the reader to bring them to life. Whereas *Amalgamemnon* focuses on the fictionality of many of the so-called discourses of 'truth', *Textermination* treats the concept of fictionality from the point of view of reception. This treatment takes two forms. The novel sets the individual reader's response above authorial determination of meaning, orthodox critical interpretations, and other 'closed' forms of response. It also emphasizes the importance of readings in which fictional texts are recognized for what they are rather than being treated as truth claims or pronouncements about the world.

The setting of the novel is the annual 'Convention of Prayer for Being' held in San Francisco. Attending the convention are characters from hundreds of works of literary fiction from all ages and all parts of the world, who convene with the express purpose of bolstering their existences and securing their continued survival. They accomplish this task by listening to papers delivered on them and by attending 'pray-ins' in which they pray to the Implied Reader. Prominent figures include Jane Austen's Emma, Emma Bovary, Dorothea Brooke from *Middlemarch*, Felipe Segundo from Carlos Fuentes's *Terra Nostra*, and Gibreel Farishta from Salman Rushdie's *The Satanic Verses*. There are also characters present from works by authors as diverse as Homer, Clarice Lispector, Mark

Twain, Milan Kundera, and Eugène Sue. The convention is organized by eminent literary critics, and support staff include 'interpreters' whose job it is to facilitate relations between the characters as well as ensuring the smooth running of the convention generally.

The novel opens with a series of quotations from well-known works of European literature loosely strung together with third-person narrative. Each quotation describes a journey in a carriage taken by the protagonists of works which are in many cases those whose titles bear their names: *Emma*, *Madame Bovary*, *Clarissa*, and others. Suddenly all the characters find themselves in an 'aerobrain' headed across the Atlantic toward San Francisco, with a stopover in Atlanta *en route*. On leaving this city the characters have a vision of its demolition by fire, or rather, as it burns we are given a series of famous fictional burnings of cities, libraries, and books. This constitutes a ritualistic burning of the books in which the characters were conceived; they are thus taken out of the 'old world' of their origins and made to embark on an adventure in the 'new world' of Brooke-Rose's novel.

The plot of the remainder of the novel revolves around a series of attempted rebellions by various factions at the convention who are critical of the way it is organized. Each of these challenges comes to nought in the end though, for, as one of the interpreters explains: 'Some will say nothing happens in this novel, in this, Convention, and they'd be dead right. It's not about events but about characters and their discourse' (148). When the delegates from Western literature meet on the first day to pray for their existence, there is an attempted disruption of the ceremony by Muslim fundamentalists who claim to object to the Christian format of the proceedings, but, as we later discover, their real target is the elusive Gibreel Farishta whom they are trying to punish for his heretical views. Order is eventually restored through the good offices of the interpreters Kelly and Jack, but no sooner are the terrorists under control than there is a second attempt to sabotage the convention by characters from television who demand representation. A quarrel ensues in which the television characters argue that they are more deserving of prayer than novelistic characters because the latter have a far longer life; the characters from novels insist that only they need their existences reinforced because only they are in danger of losing their audience.

Meanwhile Kelly begins to suspect that many of the people helping to run the convention may also be fictional. The police inspector who investigates the terrorist attack turns out to be none other than Columbo, the clerks at the hotel are discovered to be Akaky Akakievich, Badin, Devushkin, Mr Guppy, Goliadkin, Sainthomme, and Uriah Heep, and the journalists who report it include Jake Barnes, Ian Scuffling, Joe McCarthy Hynes, and Rouletabille. Her worst fears are confirmed when she finds a list, containing the entry 'McFadgeon, Kelly. From Textermination, by Mira Enketei' (92), of all the characters who have completely ceased to exist because they are no longer read. Mira herself makes several appearances, both in the first and the third persons, before also discovering that her name is on the list as the delegate from *Amalgamemnon*, whereupon she too 'dies'.[16] There follows an attempted conspiracy by 'I-narrators' in the aim of increasing their prominence and defining their specific needs, a revolt by several characters against their authors (most notably Oedipa Maas from *The Crying of Lot 49*, who declaims her views as a feminist despite Pynchon's 'macho' stance), and finally, a protest by a gay-rights group against the under-representation of homosexuality in literature. The novel ends with San Francisco going up in flames, then succumbing to a monstrous earthquake. (This recalls the burning of Atlanta at the beginning: here it is the novel *Textermination* which is auto-destructing.) The only survivors are, appropriately, the participants of the convention, who wander the streets before eventually making their respective ways home in a repetition of the opening scene.

What Brooke-Rose does with discursive and textual matter in much of her previous fiction she does here with *personae*. *Thru* and *Amalgamemnon* 'plagiarize' texts from other authors, whereas *Textermination* abducts their characters.[17] The first scene of the novel involves a paradigmatic 'crossing' of characters from different fictional worlds. When Jane Austen's Emma accidentally enters a

---

[16] While the 'death' of these two characters may be attributed to self-deprecating humour on the part of Brooke-Rose, it is also a paradoxical instance of the counter-factual nature of fictional worlds, for these are the only characters who do truly 'exist' in the mind of the real reader of the novel at this point in the reading.

[17] This distinction is not absolute of course: *Thru* imports Jacques and his Master, and *Textermination* makes liberal use of quotation. The device of *retour du personnage* is first used by Brooke-Rose in *The Middlemen*, but in this novel it functions much as it does in the fiction of Waugh, Faulkner, or Balzac: the characters transplanted are those of Brooke-Rose's own invention and they play only minor roles.

carriage containing Goethe's Lotte and Goethe himself (characters from Thomas Mann's *Lotte in Weimar*), she finds herself unaccountably thinking and speaking in Lotte's voice, for she has crossed into another fictional world. Just as in her earlier fiction Brooke-Rose fused discourses, so in *Textermination* she fuses characters by making them (and their discourses) interact.

In *Textermination* the reader's mind becomes a veritable anthology of literature which supplants the author's literary heritage as the source on which the novel draws. The narrator of Flann O'Brien's *At Swim-Two-Birds* expresses the view that: 'Characters should be interchangeable as between one book and another . . . The modern novel should be largely a work of reference' (1939: 25, cited in Brooke-Rose 1981: 114). *Textermination* is a work of reference of this kind. The idea that characters could be interchangeable units raises the question of just what a fictional character is and what is involved in shuttling it between novels. As early as *The Sycamore Tree* Brooke-Rose displayed frustration with the limitations of the traditional character, but in *Textermination* she succeeds in manipulating these limitations in such a way as to move beyond them without completely abandoning the trappings of realism. The 'reduction' of characters to functions or 'ghosts' does not threaten their vitality; as fictions they survive and 'wander the streets', even when the physical world is severely altered. Their mode of existence has changed, however: they no longer represent coherent subjects but discourses transmuted through (metaphoric) interaction into 'poems', 'gaps' in the text at which the reader is invited to intervene, or deictics with multiple and mutable referents.[18] Like the 'alien' Xorandor and the fantastic figure of Decibel, these characters are coextensive with their language, but in *Textermination* there is displacement of creative responsibility from author to reader. It is up to the reader to recognize the imported characters and thus to 'actualize' the discursive worlds the novel brings together.

In questioning the ontological determinacy of the fictional character, Brooke-Rose is striking at the mainstay of the traditional

[18] Such 'gaps' may be compared with the 'holes' in *Thru* which represent narrative functions. In *Thru* Armel writes to Larissa that 'we were a poem not a couple' (25/603), and in her article 'The Dissolution of Character in the Novel' Brooke-Rose argues that characters 'exist in any complexity only insofar as they represent ideas rather than individuals with a civic status and subtle social and psychological history . . . At best the characters are poems in themselves' (1986a: 192).

novel. If a character is not inscribed in the text, but is instead a product of the reading process, the status of the entire world the character represents is highly variable.[19] The ontological status of fictional worlds has been of interest to philosophers as well as literary critics. Roman Ingarden's seminal work *The Literary Work of Art* provided the basis for much subsequent analysis of the nature of fiction and the process of reading. Ingarden defines the act of reading as the 'realization' of the work which is accomplished as the reader progressively fills in the 'spots of indeterminacy' in it (1931: 246–54). In *Verbivore* Decibel makes an oblique reference to Ingarden's theory when she describes her own problematic existence:

Perry tried to kill me off—as if one could kill an abstraction, a measurement. Oh, I know, some of you oddball characters will say: Don't be so vague, if you're a measurement. But a few might add: you also belong to the stratum of represented objects, you have a right to be indeterminate. (177)

Wolfgang Iser points out that Ingarden's analysis implies two types of indeterminacy: that which is eventually eliminated in the process of 'realization' and that which is integral to the world of the text and a constitutive aspect of its status as fiction (Iser 1978: 173).

Brian McHale sees the foregrounding of the second type of indeterminacy as a characteristic strategy of postmodernist fiction. In his discussion of transgressions of ontological levels in which characters are instrumental, McHale remarks that: 'Characters often serve as agents or "carriers" of metalepsis, disturbers of the ontological hierarchy of levels through their awareness of the recursive structures in which they find themselves' (1987: 121). Yet novels and plays that have characters who are aware or become aware of their fictional status generally focus on the relation of the characters to their author, as in Luigi Pirandello's *Six Characters in Search of an Author*, Flann O'Brien's *At Swim-Two-Birds*, Muriel Spark's *The Comforters*, Robert Pinget's *Mahu, ou le matériau*, and

---

[19] Brian McHale observes, interestingly, that the use in *Verbivore* of characters from the 'derealized' text of *Amalgamemnon* 'has the effect of *actualizing* them retroactively. It is as if these characters, ontologically so enfeebled by their 'native' context, somehow acquired a degree of ontological robustness 'between' texts, in the passage from their home text to its sequel' (n.d.: 24–5).

countless other postmodernist texts.[20] Brooke-Rose reverses this familiar postmodernist trope by focusing instead on the relation between the characters and their readers.[21] McHale points out that 'a character's knowledge of his own fictionality often functions as a kind of master-trope for determinism—cultural, historical, psychological determinism, but especially the inevitability of death' (123). When used to foreground the character–reader relationship the same device does just the opposite. A reader is free to interpret the actions and the motivations of the characters of even the most traditional novel in a variety of ways. Knowledge of their ontological status thus functions in *Textermination* as a trope for indeterminacy.[22]

Iser expands on Ingarden's description of the reading process as the filling-in of gaps but criticizes Ingarden's belief that there are true and false realizations of a text (1978: 178). Susan Suleiman points out, however, that Iser's claim for the multiplicity of 'correct' readings is in fact not borne out by his readings themselves (Suleiman 1980: 24, cited in Brooke-Rose 1981: 35). In *Textermination* the variety of reading experiences is ensured by the fact that for each reader the 'gaps of indeterminacy' will be different. How he or she reads depends not only on what Eco calls 'passeggiati inferenziali' (1979: 204), but also on his or her specific cultural heritage, a dimension of the reading process which Iser acknowledges but fails to take fully into account. Like *Between*, in which foreign languages serve as a psychological trigger to recall the experience of incomprehension that is an integral part of travel, *Textermination* makes use of novelistic allusions which readers will be aware that they do not always understand. The interpreter Kelly functions as a surrogate for the reader who is ashamed of his or her literary ignorance: 'Gaps, so many gaps in her reading, she'll never

---

[20] See McHale (1987: 121–4) for a discussion of these and others.

[21] She anticipates this reversal in *Stories, Theories and Things* when she discusses the postmodernist trope of the narrativized author: 'if it is a truism that no character can exist without his author, it would be more philosophically interesting today, with the loss of novel-reading, to explore the notion that, even more clearly, no character can exist . . . unless he is read' (1991a: 215).

[22] Raymond Federman's *Take It or Leave It* and, in another context, Italo Calvino's *Se una notte d'inverno un viaggatore . . .* are the novels discussed by McHale which dramatize the reader. The fact that in each case the implied reader is dramatized as an actual character or a well-defined addressee eliminates the effect of indeterminacy which is preserved in Brooke-Rose's novel by figuring the reader's presence as a transcendent void or 'singularity' in the text.

catch up' (22).[23] In this novel the reader is the one irreducible gap or 'spot of indeterminacy' which roves the text at will and fills holes in his or her knowledge on whim. Because the novel relies on prior literary knowledge, each individual reading will necessarily be the idiosyncratic result of an interaction between the proper names given and the reader's capacity to 'round out' these names by furnishing them with personalities and circumstantial details (which may vary considerably even between readers who have read the same texts). The use of extraneous knowledge is a feature of all of Brooke-Rose's novels, but in this case the knowledge deployed requires that of the reader to activate it.

Textermination thus privileges active participation in the creative process on the part of the reader over authoritative readings by professional interpreters. At one point in the novel the 'implied author' intervenes to argue that in critical discourse the critic-as-reader becomes a principle of unity and semantic determination:

when came the fashion for the vanishing author, the silent author, the transparent text . . . the critics, always quick to adapt their vocabulary to the latest bandwagon, started calling the narrator both the character who narrates and the producer of the text, that is, the author . . . The author was out. All authority rested in the text. And later all authority rested in the Reader, Implied, Ideal or whatever. And so they passed imperceptibly from phrases such as 'the author's intention here is clearly' to 'the text clearly says', and then to 'the reader clearly infers'. But behind this lip-service to fads, what the author intends, what the text says, what the reader infers, is in every case what the one critic interprets. He too is Reader, he too is God. (106–7)

This type of interpretation is impossible in the case of *Textermination*, for no critic can foresee each and every one of the possible epistemological permutations put into play by the interaction between the text and its potential readers. Though deceptively easy to read, the novel resists authoritative 'readings'.

All texts must be read in order for them to 'exist'; the corollary of this is that the mode of their existence in the world depends on *how* they are read. In *Amalgamemnon, Xorandor,* and *Verbivore* the fictional or mythic nature of the simulations and abstractions we take

---

[23] The fact that we are encouraged to identify with Kelly in her role as 'interpreter' makes it all the more of a shock when she discovers that she is a fictional character herself. To the extent that we have followed her this far, we are obliged to recognize that we too have allowed ourselves to be fictionalized, to play the role of the implied reader who never coincides with any actual reader.

to be fact is demonstrated by simulations of these simulations which reveal them to be discursive constructs. Similarly, *Textermination* exposes the fictional nature of readings of texts. Like the critical readings which present themselves as accurate representations of what an author 'really' intended, what a work 'really' means, or how a reader 'really' experiences it, but are no more than interpretations or simulations of these supposedly verifiable facts, readings of 'non-fictional' texts are also in part fictitious constructs.

In a recent article (1990a) Brooke-Rose addresses the issue of determinate versus indeterminate readings of texts and the consequences this has for people's world-views. She brings together under the heading 'palimpsest history' both *Terra Nostra* and *The Satanic Verses*, for both novels provide creative or poetic readings of discursive traditions—the history of the Spanish empire and the history of Muslim heritage. That these 'alternative histories' should be deemed in some sense heretical is a consequence of a perceived transgression of the firmly grounded distinction between secular and sacred exegesis on the one hand, and novels on the other. The fundamentalist outrage directed against Salman Rushdie (parodied in *Textermination*) is a real-life consequence of a failure to read the novel as a novel, that is, as a plotted confrontation between people with different points of view, not as a tract or a credo. This 'mistake' is itself the result of a failure to recognize the ontological status of the novel, that is, the irreducible indeterminacy which leaves it open to multiple interpretations.

Brooke-Rose describes *The Satanic Verses* as 'a different, a poetic, re-creative reading, of what is in the Qur'an' (1990a: 25). Readings such as this must be situated *between* sacred or received texts and those of their official interpreters:

the novel's task, unlike that of history, is to stretch our intellectual, spiritual and imaginative horizons to breaking point. Because palimpsest histories do precisely that, mingling realism with the supernatural and history with spiritual and philosophical reinterpretation, they could be said to float half-way between the sacred books of our various heritages, which survive on the strength of the faiths they have created . . . and the endless exegesis and commentaries these sacred books create. (1991a: 189)

The view that certain types of fiction occupy a mediatory position between the 'reality' of a cultural heritage and contemporary 'true' accounts of it elevates these texts to a status which the novel has not held for quite some time. The novel's role could then be said to be to question the way we think about culture. This role is assumed in *Textermination* vis-à-vis the genealogy of the novel itself; Brooke-Rose's novel can thus also be included in the generic category of 'palimpsest history'. By using characters from other such works, she draws an implicit parallel between religious or historical fundamentalism which enforces a single interpretation of the discourses of the past, and literary critical 'fundamentalism' which arrogates an individual reading of a text to the status of a general truth. The obviousness of the creative misreading of world literature offered by the novel highlights the idiosyncracy of reception and demonstrates that 'perpetual immanent metamorphosis' is inherent in reading as well as writing.

The relation between contemporary modes of communication and the contemporary novel may not always be obvious or straightforward, but it has profoundly changed the ways in which people think about fiction and the value they attach to reading. At one extreme is Calvino, who views technology as the occasion for a radical reconception of the act of reading. He foresees the disappearance of the author in favour of a cybernetic combinatory which will shift the decisive moment of a text from its production to its reception. The reader will, he predicts, find in a machine-produced text the quintessentially human 'ghosts' that haunt the collective unconscious (1967). Christine Brooke-Rose does not go so far as to disavow authorial creativity altogether, but she too sees technology as the possible key to a breakthrough in how we think about the human subject. In 'The Dissolution of Character in the Novel' she expresses her faith in the power of the computer as a concept to change literature in the same way that print did nearly five hundred years ago:

perhaps the computer . . . will alter our minds and powers of analysis once again, and enable us to create new dimensions in the deep-down logic of characters. I do not mean computers with human emotions or humanoids with computer brains . . . I mean a completely different development arising from computer logic but as unimaginable to us now as a Shakespearean character would have been to an oral-epic culture, and a different way of thinking about and rendering . . . all worldly phenomena, as revolutionary as the scientific spirit that slowly emerged out of the Renaissance and the Gutenberg galaxy. (1986a: 195)

The 'Intercom Quartet' represents an attempt to move in this direction by exploring the cognitive and cultural consequences of contemporary developments in technology. Modern technology and the discourses of knowledge associated with it represent both a threat to society and a possible means of expanding human consciousness. The role of the novel at this juncture is seen by Brooke-Rose to be crucial. Its status as written narrative fiction and its function as a means of communication provide it with the wherewithal to participate actively in present-day debates about the future of social institutions. Whether it will rise to this task is, the Quartet suggests, a question of its ability to recognize its potential and adapt itself accordingly.

Part 2

5. Contexts, Traditions, and Placing Christine Brooke-Rose

> ... the writer is anyway in perpetual exile.
>
> (Brooke-Rose 1973b: 614)

Up to now I have analysed Christine Brooke-Rose's fiction on its owns terms according to broad divisions in the techniques and themes which characterize it. I demonstrated in Part 1 that a grasp of contemporary French thought is crucial to an understanding of the intellectual context of Brooke-Rose's novels. But it is also necessary to view them in terms of the British literary institutions which produce, market, and evaluate them, and through the eyes of the public which does or does not read them. Her novels consciously position themselves on the borders between semantic fields, a topos which invites comparison with her own situation as a writer: since the 1960s she has participated in the literary cultures of both Britain and France, and the implications of this liminal position are numerous. The present chapter will examine Brooke-Rose's position *vis-à-vis* the institutions of literature in which her writing has been involved. Chapter 6 will then study the relationship between her novels and post-war experimental fiction in the two countries.

The sense of national identity is weak in Brooke-Rose's writing. She looks to Europe as her cultural home and as a point of reference for her public image. She is described in the blurb of the *Omnibus* as a 'European humanist'; in 1987 Ian Hamilton on BBC television's *Bookmark* introduced her to the British viewing public as a foreign-born novelist who 'has never minded being thought of as a European'; and the *Cambridge Guide to Literature in English* labels her a 'European intellectual' (1988: 128). Even before her definitive emigration to France in 1968 she wrote her novels while abroad. In an interview given in 1965 she explains that this is because even temporary exile makes what is being written about 'peculiar': 'I go abroad to write, because there I see everything differently. Even if I'm writing about London, I see it with a peculiar focus' (1965b: 3).

Because of Brooke-Rose's 'French' upbringing, she is perfectly bilingual and has been able to integrate herself easily into French culture.[1] Her training as a comparative philologist and her interest in the *nouveau roman* in the 1960s also took her out of England conceptually, and the feeling of being an outsider, of being ambiguously positioned, pervades her work. But though she has adopted France as her home, she has chosen to retain English as her language of composition. In this sense her exile is linguistic more than it is cultural. The language in which she lives is at one remove from the language in which she writes. She describes French as her 'material language' (1977a: 131) as opposed to English, which is her professional, adult language.

Within 'English' literature, the class of 'exiled' writers may be divided into those who have come to England and those who have left it. Though not truly exiled from British culture, Brooke-Rose falls into both categories. She came to England at the age of 13 and left at the age of 45. The intervening thirty-two years were formative: she came to be taught and she left to teach. England was a country of initiation, apprenticeship, and definition, both for her as a writer and for the nature of her literary project. Curiously, her fiction charts a reverse migratory path. Her *œuvre* leaves England after *The Middlemen* and does not definitively return until *Xorandor*, and when it comes back it does so as she herself first came, as a child. But one must beware of treating this return as that of a prodigal daughter, for if *Xorandor* also marks a reversion to the traditional generic and discursive conventions of the English novel, these have lost their innocence. They are adopted strategically in an attempt to translate concepts derived from post-structuralist philosophy into the language of the British reading public. Though there is a certain amount of self-ridicule in the quasi-messianic nature of this mission, the fact remains that Brooke-Rose's prolonged residence in a geographical and literary elsewhere has determined her subsequent novels' approaches to their projects.

The relation of Brooke-Rose's fiction to geographically and culturally defined national literatures is complex. In her early novels she gives the impression of being a very 'English' writer. With the exception of *The Dear Deceit*, these novels all have a strong sense of

---

[1] It is significant that she was one of the first non-French people to be made a tenured professor and head of a French university department.

London as a geographical presence. If the characters they portray are not all English, they nevertheless all participate in an intellectual and literary culture steeped in English mores and traditions. Moreover, the novels all fall within the realm of the very English genre of social satire—Brooke-Rose herself has described them as 'sub-sub-Evelyn Waugh' (1988c)—and a society satirized must be deftly portrayed. But already in the 1950s reviewers sensed that her work fitted uncomfortably into the contemporary norms for English fiction, and the problem of reception has been compounded since her break with realism.[2] While the later novels are set within the cultural parameters of the West, Brooke-Rose largely abandons the use of explicit cultural markers. The condition of the colourless in *Out* afflicts the entire race indiscriminately. As in Beckett's fiction, the guiding topos is clearly not geographical, but the site of philosophical and cultural problems that have been developed within Occidental discourse over the last 2,500 years. The same can be said of *Amalgamemnon* in which the question 'shall we ever make Europe?' (5, 24, 28) echoes like a refrain. The allusion to Herodotus and the Europe of Greek mythology which accompanies this phrase relocates the problem at the start of Western history as a discourse. Geographical references from Herodotus are counterpointed in *Amalgamemnon* with descriptions of modern-day superpowers, creating an effect as disorienting as the place names 'Chinese Europe' and 'Afro Eurasia' in *Out*. The spatio-temporal reference-points in these two novels mark the beginning and the projected end of the hegemony of Occidental culture and the Western literary tradition (art, it will be recalled, is banned in the world of *Out*); they indicate an awareness of the contingent and provisional nature of attempts at national self-definition.

On a practical level, however, novels are read and evaluated through the grid formed by geographically grounded institutions of literature such as the publishing industry, literary journals, the reviewing establishment, and academic criticism, which act collectively as a mechanism for placing them. While a writer may conceivably write in isolation, no book is published in a void, nor is

---

[2] The reception of Brooke-Rose's first four novels has been dealt with separately because an awareness of the literary context out of which they arose is crucial to an understanding of their propensity to strain fictional convention. The same basic problems have, however, characterized the reception of her entire *œuvre*, as will become evident over the course of this chapter.

it read in one. The very act of going into a bookshop or a library entails witnessing a book's insertion in the world of other books, and comparison is inevitable. By the fact of choosing to publish his or her novels in a given country, an author is committed to being placed within the context of that country's literature, whatever other contexts the work may also call to mind. Moreover, the rite of being placed in a literary context is a condition for an author's entry into critical discourse via the institutions of literature which regulate the production, distribution, publicity, and reception of literary works. It is nevertheless not a sufficient condition, and the process whereby a work is integrated into a tradition has a direct bearing on whether it is read, by whom, and how. A literary context can thus be understood as a historically specific force field which provides a set of assumptions about the relevant issues, questions, and problems which govern the reading of a work of literature. When a work is read through or in terms of a given context, this context organizes the reading and makes certain aspects of the work stand out.

The questions raised by the concept of context are particularly interesting in Christine Brooke-Rose's case, for it is not immediately obvious where her work fits in, whether it fits in at all, and what it might mean if it did not. We saw in the last chapter that *Textermination* takes advantage of the variety of individual response, and that in so doing it resists the determinate readings which form the basis of classification. This novel is obviously an extreme case, but to a certain extent all Brooke-Rose's novels question the categories we generally use to describe contexts: the national tradition, experimental literature, women's writing, postmodernism, science fiction, and so on. These categories all assume a certain dividing up of the field of literature according to a given conception of the most important features of a work. Throughout her career as a novelist Brooke-Rose has participated in the literary culture of the country in which she has written, first as a literary journalist in London, and then as a university lecturer in Paris. Her experience of her mediatory position is that of seeing each culture and each language through those of the other countries, but her position as it is perceived in Britain and France may be summed up by the formula that she represents Anglo-American fiction in France, while in England she represents contemporary French fiction. In each case she marks the position in one culture of that which is alien to it. Because of the difficulties this situation poses for anyone who would endeavour to place Brooke-Rose, her *œuvre* demands a less straightforward approach than that commonly adopted by readers and critics. Her writing complicates the act of placing because it works to defamiliarize culturally bound categories, and because both as a process and as a product it is informed by a number of very different contexts.

Yet with the increasing mobility of writers over the last forty-five years, Brooke-Rose's apparently anomalous position is beginning to become the norm rather than the exception. In the 1960s disaffection with the post-war welfare state and the taxes it entailed caused several British writers who had begun to make their mark in the 1950s—Anthony Burgess, John Fowles, Muriel Spark—to leave England. Equally, this period saw the emergence of a number of émigré writers such as V. S. Naipaul, Doris Lessing, Gabriel Josipovici, Dan Jacobson, Salman Rushdie, Kazuo Ishiguro, and Ruth Prawer Jhabvala who began to be taken seriously as British novelists. The net result is that much of Britain's fiction is being written by exiles and expatriates. If an adequate way of understanding the relation between Brooke-Rose's writing and the larger field of post-war literature could be found, this might provide a paradigm for dealing with the complexities involved in the placing of much contemporary fiction, and indeed of any work.

National Traditions and Literary Contexts

Unlike some writers, Christine Brooke-Rose does not develop a philosophical system or an autonomous symbolic world in her fiction. It has therefore been necessary to analyse how her texts interact with the theoretical constructs they invoke and manipulate. One such concept, employed particularly in *Out* and *Such*, is the uncertainty principle, according to which the practice of scientific observation itself affects the results obtained. This reinsertion of the perceiving subject as a constitutive aspect of scientific knowledge about the world has led to a conception of the analytic tools of science as frames of reference which enable data to 'make sense'. Similarly, the context of 'English literature' has traditionally served to situate the British reading subject in relation to the textual object. A whole matrix of categories is deployed in the acts of choosing, reading, and interpreting a book, and the myth of the national literary tradition often serves as the frame of reference within which literature is evaluated. I shall be arguing that the concept of the national tradition is not able to cope with a novelist such as Christine Brooke-Rose, and that an alternative framework must be found if we are to succeed in understanding the relation of her fiction to contemporary literature.

The myth of the national tradition which I would contest is, from the point of view of literary institutions, a lineage that acts as the historical background for contemporary literature and provides a system of landmarks against which to measure candidates for admission to it. However the process of succession is construed, be it as a cycle (Frye, Bloom), or a progressive accumulation and modulation (Eliot, Hirsch) it is governed by the idea of *handing* something *down* from one generation to the next. At the most abstract level, what is handed down is the idea of literature itself, but there is also a certain more specific set of technical acquisitions, value assumptions, hermeneutic methods, and networks of association which function as a guarantee of ongoing decipherability. At the most basic level, what is seen to be handed from generation to generation is a corpus of works, defined differently by different people, and variable over the ages, but sufficiently coherent to include a core of so-called masterpieces.

While this 'canon' has been largely desacralized of late as critics, teachers, and writers have sought to reform or 'deconstruct' it, its effective presence is undeniable. The value of such projects lies in the fact that they demonstrate the canon to be constructed rather than given. In practice, however, where once there was a single corpus, clusters emerge at the periphery which must also be read and taken into account for any new text to be deemed 'readable'. The ways in which a tradition is invented or constructed, by whom, and for whom, have a direct bearing on the likelihood that a given work will be eligible for inclusion in it. As we shall see, the dominance of the concept of the tradition has prevented Brooke-Rose's work from finding a stable place within any prevailing canon.

The second aspect of the national tradition which needs to be considered is precisely its national affiliations. In a recent article Timothy Brennan rehearses the arguments for the historical links between nationalism and narrativity. The novel has traditionally 'mimicked' the nation, in that it is a composite genre which reflects the cultural heterogeneity within a nation (1990: 51); the novel·is also one of the primary means of disseminating the myth of the nation as a coherent whole. Historically, the rise of the nation-state in the eighteenth and nineteenth centuries coincided with the rise of the novel, and Brennan argues that the strategies employed in fiction are manifest also in the 'narrative' of a nation-state as an official self-representation (49). This intriguing hypothesis nevertheless raises some doubts. Is it not a facile analogy? Does it apply to all novels?

A contrary view is offered by Mikhail Bakhtin in his essay 'Epic and Novel' (1981: 3–40), which traces the origin of the novel to a bilingual consciousness of national and cultural alterity and a tendency to question the official story of the national tradition embodied in epic and other 'completed' genres. The novel relativizes these genres by taking them as its object of representation and revealing them to be foreclosures of a cultural tradition that is infinitely more rich, diverse, and alive than the consecrated symbols and myths which nominally represent it.

The discrepancy between the two positions can be explained by the fact that Brennan and Bakhtin describe different texts. Brennan focuses on the nineteenth-century manifestation of the novel and its direct descendants, while Bakhtin traces the genre back to what he takes to be its origins in antiquity. The opposing conclusions drawn from these two analyses demonstrate that the novel is intrinsically neither a nationalist genre nor a genre which transgresses the frontiers of national cultures, but that it can be enlisted to play both these roles. Many present-day nations possess the lauded qualities of heterogeneity and openness characteristic of much contemporary narrative fiction, but the causal relation between these two phenomena is at best tenuous. The most that can be asserted with confidence is that there is a parallel between the perspective on a nation afforded by critical distance, be it internal or external, and the distancing effects of certain types of narrative which disorient the reader by portraying culturally bound myths from an alien point of view.

In contemporary Britain the heterogeneity of race, class, language, and ethnic origin among both writers and readers makes for an extremely complex literary situation. Not only can a single canon no longer be assumed, but the mechanisms by which canon formation has traditionally functioned are themselves being questioned as the definition of 'English literature' is opened to debate.[3]

---

[3] See Doyle 1989, Ashcroft *et al.* 1989.

Furthermore, individual readers and writers can no longer be assumed to share a canon; in Brooke-Rose's case, the concept of 'English literature' plays a relatively minor role compared with that of European literature broadly conceived. Critics have begun to extend their view of contemporary writing to include an international frame, but until very recently there has been a strong Anglocentric bias among critics of the contemporary novel which has had the effect of marginalizing writers such as Brooke-Rose, whose 'Englishness' is not immediately apparent.

In the 1950s the legacy of F. R. Leavis's adamantly Francophobic tradition-making enterprise was evident in many writers' preoccupation with the 'English' novel as a characteristic expression of the national consciousness.[4] In the 1960s the literary mood became less insular with the rise of the New Left and an increasing interest in literary developments taking place in France and America. But as late as the 1970s David Lodge maintained that while offshoots into the realms of fabulation and non-fiction are to be tolerated, they do not form part of the 'main road' of English fiction which is realist (1971: 8–34). Criteria such as this, though superficially more broadminded than Leavis's narrowly prescriptive stance, are nevertheless equally limiting in practice, for they set boundaries on what is to qualify as English, and they implicitly valorize the most culturally representative or pure manifestations of a genre as the most worthy. It is becoming increasingly obvious, however, that the myth of an uncontested unilinear national tradition provides an inadequate background against which to evaluate new texts. The contemporary cultural diversity of 'English' literature questions the validity of the notion of tradition itself.

An alternative, and in Brooke-Rose's case more suitable, approach to the problem of situating a work of fiction is a more strictly

---

[4] Francis Mulhern (1990) demonstrates that Leavis's Great Tradition is haunted by the spectre of the French novel in opposition to which it is constructed. Characteristic attitudes of the 1950s are exemplified in Karl Miller's description of the pernicious (if limited) influence of the *nouveau roman* on the fiction of the period as the 'French flu' (1968: 26), and William Cooper's denunciation of experiment and implicit attack on Robbe-Grillet in 'Reflections on Some aspects of the Traditional Novel' (1959). When in 1963 Frank Kermode interviewed seven major novelists of the 1950s (Iris Murdoch, Graham Greene, Angus Wilson, Ivy Compton-Burnett, C. P. Snow, John Wain, and Muriel Spark), he remarked that they were unanimously opposed to developments in contemporary French fiction: 'Not for the English novelists the sophisticated epistemology of the new French writers (of whom few of our subjects were willing, by the way, to speak)' (1963: 112).

contextual view in which the legacy of the past is seen as part and parcel of the present situation of literature. The argument that our understanding of texts we dub literary is determined by the context in which they are produced and read is akin to the postulate of information theory according to which all messages may be disambiguated given sufficient knowledge of the relevant circumstances of the communicative act. The obvious objection to this view is that the act of utterance and the act of reception are bound, in the case of written texts, to be performed in a variety of situations, and that there is therefore never only one context for any work. This is the objection to the notion of the contextual determination of meaning that Derrida articulates in 'Contexte, signature, événement' (1972*b*). Writing, he argues, necessarily implies a rupture with context because of its inherent iterability and 'citationality'. The written text is condemned to a perpetual exile from the circumstances of its production by its very nature as transportable, transposable message. The impossibility of confining writing to one spot would seem to demand that it be understood as that which undermines the determining effects of context.

Brooke-Rose's novels could be seen in this light to be prime examples of the rupture with context which characterizes all texts. The metaphoric technique that runs throughout her fiction serves to confuse linguistic domains by bringing them together in unconventional ways involving flagrant transgressions of frames of reference and the manipulation of situationally determined meanings. Brooke-Rose's career as a novelist and critic embodies the same principle: she has physically displaced herself a number of times, and she has allegiances to several different cultures. The very task of placing her as a writer might therefore seem at first to be a perverse effort to pin down for the sake of an orderly view of literary history an *œuvre* which makes the process of uprooting its principle mechanism and its underlying aim. She could be characterized as a novelist who defies placement altogether; the problem of the literary context of her work would then become a matter of its deconstruction.

But while this approach has a certain appeal, it is limiting in that it fails adequately to account for the specific nature of the discursive settings in which she has written and which her writing invokes. If Derrida objects to the limited polysemy proposed by information theory and semantics, it is not because he rejects the notion of context altogether, but because he recognizes that it does not entail finitude: his theory 'ne suppose pas que la marque vaut hors contexte, mais au contraire qu'il n'y a que des contextes sans aucun centre d'ancrage absolu' (1972*b*: 381). By no means does this lessen the importance of the mode of intervention of a text in the historical field of the 'general text'. For this reason, an analysis of the situation of an author such as Brooke-Rose will need to examine circumstances of writing in relation to circumstances of reception, which will always be more diverse, and it will be necessary to take into account the historical specificity of each.

In his analysis of exile and the twentieth-century writer, Andrew Gurr follows Mary McCarthy's distinction between expatriates, who choose to leave their native country, and exiles, who leave because for some reason they feel unwelcome there. Expatriates, Gurr argues, are generally those who move from metropolis to metropolis, and they tend to be poets, while the characteristic move of the exile is from colony (or province) to metropolis, and exiles tend to write realist fiction. The reason for the different modes of artistic expression in the two categories is explained by Gurr as a difference in attitude toward the country left behind. In the case of the exile, an urgent need to communicate the identity of that country drives him or her to the more 'explicit' form of realism, while the lack of this need in the expatriate allows for more abstract and allusive forms (1981: 19). Clearly Christine Brooke-Rose bears the marks of the expatriate more than those of the exile: she has migrated from European metropolis to European metropolis, and she has rarely, if ever, demonstrated the need to recreate the various homes of her youth. It is perhaps for this reason that she abandoned realist modes relatively early and moved into the areas of abstraction and allusion more characteristic of Gurr's expatriate poets.

Gurr's definition of the expatriate may be extended to include his or her relation to the concept of the nation. While the exile typically identifies strongly with the myth of the fatherland or the mother country, the expatriate is more often an ex-patriot. As with the narrator of *Between*, loyalty to any nation in particular remains in a state of suspension above frontiers. The exile's nostalgic longing for home, for a centre on which to fix identity, has given way in the expatriate to a continual circulation or displacement of identification. In the case of Brooke-Rose place becomes either indeterminate (*Out, Amalgamemnon*), variable (*Between, Verbivore*), or motivated by factors internal to the novel's conceptual structure (*Such, Thru,*

Xorandor, *Textermination*). The contemporary expatriate identifies with transnational institutional frameworks. In Brooke-Rose's novels these include universities, networks of scholars, networks of scientists, the European Parliament, and so on. Though he does not make this explicit, Gurr implies that whereas exiles seek to recreate in their writing an image of home that is tied to a physical place and the identity of a regional culture, expatriates (he cites James, Eliot, and Auden) tend to establish a literary identity linked rather to a corpus of texts which is by nature transportable. This capacity for transportability (or 'citationality') is thus characteristic of the modern expatriate's sense of the relation of the individual to his or her cultural origins.

But the distinction between the exile and the expatriate is not as easy to make as it may first appear. How, for example, is one to decide whether or not a given writer left home because he or she felt unwelcome there, and to what extent other factors were at play? Gurr follows McCarthy in implicitly valorizing the 'true exile' over the expatriate motivated by a lust for hedonistic escapism (18). The examples he gives of the latter category are Hemingway and Fitzgerald, but among contemporary writers the choice to settle abroad often has to do with more down-to-earth considerations, such as job opportunities or the rate of taxation. In Brooke-Rose's own case it was the offer of a post in Paris that led her to leave England, yet one could equally argue that she was motivated to a large extent by her dissatisfaction with the British intellectual scene and by the feeling that what she was writing was unwelcome in the provincial climate of the city that spawned her artistic aspirations.

Several years after her emigration to France, Brooke-Rose described for the *Times Literary Supplement* what it was like to live and work in Paris. The fact of living abroad she discounts as insignificant, in that many writers live abroad and she is of 'French' origin anyway. Furthermore, she agrees with Gurr that 'the writer is anyway in perpetual exile' (Brooke-Rose 1973*b*: 614); the act of writing fiction places her at one remove from the day-to-day life of any country.[5] Her physical displacement is thus a 'non-problem' which 'vanishes' in the face of 'the tremendous stimulus, the

---

[5] There is an interesting relationship between the idea that exile is necessary to writing and the idea expressed here that writing is itself a form of exile. Writing would seem to be an exile within an exile, an exile that mimics the conditions it demands for its accomplishment.

stretching of [her] mental horizons almost to breaking point' that she experienced in the climate of the French *nouvelle critique*. She describes the continual *recyclage* or renovation of ideas which French literary critics undergo as something lacking in the English intellectual environment, complaining that the distinction between academic and journalistic criticism in England impoverishes both.[6]

Though one could hardly describe the move from London to Paris as a flight from colony to metropolis, in retrospect Brooke-Rose felt the intellectual terrain of 1960s Britain to have been relatively stagnant compared to what she discovered upon her arrival in Paris. As a crossroads for contemporary European intellectual trends, Paris provided the conceptual tools which enabled her to turn back to concerns that had germinated while she was in London, and to formulate them within the broader perspective of structuralist and post-structuralist theories of language, subjectivity, and culture. The pattern Gurr discerns among exiled writers who move from colony to metropolis may be traced in Brooke-Rose, the expatriate, on another level. The move does not instigate an effort to put her national or regional cultural identity in perspective, but rather her intellectual identity. In all her novels from *Out* on, the values and assumptions of liberal humanism are confronted with the post-humanist enterprise of continental philosophy. The result of this interaction is never articulated as a solution or a formula; rather, by filtering her novels through theories developed in France, Brooke-Rose displaces the discursive matrices in which the novels are embedded. This displacement involves the traditional material of the (English) novel in a lateral detour through a contemporary set of epistemological constructs that are radically extrinsic to it. This idea of passing through, or *handing over and back*, in order to achieve the sense of difference necessary to reveal the specificity of a given culture may be contrasted with the notion of the national literary tradition as a process of *handing down*. From the point of view of the native cultural milieu, this passage through the other is perceived as a removal or an 'ex-tradition'. But far from being a flight from the

---

[6] This article was written in 1973 in the heyday of the *nouvelle critique* in France, when it had not yet had any significant success in crossing the channel. The situation had changed somewhat in 1986 when Brooke-Rose was interviewed on *Bookmark*, but still she said she thought the reviewing establishment and cultural programmes in the media were 'thirty years behind' (1987*d*). In an interview in 1990 she again referred to 'this slightly provincial literary life', but conceded that 'it's getting better now' (1990*c*: 31).

concerns of one's native society, the displacement of contexts functions as a generative principle which reinvigorates that society.

In describing the overwhelming nature of the multitude of theories she encountered upon her arrival in France in the late 1960s, Brooke-Rose lists one possible strategy for coping as 'hibernation' from the intellectual context of the times. She notes, however, that even temporary seclusion leads to eventual reintegration, and that it is impossible to ignore changes in one's circumambient culture. She cites as an exemplary illustration of the effect of 'hibernation' Washington Irving's story 'Rip Van Winkle' in which the eponymous protagonist is put to sleep for twenty-odd years under the force of a spell. When he wakes and returns to his eighteenth-century American village he is confronted with the fact that while he has been asleep the American War of Independence has occurred: without physical displacement he has returned to a different country. This literal effect of *dépaysement* necessitates an explanation of Rip's disappearance, and the latter half of the story recounts his attempts to adjust to this new national situation, which in turn motivates the telling of the tale. Brooke-Rose concludes her discussion of the story with a recognition of the impossibility of true evasion of context, for context is encoded in language itself: 'the writer cannot, in fact, cut himself off or do without some system, some patterning or structure if only that of language' (1973b: 614). Even the most radical decontextualization becomes in the end a matter of accounting for the gap, and the effort to do so produces narrative.

Another example of this phenomenon can be traced in *Xorandor* when the twins are sent to Germany by their father at the height of the scandal over the 'alien' stones. From their narrative limbo they complain bitterly that they cannot possibly record the events that have transpired in their absence. Because they have been 'dropped from the story' (154) they are in a narrative fix. But the very fact of being cut off awakens them to the realization that: 'Even storytellers can change, during the story' (159). The 'gap' they experience, like that of Rip van Winkle, leads to an understanding of the nature of time and narrative. Again an enforced hibernation retroactively yields a story, and the eventual return to the locus of action affords a new perspective on events.

The circuit of alienation and return acted also as a determining factor in the composition of the novel. The hybrid dialectic of computer jargon Brooke-Rose invented for the children's use was partly a consequence of her own expatriation. She claims that she was obliged to invent this language because, having been away from England for so long, she no longer knew how children spoke and could therefore not faithfully recreate contemporary adolescent slang.[7] Her own 'hibernation' in France meant that the concepts she brought 'back' and transposed onto English generic conventions were mined in French philosophical systems, but also that the England she 'returned' to in *Xorandor* was different. Her efforts to cope with the disparity between the England she knew and the England to which she returned resulted in formal experimentation. The discursive effects of alienation and reintegration are thus evident both within the novel and in the conditions out of which it arose. In both cases the primary effect is the generation of narrative and a reflection on the very conditions of possibility of the narrative act. This is just one example of the effect of 'ex-tradition', the detour through another cultural context and another language, which can be seen as a fundamental component of Brooke-Rose's writing.

There is a complex relationship in the history of twentieth-century literature between the role of the nation in a writer's work and the condition of writing across cultures and across languages. Edward Said (1984: 162) argues that the relation between exile and nationalism is dialectical. As demonstrated above, the notion of a unilinear national tradition likewise implies a continuity of orderly succession and a cultural unity that is belied by the diversity of influences, both internal and external, which in our post-colonial era are becoming ever-more prominent. The countries of Western Europe are exceptional in their linguistic homogeneity. The majority of people in the world speak more than one language in the course of their daily lives, and the impossibility of writing in one language alone has been a defining characteristic of the literary production of many writers. While for Brooke-Rose the political implications of such problems are greatly reduced, her knowledge of other languages has been an important determinant in her writing. Multilingual puns were common in her childhood home, where French, English, and German were all spoken (1989*e*: 84), and her doctoral dissertation was a comparative study of the linguistic influences of medieval French literature on its English counterpart.

---

[7] 1989*d*: 104. See also Brooke-Rose 1990*c*: 30.

She is keenly aware of the multiple linguistic 'invasions' that went into the formation of what eventually came to be the heterogeneous language she has chosen as her primary medium of composition:

Viking and Norman invading Anglo-Saxon, Latin and Greek invading English, American invading French, the wheel coming full circle, enriching, cluttering, doubling, complicating and simplifying the navigational genius of the language that keeps only what it wants, absorbing it, concealing it in its own phonetic system and throwing out the surplus into the winedark sea. As Pound the poet said that Ino said to Ulysses: 'get rid of the paraphernalia'. (1977a: 131–2)

In likening the development of language to Pound's advice to the poet, Brooke-Rose also alludes to her own penchant for combining diverse 'languages' from different specialized fields. Though this technique is only brought to bear extensively on natural languages in *Between*, sensitivity to multiple alternative codes is undoubtedly the result of Brooke-Rose's exposure at a young age to linguistic and cultural diversity. Bakhtin connects polyglossia to heteroglossia (linguistic diversity within a language), seeing in these hybrid forms the key to an 'objectivized' view of one's 'own' language: 'it is possible to objectivize one's own peculiar language, its internal form, the peculiarities of its world view, its specific linguistic habitus, only in the light of another language belonging to someone else, which is almost as much "one's own" as one's native language' (1981: 62). The process of language formation and the cultural evolution it reflects provides a model for Brooke-Rose's compositional technique as well as a reminder of the variety inherent in all language use. Far from being an ornamental effect, cultural and linguistic heterogeneity are for her the very condition of creativity.[8]

It seems evident that any attempt to circumscribe a literary context will fail if it is based solely on the notion of a national tradition, or even on linguistic criteria. In choosing a nation or a language as an organizing principle, the ethnic diversity of individual writers is invariably overlooked. The great movements of twentieth-century French and English literature have been extremely heterogeneous with respect to the cultural origins of their

---

[8] Ashcroft *et al.* (1989: 58–9) note that often the poly-dialectical fiction of post-colonial societies creates hybridized forms of language which do not represent any actual instance of possible language-use. The same may be said of Brooke-Rose's combination of diverse discourses to produce 'unrealistic' language which is nevertheless highly evocative of a variety of usages encountered daily.

adherents. It could even be argued that the most significant literary developments of the last eighty years have resulted from a break with national tradition, either as a consequence of war (Surrealism, English Modernism, the Movement in England, and the *nouveau roman* all materialized after world wars) or as an intellectual grounding that acts as an alternative to a native heritage.[9] Geographical considerations play a significant role in both cases, and the effect of 'ex-tradition' has had a formative influence on many of the period's most significant writers. Literary institutions, however, operate almost exclusively at the national level, as they are determined in large measure by the resources made available to literary production by state-run bodies and by the laws and codes of conduct that govern the production and marketing of books. Furthermore, place, in the geographical sense, works as a literal conjunction in space of ideas and trends disseminated through the media, symposia, societies, and personal contacts. These factors combine to lend a certain coherence and orientation to the variety of literary activities that prosper in a given place at a given time.

A number of different physical and conceptual spaces have contributed to the development of Brooke-Rose's fiction. The analyses that follow will attempt to delineate first, the type of reading her novels demand, and second, the ways in which the literary industry and the academic establishment in Britain have prevented them from receiving this type of reading, subjecting her and her fiction instead to a set of geographically bound cultural distinctions that fail to do justice to either.

Placing Christine Brooke-Rose

The situation Christine Brooke-Rose occupies in the field of contemporary literature must be understood in part as a function of her readers' own acts of 'ex-tradition', of their desire to locate her within their spheres of knowledge. Despite the infringement of national identity exhibited in her fiction, readers have been reluctant to abandon the national paradigm. Brooke-Rose's novels are generally thought of as difficult, 'resplendently unreadable' (Hope 1964: 742) as one reviewer phrased his hermeneutic frustration. This

---

[9] For example, Dadaism, Imagism, Vorticism, and the movements that grew around expatriate magazines during the twenties and thirties, as well as later 'isms' such as feminism and postmodernism.

is because they try to break people's reading habits; Brooke-Rose says that she writes the way she does 'to teach people to read' (1989e: 87). An analysis of the reception of her fiction will need to consider both this goal and the extent to which it is achieved. Questions that will need to be answered include: How have her efforts and those of her publishers to·publicize her fiction oriented it toward the reading public? How have individual readers' perceptions about her novels (gleaned from advertising, reviews, criticism, knowledge of the author's reputation, and so on) influenced the way in which it has been read and understood? And what are the mechanisms whereby the literary-critical establishment has determined the reading her work has received?[10]

A number of factors have combined to prevent Brooke-Rose from being fully accepted as a British novelist. She has been read *as* French rather than *through* French writing; readers and critics alike have balked at the intellectual effort demanded by her work; and the world of publishing and reviewing has found her novels difficult to process according to the expectations of a book encoded in its practices. The constraints these practices impose on the evaluation of literature place certain forms of writing at a disadvantage, notably those forms that do not conform to generic norms. The literary industry is ill-adapted to cope with an author as original and as protean as Christine Brooke-Rose, not because it is unable to tolerate novelty, but because the specific type of novelty her work offers challenges the cognitive processes which the industry assumes the reading of fiction to involve. It is the aim of Brooke-Rose's fiction to disorient the reader by encouraging him or her to survey the familiar terrain of fiction from a new perspective. The type of reading her novels demand entails a displacement of the categories around which the literary industry is structured. For this reason they have been slow to reach a readership willing to evaluate them on their own

---

[10] In Hans-Robert Jauss's terms, Brooke-Rose's goal is to change people's 'horizons of expectations'. But Brooke-Rose is uneasy with Jauss's *Rezeptionsästhetik* for the same reason that she has reservations about Iser's reader-response theory, i.e., the fact that both approaches are normative. She criticizes Jauss for assuming the possibility of a unified horizon of expectations shared by a given group of people at a given time (1981: 43). I do not want to imply, as Jauss would, that the objective qualities of Brooke-Rose's fiction can be ascertained through recourse to the reactions they have provoked in their readership. What I wish to examine are the processes by which readers have attempted to place her, the inadequacies of these moves, and (in Chap. 6) possible alternatives.

merits and have instead been deemed unsatisfactory because uncategorizable.

Reading and Readability

The diversity of the fields of knowledge on which Christine Brooke-Rose's successive novels draw is undoubtedly one of the factors which has prevented her from garnering a wide readership: those who delight in astrophysics may not be so keen on literary theory, and the followers of Derrida may not all be science-fiction fans. But Brooke-Rose's fiction has also been the victim of the unwillingness of many readers to allow it to alter their conception of what fiction is and what it might be capable of doing. Before examining the consequences of the notorious 'difficulty' of Brooke-Rose's fiction for her literary reputation, I shall therefore analyse in some detail just what the supposed obscurity of her novels entails from the point of view of the reader.

When asked recently to write an article on her 'aesthetics', Brooke-Rose interpreted the word according to its etymological origin as the reaction to a work of art; she consequently chose to analyse the bewilderment many readers express as an initial reaction to her novels. In discussing George Steiner's typology of difficulty in terms of her own work, she identifies two of Steiner's four types as pertinent. The first is the contingent: that which can be overcome if one 'does one's homework'; and the second is the tactical: intentional difficulty on the part of the author based on a desire to change readers' thought processes (1989d: 105–8). The same pair can be traced in her comment several years earlier that the difficulty in reading Pound is 'not in his language, but in his orchestration and archaeology' (1991a: 142). Like Pound, Brooke-Rose is fascinated with language, but the difficulty of her novels is not lexical or syntactic (with rare exceptions which are elucidated through repetition). The two areas of difficulty are, as in Pound, a matter of 'archaeology': the use they make of specialized knowledge and allusion, and 'orchestration': the highly complex interweaving through which textual material is put together and manipulated in unexpected ways to generate incongruous combinations and parallels.

Brooke-Rose's fictional project is conducted in accordance with Horace's dictum that literature should both please and instruct. Her didactic aim to teach people to read notwithstanding, her primary goal is to please: 'I still think that people should take pleasure in reading, that it is up to the writer to write in such a way as to direct the attention of the reader to the richness of the possibilities of language' (1989e: 89). She distinguishes between the 'pleasure of recognition' which most novels provide, and the 'pleasure of discovery' which is her goal (1987d). Yet she was aware as recently as 1990 that she still did not 'pierce through to the general public' (1990c: 31). The problem, as she sees it, is not so much a matter of readers' inability to understand her novels as the desire on the part of most for effortless consumption: 'People want the familiar. They want to be *sécurisés* as the French say, they want to be made secure, they want to be made to recognize everything. It's the pleasure of recognition, not the pleasure of discovery, and I prefer the pleasure of discovery' (1987d) The two types of difficulty can be roughly broken down according to the two types of pleasure that are attained in overcoming them. If and when a reader recognizes an allusion or quotation, the self-congratulatory delight is clearly of the first type. But because of the determining effects of context, the initial pleasure of recognition soon changes into the pleasure of discovery as the well-known reference is subtly made peculiar by its new setting or by the slight alterations and adulterations it may have undergone. This is part of the work's 'orchestration' which, when grasped, yields the pleasure of discovering a new way of conceiving of old material and delight in the disruption of expectation.

Yet the initial pleasure of recognition depends on the reference being familiar. One may well ask of any highly allusive author to what extent intertextual references rely on prior knowledge, and to what extent they act as a substitute for it. When a reference is unfamiliar there is a block; the reader is confronted with his or her own ignorance.[11] *Textermination* plays with this problem; it suggests that the ideal reader is not necessarily the reader who recognizes all the allusions, and the genius of the novel lies in this indeterminacy. *Thru*, on the other hand, ends with an 'index' of all the writers alluded to, with each name accompanied by a 'degree of presence'.

---

[11] In certain cases this can lead to the pleasure of recognition through identification. Brooke-Rose says that in *Between* she was 'exploring what it's like to be bilingual, and what it's like also *not* to know all the languages' (1990c: 30). She wrote the book upon her return from a trip to Eastern Europe, and the experience of the traveller who is confronted constantly with an incomprehensible code will itself be recognizable to anyone who has travelled abroad.

This device allows the reader to look up all the references if he or she so chooses, but it also serves as a wink to the over-eager critic. In her book on Pound Brooke-Rose recommends the first-time reader not to be worried about catching all the allusions but to 'let it just roll over you' (1971: 3). Similarly, in Brooke-Rose's novels allusions *represent* texts of the past; *how* the incorporated fragment is presented is of more significance than its precise origin. Brooke-Rose's novels are not only for the erudite. They generally repeat the references they make use of, explain them, and define them in a number of different contexts in such a way that the uninitiated will end up recognizing them and at the same time be forced to rethink them with each fresh instance. The pleasure of recognition is thus an added extra; the main aesthetic pleasure to be gained from her fiction is that of exploring the unfamiliar. Hers is 'not so much a wicked intention to thwart . . . readers as a positive desire to shift fictional conventions' (Brooke-Rose 1989*d*: 102), and it is for this reason that her novels cater to a specialized audience. Despite widespread belief to the contrary, this audience is not that of the intellectual élite capable of appreciating all the intertextual subtleties of her novels; it is composed rather of those readers with a taste for a certain form of cognitive stimulation not to be found in conventional realist fiction.

In some cases, however, the targeted audience does indeed become so narrow as to be exclusive. Brooke-Rose decided after the publication of *Thru* that she had 'gone too far', and *Amalgamemnon* was, she claims, 'the beginning of an effort towards more readability' (1990*c*: 30).[12] Yet the 'difficulty' of Brooke-Rose's writing up to this point has been partially obviated by the fact that as time passes her fiction is coming increasingly to depict the quotidian culture of its likely readers. Today many more people lead the type of life described by the narrator in *Between* than in 1968 when the novel was first published. With the expansion of multinational corporations in the 1970s and 1980s and the consequent increase in international air travel, and with enforced bilingualism imminent in the EC, the narrator in *Between* comes less to resemble a member of the jet-set élite and more to figure as a hyperbolic representation of what many frequent travellers experience in their daily lives. While the mythical type of the 1960s novel-reader read novels in a

[12] It may be added that this only becomes truly apparent with *Xorandor* and *Verbivore*, and that *Textermination*, though eminently readable, clearly hails the lover of literature.

dilapidated armchair in a shabby flat in Chelsea, the novel reader of the 1990s is more likely to read in airplanes, airport lounges, and hotel rooms, between countries, between flights.

Like *Between*, *Thru* re-creates both the act of reading and the conditions under which it is read. The 'radical' university featuring courses in 'The Inscription of Protest' and 'Narrative as Object of Exchange' was an anomaly in the early seventies when courses such as these were truly 'radical' in pedagogic terms, whereas now the teaching approaches figured in the novel would be, if not the norm, at least *a* norm among others. Moreover, because of the specialized nature of the conceptual material the novel deploys, the conditions under which it is most likely to gain wide readership are precisely those of the university class-room it portrays.[13]

The narrator of *Amalgamemnon* is another figure of the contemporary reader. She is a consumer of mass culture, and like the narrator of *Between* who reads the world around her according to conference schedules, and the academic readers in *Thru* who read according to course timetables, she reads discontinuously, between snatches of radio programmes and amorous interventions from her various lovers. The conspicuous intrusion of the radio into the time and space of reading is a concrete depiction of a generalized infringement by the mass media of reading's traditional role as a primary source of entertainment. The contemporary reader is torn, she has other allegiances, the book does not, cannot, captivate her full attention. She feels the pull of the oral/aural medium of the radio just as Herodotus's first 'readers' felt the force of the spoken word as he read out his *Histories*. The phenomenon of the printed book that occupied the intervening centuries is thus sandwiched, like the narrator's reading, between other forms of communication.

These three novels provide a model of the act of reading as it pertains to the book in all its physical and sociological specificity. They also posit it as a paradigm for cognitive activity and dramatize its place in the contemporary world. The label 'difficult' which is

---

[13] To Brooke-Rose's own chagrin, the novel lost some of its radical edge even in the time it took the printer to set it. She laments shortly before its publication in 1975 that since it was first conceived and written, Lacan's theory of the mirror stage had become somewhat of a 'banality' (1976k: 11). But what the novel loses in originality by this lapse it gains in accessibility. The two-year gestation period during which it was being laboured over by typesetters was also a crucial period of gestation for what came to be known by the general appellation of 'theory', and concepts such as the 'mirror stage' had by then gained wide currency.

attached to Brooke-Rose's fiction can be seen as a symptom of the reluctance on the part of many readers to accept the relevance of the intellectual movements which have attempted to come to terms with this world as much as it is a resistance to the experimental character of the novels themselves.

Christine Brooke-Rose and the Literary Industry

The recalcitrance on the part of many of Brooke-Rose's readers to change their reading habits is reinforced by the publishing industry. Viewing her novels through what it takes to be the eyes of the average reader, the publishing industry classifies them as both difficult and experimental. Furthermore, the type of experiment they engage in is particularly refractory to assimilation as a marketable product because the industry founds its coherence on 'recognizing', not, as some might believe, on 'discovering'. Fortunately, small presses such as those which have published Brooke-Rose's work tend to be less concerned with short-term profitability than their counterparts in other spheres of commerce. This is partly of necessity. A work of literature is an unknown quantity; even if it is highly praised by its first readers, a publisher has no means of establishing with any certainty what its future prospects are. This accounts for the well-known peculiarity of publishing practices that the majority of books printed lose money and are subsidized by occasional successes. Consequently, publishers can afford to take risks, but they must be able to rely on some regulatory mechanism that will ensure a minimum number of successes and a reasonable return on their investment. Despite their good intentions, publishers cannot afford to be philanthropic patrons of the arts, they must standardize their means of evaluating and selling their products. To do this they depend on the collusion of other branches of the 'literary industry': the literary press and academia. Because both Brooke-Rose's position as a writer and her fiction itself resist this standardizing process, she has long had an uneasy relationship with the literary establishment. In order to understand precisely how this uneasiness translates into specific constraints on the production and reception of her work, I shall analyse the four stages of this process: firstly, the enabling factors that put a novelist in a position to write; secondly, the processes of publishing and marketing; thirdly, reception as measured through reviews and published or broadcast interviews; and finally, reception by professional critics and the pedagogical establishment.

Enabling Conditions

There are important differences between the patterns of production and consumption of novels in France and Britain which have a significant impact on the fiction produced in these countries. In Britain, public lending libraries have since the war played a major role in the fiction industry. Between 1960 and 1968 state expenditure on libraries doubled. During the 1970s 30 per cent of the population were registered borrowers, and since the demise of private libraries in the 1950s fiction has represented the vast majority of books borrowed. In the early 1980s over 90 per cent of the people who read hardback fiction were library users (S. Laing 1983: 139–40). In social terms, these statistics mean that the average British novel reader is between 45 and 65, with well-established literary tastes. Consequently, libraries are generally conservative; John Sutherland goes as far as to claim that they have a 'provable bias' against the avant-garde (1978: 18).

In France, however, the situation is completely different: 13 per cent of the population buys 75 per cent of the books (Sutherland 1978: 179). As library borrowing plays a very minor role—only 4 to 5 per cent of the population are active borrowers (22)—it can be assumed that this figure is fairly representative of the number of people who actually read books in France. The French market is dominated by young, urban, educated buyers, and Sutherland comments that 'it is the *élite* nature of French reading–buying patterns which has enabled movements in "pure" literature like the *nouveau roman* to flourish' (23). Writers who publish in France are able to target an audience with élite tastes and can thus *afford* to write experimental fiction. From another point of view, the rise in France of the *nouvelle critique* meant that certain writers, Philippe Sollers for example, could write extremely difficult texts with the assurance that there would be critics such as Julia Kristeva, Jacques Derrida, and Roland Barthes poised to provide timely response. The guarantee of mediation by sympathetic critics can thus be seen as an enabling condition for much of the innovative writing in France in the 1960s.

The type of novel that will be published in a given place at a given time depends on the composition of the novel-reading audience, on the amount of income generated by various types of novels and on their sales potential over time, and also on the resources available to the novelist in the form of state subsidies, private wealth, advances from publishers, and so on. But the type of novel that is *written* in a given place at a given time, though influenced significantly by its likelihood of being published and therefore by the factors that contribute to this, is also determined in large measure by another set of factors which have to do with the role of novels and novelists in society at large. Writing in *The Author* in 1965, John Weightman compares the prestige of the author as a public figure in France with that of his or her British counterpart, and suggests that the author's sense of self-importance in France may have contributed to the rise of self-reflexive fiction in that country (1965: 4–5). In order for the writing of novels to be considered appropriate subject-matter for fiction, the act of writing must itself be held in high esteem, and with it the novelist as a figure. The situation in Britain is, of course, slightly different: the novelist does not enjoy the prestige of the French writer, nor can he or she afford to cater to as select and rarified an audience. In Britain the paucity of institutional backing and the nature of British reading habits condemns novelists to write highly accessible fiction if they are to live off their pens. This means that experimental writers are, in the main, people who can support themselves in other ways.[14]

For an English-language author publishing and selling books in Britain to write 'like' the French writers in fashion in the early 1960s is, therefore, for her to write as if she were publishing and selling her novels in France, as if she were writing under radically different cultural and institutional constraints from those that in fact impinged upon her scriptorial activity. But if the contradiction of Brooke-Rose's situation as a novelist surfaces in her writing as a sense of having no validated place, it is also, for this very reason, a source of creativity. It allows her to occupy a privileged position between the two cultures which affords her a critical perspective, incorporated into her novels' formal strategies, on both of them; her novels internalize and defend the ambiguous site from which they are written through the process of 'ex-tradition' discussed above. This does not, however, prevent them from being mis-placed by the very institutions they would dis-place.

[14] Though Hamish Hamilton did receive a bursary from the Arts Council to help finance the typesetting of *Thru*, between 1966 and 1970 only four other works were subsidized by individual grants from that body (S. Laing 1983: 142).

Publishing and Marketing

Christine Brooke-Rose could not have chosen a better moment than 1964 to publish her first experimental novel. The 1960s were a time of plenty for the publishing industry in Britain. The increase in grants for education following the Second World War increased the market for 'quality' fiction, and public lending libraries were being liberally funded. Small presses were in a position to undertake 'imaginative publishing ventures' with the knowledge that libraries 'could be expected to buy a commercially reassuring number of any novel emanating from a respectable publisher' (Sutherland 1978: 12). Even with relatively short print-runs, Brooke-Rose's novels were potentially able to turn a profit. Given the fact that she had established her literary reputation in the 1950s both as a journalist and as a novelist, she was a 'safe bet' no matter how obscure her work was considered to be.

Secker and Warburg, the publishers of her first four novels, nevertheless rejected *Out* in 1963. The novel was accepted by Michael Joseph, who also published *Such*, *Between*, and *Go When You See the Green Man Walking*. The print-runs of the novels became successively shorter: 3,000 copies were printed of *Out*, and despite the fact that it won the Society of Authors Travelling Prize, with the publication of *Such* the figure was reduced to 2,500. Again, the James Tait Black Memorial Prize conferred upon *Such* evidently did little to boost sales.[15] But though *Between* had an edition of only 2,000, all the copies were sold (Brooke-Rose 1983*b*: 209). When Raleigh Trevelyan, Brooke-Rose's editor at Michael Joseph, moved to Hamish Hamilton, he took her with him. Hamish Hamilton published *Thru* in 1975 with a print-run of 1,500, of which slightly over half were sold and the rest remaindered in 1978. Unfortunately, Trevelyan was unable in 1979 to convince Hamish Hamilton to publish an early version of *Amalgamemnon* entitled *Soon*. Brooke-Rose rewrote the novel extensively over the next four years, before sending the *Amalgamemnon* manuscript to Carcanet, which since 1981 had been publishing a small range of what its editor, Michael Schmidt, describes as 'modernist' fiction.

In 1984 Brooke-Rose had not published a novel in nine years and had only published one since fiction's boom period of the 1960s. The

---

[15] Michael Joseph was unable to provide statistics on sales figures for *Out*, *Such*, or *Go When You See the Green Man Walking*.

intervening sixteen years had witnessed a number of changes within both the fiction industry and her particular audience. In the early 1970s the industry experienced a crisis as a result of soaring production-and-distribution costs due to inflation, and falling sales due to a depressed economy. As a result it was forced to reconsolidate and find new ways of turning a profit. The paperback revolution of the 1960s and the rise of conglomerates in the 1970s meant that many small presses were bought out by larger, more diversified firms, which put pressure on them to abandon their traditional patrician attitudes so as to become more profitable. This encouraged the publishing of best-sellers, classics, and other 'safe' forms such as genre fiction, which began to enjoy increasing popularity. The publishing of genre fiction then led to generic marketing and the targeting of specific audiences, a practice which left nonconformist forms such as technically experimental fiction in danger of falling through the cracks of the industry.[16] Though the industry has since experienced a remarkable recovery, partly attributable to the renewed interest in fiction brought about by the establishment of literary awards such as the Booker Prize and partly to the increased importance of literary agents, the tendency toward generic categories has persisted. (It is perhaps for this reason that in 1986 Brooke-Rose began to publish genre fiction herself, for the pressure to fit into a category defined by the industry had increased dramatically.)

The literary world to which Brooke-Rose returned in 1984 had changed in another way as well. Not only had the audience Brooke-Rose enjoyed in the 1950s and 1960s aged considerably, but a younger generation of educated readers was beginning to internalize some of the theoretical concepts that had become second nature to her ten years earlier. This audience had been broken in on 'postmodernism' with the popular success in the 1970s and early 1980s of novels by Angela Carter, Alasdair Gray, Robert Nye, and Salman Rushdie, and the sophisticated fiction printed in paperback by Picador. Reviewers could no longer complain shamelessly as they had in the 1960s that 'the reader needs to work too hard, intellectually, all the way' (Seymour-Smith 1966: 593). Readers were more attuned to the issues Brooke-Rose was addressing and were better equipped conceptually to handle her novels.

[16] The foregoing portion of this paragraph relies heavily on Sutherland 1978: Chap. 2.

At the same time as the manuscript of *Amalgamemnon* was under consideration at Carcanet, Raleigh Trevelyan also sent it to her former publisher, Secker and Warburg, who, should they have launched her come-back, would have given her ample publicity and the security afforded by a large press. Secker and Warburg in fact made her an offer, but she chose Carcanet when they agreed to reprint her four previous novels in paperback. Though Carcanet is a small firm and cannot afford to advertise widely, Brooke-Rose received extensive behind-the-scenes publicity designed to reawaken interest in her fiction among well-known reviewers and critics who were already familiar with her work. In 1986 *The Christine Brooke-Rose Omnibus* appeared after considerable delay. *Xorandor* was published the same year and met with sufficient success for it to be bought by the paperback firms of Paladin (UK) and Avon (US) the next year.[17]

Amalgamemnon, the *Omnibus*, and *Xorandor* were also published in the US by Carcanet New York, opening up the American market to an author whose only other American publications—*The Sycamore Tree* in 1959 and *The Dear Deceit* in 1961—had long since been forgotten. The sudden availability of all Brooke-Rose's work together triggered a spurt of interest among American-based critics which marked the beginning of her acceptance as a significant writer. Unfortunately, the New York branch of Carcanet has since closed, but *Textermination* was published in the US in 1992 by New Directions, and the Dalkey Archive Press is to reprint *Amalgamemnon* there in 1994.

While *Amalgamemnon* and *Xorandor* sold relatively well in hardback, neither the *Omnibus* nor the paperback edition of *Xorandor* achieved wide sales in Britain. *Verbivore* also failed to live up to Carcanet's expectations; *Textermination*, on the other hand, was a considerable success in hardback. If one can assume that the market for paperback fiction is younger than that for the hardback equivalent, these figures suggest that through her association with Carcanet Brooke-Rose has largely recaptured her former audience, but that she is only now beginning to reach an international audience and the younger readership in Britain which is potentially more receptive to her work than was the corresponding generation of the 1960s.

[17] The information in this paragraph was obtained from Michael Schmidt of Carcanet.

The presses which have published Brooke-Rose's fiction have tried to overcome the difficulties inherent in marketing her fiction in a number of ways. The two means of marketing which a small press has at its disposal are the physical presence of a book in bookshops and the descriptions of it in their catalogue.[18] Carcanet does not advertise in the media, and newspaper advertisements for new novels by Michael Joseph and Hamish Hamilton generally consist of lists of a season's books, with little if anything to differentiate them. The dust-jackets of hardcovers and the covers of paperbacks are thus the most direct form of contact the reading public has had with Brooke-Rose's fiction. The most successful jackets of Brooke-Rose's novels have been characterized by two features: bright, bold graphics (usually composed solely of text) which draw the bookshop browser's immediate attention, and mystery as to the title of the book.[19] Such enigmas draw the inquisitive reader who is attracted by the unusual and is willing to make the effort to work out logical puzzles. *Between* is perhaps the most striking example of this technique: there is no lettering on the cover at all. The title and author's name appear only on the spine, so that when the novel is displayed they are not in evidence, an absence which is perhaps a subtle allusion to the novel's proscription of the copula. The jacket of *Amalgamemnon* has as its background an extract in Greek from Herodotus's *Histories*. This is overlaid with the title itself in cybernetic-cubic characters. Without any pictorial 'representation of content', the jacket represents textually the imposition of computer-age technology on the classical humanist tradition. This palimpsest juxtaposition of the ancient and the futuristic is disorienting; it is designed to spark curiosity in the potential buyer and a desire to read the book in order to discover what the connection between the two could possibly be. Arousing the curious reader's interest through the use of intriguing graphics is a relatively straightforward task, however. Once the book has seized his or her attention, persuading him or her to actually buy it is another matter. This is the function of the blurb.

[18] The descriptions given on the dust-jacket are in most cases virtually identical to those given in publishers catalogues and in press releases. They will be treated as such in the following discussion except where otherwise noted.

[19] In a letter to Carcanet in 1985 concerning the jacket design of *Xorandor*, Brooke-Rose makes two requests: she wants the design to be composed solely of lettering with 'no representation of content'; she also asks that the lettering be 'clear and large and call the potential buyer from the other side of the shop' (1985d).

The marketing of a novel involves the targeting of an audience. In the case of an experimental or difficult novel, the publisher promotes the fact that it is new and different and ought therefore to be read by anyone with a serious interest in literature. In order to reach the audience of 'serious fiction', Michael Joseph focused on Brooke-Rose's originality. In the blurb for *Such* this is quite explicit: 'In this country we have virtually no modern writers exploring fiction beyond the conventional forms. By attempting such a bold and complex theme, by bringing to it her usual qualities of humour, high seriousness and poetic precision, she stands almost alone.' The blurb descriptions of *Out*, *Such*, and *Between* all exploit the continuity with Brooke-Rose's earlier fiction evident in the consistency of her humour. *Out* is described as being 'full of the humour and wit always associated with Miss Brooke-Rose's earlier work', but it is also labelled 'a most unusual novel'. Likewise, *Between*'s jacket refers to Brooke-Rose's 'unique analogical style'. This emphasis on originality is tinged with a sense of the bizarre and outlandish in order to lend it a specific character. *Out* and *Between* are both qualified as 'strange', while Brooke-Rose's technique in *Such* is characterized as 'most unreal'. It is difficult to convince people that they ought to read something experimental or unique for that reason alone. Another selling-point is necessary, and this Michael Joseph largely failed to provide. Their technique of defamiliarizing the novels may well have had the effect of alienating the reader before the point of sale.

Hamish Hamilton appealed in the blurb of *Thru* to 'admirers of *Between*, *Such*, and *Out*', but warned even this restricted audience that 'they are liable to be both dazzled and teased', and that it was Brooke-Rose's intention 'to make demands on us, even to baffle us'. The audience to which the novel is likely to appeal is thus clearly targeted, but at this low point in the book trade, the novel did perhaps not have a very large potential buyership to begin with.

In the 1980s Carcanet recognized that the 'serious reader' also had serious moral concerns. It therefore attempted to defuse Brooke-Rose's reputation as an artificer of pure form. The blurb on the back of the *Omnibus* claims that Brooke-Rose's novels are written 'not in a spirit of innovation for its own sake but to engage with central tensions and contradictions in our culture'. The aversion to gratuitous experiment is also anticipated through pre-emptive strategies on the jacket of *Amalgamemnon*, where a description of the author's 'creativity of wit and invention and an infectious joy in language' is followed by the proviso that: 'These are themselves part of a much larger crisis, that of humanism and print-culture facing, trying to outface, the electronic culture and the global crisis together.' Carcanet's approach thus has been to convince readers that there is a solid reward to be had in making the effort to read Brooke-Rose's work, and that this reward is one they habitually seek in fiction.

In choosing material for the blurb of *Xorandor*, both Carcanet and Paladin have relied on parallels drawn between Brooke-Rose's novels and exemplary instances of ground-breaking works which have proved successful in the past. This strategy takes the form of the identification of an as-yet ill-defined and untapped audience brought to light as a potential market by an unexpected recent best-seller. Thus the paperback edition of *Xorandor* bears on its cover a quotation from a review comparing it to Douglas Hofstadter's *Gödel, Escher, Bach*, which by its huge success identified as a distinct group of readers those who have a taste for amusing intellectual mind-games. A quotation on the back cover compares the novel to Anthony Burgess's *A Clockwork Orange* and to Russell Hoban's *Ridley Walker*, both also slightly unusual novels which gained wide readership. Though these comparisons may be inexact and even misleading, their primary function is not to tell potential readers that *Xorandor* is *like* another book they have enjoyed, but that if they have enjoyed another book, they will enjoy this one too.

There is a danger, however, that the advertised content of a novel might appear to limit its audience to the cult-following of certain sub-genres. To prevent this, Carcanet's jacket praises *Xorandor* as Brooke-Rose's 'most excitingly topical novel yet', and attempts to pander to as many tastes as possible by emphasizing the novel's multi-generic qualities: 'high-tech and nuclear energy mingle with myth, children's adventure stories, thrillers, fabulations and philosophical speculations'. Again with *Verbivore* genre is used ambiguously. The press-release for the novel describes it as 'only just science fiction' so as not to alienate readers who might be put off by the generic classification, but at the same time to build on the science-fiction audience garnered through *Xorandor*'s success. The strategy is a 'xorandoric' effort to have it both ways. Likwise, the blurb on the jacket of *Textermination* stresses that the novel is 'a good read', while also appealing to those interested in literary theory by indicating that it 'raises a multitude of questions about reading itself'.

With the increased image-making and packaging of authors that has become the norm over the last fifteen years, Brooke-Rose is at a considerable disadvantage. She does not have an agent, she has published irregularly, she has not been taken up by a major highbrow paperback publisher such as Picador, and her novels do not fit easily into the categories publishers use to sell fiction. Moreover, the fact that she lives abroad takes her out of day-to-day contact with people who might help re-establish her reputation. Her novels have not met with large popular success, nor have they been recuperated to any great extent into the professional intellectual discourses of literary criticism. In order to understand their apparent failure on both fronts, I shall now examine the specificities of the institutions that govern these two domains, and how Brooke-Rose's fiction has fared in each of them.

Reviews and Interviews

If marketing practices map out a potential audience for a novel, reviews effect a redefinition of this market, and over the last thirty years there have been significant changes in book-reviewing in Britain. The split Brooke-Rose so deplored between academic journals and the popular literary press occurred in the late 1960s, when the demise of the literary magazine effectively destroyed what forum there was in Britain for the exchange of ideas.[20] Stewart Laing describes the mediation of literature by the literary press as 'a whole process of filtering of knowledge and opinion' which was in the 1960s the mechanism whereby 'readers identified themselves as literary and producers identified the readers as a market' (1983: 134). New mechanisms were required in the 1970s and 1980s for the identification of a market. The most significant of these was genre reviewing, in which the reading public was implicitly divided up into taste-groups and books were reviewed according to standards established for each group. In such a situation most of Brooke-Rose's novels are clearly at a disadvantage.

The plot of *Xorandor*, in which an unfamiliar alternative life-form is mistaken for an alien and expelled from his native planet, can be

[20] Brooke-Rose began to have difficulty publishing her criticism in the literary sections of Sunday papers at this time (see Brooke-Rose 1970), and her frustration with the changes that were taking place in British literary journalism may have contributed to her decision to move to France in 1968.

read in the light of Brooke-Rose's reception in England as an allegorical literary autobiography.[21] She has been described as 'England's most experimental novelist' (*Radio Times*, 2–8 May 1987: 62), and her peculiar form of discursive innovation finds no parallel in contemporary British fiction.[22] Because she lives in France, her work is assimilated to that of a foreign literature which is less familiar and more hazily characterized. Until recently she has been consistently associated with the *nouveau roman* and rejected in the minds of the reading public from the 'English novel'. In Jenny Turner's phrase, Brooke-Rose's writing 'falls between too many stools' (1990: 91).

There were occasional favourable comparisons, however. John Whitley described *Between* in the *Times Literary Supplement* as a 'near-parody' of the *nouveau roman*, a combination of the French talent for precise linguistic choreography and the 'pathos and high farce' which French fiction lacks:

The rare achievement of *Between* is to put the abstract etymological theorising of Lévi-Strauss and the Structuralists into tangibly crumpled light-weight suits, sawdust cafés; for once the characters of a *nouveau roman* are alive and well and living in free association. Better still, they have a sense of humour. (1968: 62)

In tying Brooke-Rose's theoretical preoccupations and her linguistic techniques to the human concerns she addresses, Whitley hits on a connection that is central to her work but which most reviewers have ignored. They generally view her narrative and linguistic innovation as a deterrent which dazzles through its cleverness but is incompatible with an adequate treatment of moral or ethical matters.

In the 1960s and 1970s reviews of Brooke-Rose's fiction tended to be subjective. Reviewers were unafraid to voice personal likes and dislikes and to judge her work accordingly. Between 1964 and 1975 approximately two out of three reviews made an explicit connection

---

[21] See Birch 1991 for bibliographical references to a fuller selection of reviews of Brooke-Rose's fiction.

[22] She has been compared with Anthony Burgess for her lexical inventiveness (Disch 1986: 10), with Brigid Brophy for her typographics (Stevenson 1986: 212), with B. S. Johnson for her self-imposed technical constraints (Turner 1990: 91), with John Fowles for her concern with the problems of 'formulating the world' (Clute 1986: 52), and she has been consistently lumped in with the American school of postmodernism, but these comparisons often reveal only superficial likenesses and fail to account for Brooke-Rose's originality (see below, Chap. 6).

between Brooke-Rose and the *nouveau roman*. Because of the constraints inherent in the practice of book-reviewing, reviewers are not at leisure to ponder over a novel, nor can they put it down and come back to it a week, a month, or a year later when they are in a more appropriate frame of mind to appreciate it. As a result, a demanding novel is likely to frustrate reviewers far more than it would those who purchase it and have the time to savour it slowly.[23] This frustration surfaces in the reviews themselves in various guises, as, for example, when Francis King admits of *Thru* that: 'After struggling off and on for a week to unravel its intentions, I suspect that it is the kind of work that ends up on the desks of grateful thesis-writers' (1975: 12). Perhaps the fact that nearly all the negative reviews of this novel took issue with the blurb on the dust-jacket more than with the novel itself is indicative of the lack of sufficient time for reviewers to digest their weekly consignment of books. *Thru* was likened in almost all cases to French experimental fiction, and usually rather inaccurately to the *nouveau roman*.

In the 1980s critics were better-equipped technically to appreciate Brooke-Rose's fiction; it is perhaps for this reason that they tended on the whole to withhold judgement. Her novels are described in reviews and the audience that is likely to appreciate them is defined, but the element of personal response is less apparent. This can be partly explained by the gradual change in reviewing practices over the last thirty years, but it is also due to the increasing accessibility of Brooke-Rose's work and to the fact that she has been recognized by several influential critics as an important writer.

An effort was made in the 1980s by some reviewers to reclaim Brooke-Rose for British fiction. Bob Marshall gave *Amalgamemnon* a short but highly laudatory review in the *Bookseller*. He writes of the novel's 'delight in language and wordplay that attracts the pejorative label "experimental" (authors should not display too much inventiveness and intelligence or be influenced by French modes if British)' (1984: 2,159). By making explicit the hidden imperative that had conditioned reviewers' reactions to Brooke-Rose in the past, Marshall both contests it and uses it to define the type of reader who will *not* like the novel. Brian Morton's *TLS* review of *Xorandor* goes even further, and tries to disentangle her work from French

---

[23] There is evidence to suggest that Brooke-Rose's novels 'age well'. As she herself remarks, there is often 'a *décalage* of retrospective appreciation' by reviewers who praise her earlier novels but criticize the one under review (1979).

fiction: 'Brooke-Rose has been quietly dismissed as an unEnglish figure, disturbingly cerebral and "experimental". But she resembles Robbe-Grillet less than Ivy Compton-Burnett' (1986: 767). In between these two positions, Jenny Turner analyses Brooke-Rose's reputation and attributes it to her 'mystique-ridden profile': 'among general readers she is thought of, if at all, as a sterile academic prankster, not for the likes of you or me' (1990: 91).

The novel under review in this article is *Verbivore* which, with *Xorandor*, required the reviewing world to rethink Brooke-Rose's place in British fiction and the audience she is likely to attract. The fact that these two novels were written and marketed as science fiction ensured that they would be reviewed in science-fiction magazines and thereby gain exposure to the wide but select audience which would be most likely to be sympathetic to them. This move succeeded in breaking the link that had chained Brooke-Rose to the *nouveau roman* and admitting her to the category of mainstream fiction. But though reviews in the 1980s and 1990s have been by and large more sympathetic and less judgemental than they were in earlier years, this is primarily because the range of acceptable forms has increased and because Brooke-Rose has made an effort to conform to them, not because reviewers have been more wary of classification as an approach to reviewing.[24]

Brooke-Rose is aware that acceptance within a group or an 'interpretive community' guarantees the writer, like the intellectual, a means of gaining recognition and sanction: 'Il est toujours plus facile d'être acclamée comme représentante d'un groupe, même large, que comme représentante de la race humaine, ou, dans notre cas, des écrivains en général' (1986d: 394). Yet she obstinately refuses to write in such a way as to fit comfortably into a group or a type. Reviewers have consistently responded to the wit, verbal

---

[24] American reviews of *Amalgamemnon* demonstrated that the American attitude toward linguistic virtuosity is even more resolutely inimical than that of the British: 'In her effort to offer an alternative to technological impoverishment of the humanistic tradition, Brooke-Rose veers off into extravagant display' (Kendall 1985); '[the novel is] nearly unreadable and less profound' (*Kirkus Reviews* 1985). *Xorandor* was well received on the whole. Thomas Disch praises the novel for its economy and contrasts it with Brooke-Rose's earlier style, which 'only very earnest Ph.D. candidates are likely to mistake for good prose' (1986: 10). It is significant that both novels were given prominent coverage in the *New York Times Book Review* which, as Richard Ohmann (1984: 380–2) has shown, is the gateway to the canonization of fiction in America. (In America, as in Britain, reprints are not widely reviewed, and in neither country did the *Omnibus* receive significant mention in the mainstream press.)

ingenuity, and supposed difficulty of her writing, but efforts to place her have worked to her detriment because they have been based on preconceived ideas that reviewers have passed on to readers who have, as a consequence, been alienated from her fiction even before they have had a fair chance to appreciate it. When she gives public readings, Brooke-Rose remarks, 'the audience laughs in the right places and seems to have no difficulty in understanding' (1989*d*: 102).

This fact suggests that, were Brooke-Rose allowed to present her novels herself, those in a position to evaluate them might be less inclined to reductive classifications. Yet the nominally interactive mode of the published interview has tended, on the contrary, to bypass the issue of her novels' place altogether, and it has been in recent radio and television interviews that Brooke-Rose has been best able to put forward a case for the contemporary relevance of her writing.

No matter how the task is construed, the duty of the book review is to advise readers whether or not it is worth their while to read the most recent crop of books. An interview, on the other hand, either assumes a pre-existent interest on the part of the potential reader or aims to stimulate curiosity. One may assume that the interviewer will choose topics of discussion which will most appeal to the audience at large. It is not surprising, therefore, that interviews with Christine Brooke-Rose have passed over her relation to the *nouveau roman*, concentrating instead on her views on writing, the novel in general and, to a lesser extent, her own work. Brooke-Rose has been the subject of four interview-articles since the publication of *Out* in 1964. In addition, she has appeared on BBC Radio 4's *Woman's Hour* (1984) and on BBC 2's *Bookmark* (1987).

Brooke-Rose's first interview-article, published in the *Guardian* in 1964, is one of the few in which she is allowed to represent herself to any great extent. A good half of the 1,200-word article is in her own words, with the focus firmly fixed on the soon-to-be-published novel *Out*. The interviewer, Myrna Blumberg, is sympathetic but discreet, providing mainly factual information rather than evaluative commentary. *Out* is also the nominal subject of an interview in 1965 with 'Boswell', published in the *Scotsman*, but there is very little in the article about the novel itself. In the 600 words out of 1,250 that are hers, Brooke-Rose discusses the reviews she has received, readers' reactions to experimental fiction, her attitude toward being a female writer, her taste in fiction, and the conditions under which she writes. While these are undoubtedly relevant to her work, they are only meaningful in the context of a discussion of the novel itself.

Again in 1970, John Hall's *Guardian* interview conveniently bypasses Brooke-Rose's fiction and emphasizes instead her role as a critic and her theories of the novel as a genre. Written to coincide with the publication of *Go When You See the Green Man Walking*, the article opens with a quotation from 'The Foot' which Hall commends for 'exploring a form to its limits' (Hall 1970: 9). He then abandons her fiction altogether, going on to recount the resistance Brooke-Rose's critical stance met with when she worked as a literary journalist in London, and her eventual move to France. Nearly all of the remaining 800 words in the 1,200 word article is comprised of Brooke-Rose's own discussion of her views as a critic on contemporary fiction and how these have been modified as a result of her immersion in French literary culture. Again, these are relevant to an understanding of her fiction, but since the fiction itself is not well represented, the context they create is virtually meaningless.

Published in *City Limits* in 1990, Jenny Turner's article is a combination review-interview-article. Of a total of 1,350 words, Brooke-Rose is allotted only 150. The article begins by describing Brooke-Rose's reputation and goes on to give an overview of her fictional output since 1964. This is followed by a critical review of *Verbivore* which depicts it as 'old-fashioned and backward-looking' (Turner 1990: 91). Quotations from Brooke-Rose's responses to questions are fragmentary. They are interspersed at irregular intervals to complement Turner's analysis, but they prevent Brooke-Rose's portion of the article from establishing a coherent point of view.

In all but one case the interview-articles are concerned not with Brooke-Rose's fiction as such but with her role as a public figure, a critic, and in the last instance a novelist who has had her day. They do not permit Brooke-Rose herself either to discuss what she is trying to do in her novels or to counter myths that have evolved around her.[25]

Ironically, Brooke-Rose has fared better in interviews on radio and television than she has in her own medium. In the *Woman's*

[25] As the interviews she has given in academic journals and the articles she has written on her own work demonstrate, this is not out of reluctance on her part to address these issues.

Hour programme, broadcast just before the appearance of *Amalgamemnon* in 1984, approximately one-third of the ten-minute interview is devoted to the novel itself. The other two-thirds is comprised of discussion of related subjects such as what it is like to live in France, the French media, and so on. Brooke-Rose is thus granted an opportunity to outline the basic themes and textual strategies of her work, and at the same time to relate them to daily experience in such a way as to provide a context for the novel. Rather than confronting stereotypes about her past work, the interview serves as a springboard for the fresh start which was Carcanet's aim in relaunching her as a novelist.

The *Bookmark* interview is considerably longer (approximately twenty minutes) and more revealing. It can be described as 'dialogic' in that, as in the novels which are its subject, different voices are allowed to interact freely. The film is composed of a mixture of passages read from Brooke-Rose's novels (either by her or by actors), fragments of the interview in which she discusses them, and fragments of an interview with A. S. Byatt. Byatt's portrayal of Brooke-Rose is on the whole sympathetic, yet in the final section Byatt confesses a deep unease with the theories she attributes to Brooke-Rose and presents the typically English view that 'we can't act morally, or politically, or even as animals if we are constantly problematizing the world and constantly saying all this is simply a fiction'. No arbitration of these contrasting views is supplied, and the differences between them are left unresolved.

The film is also dialogic in that it consciously 'deconstructs' itself. The final image of A. S. Byatt is followed by a coda in the form of a letter written to *Bookmark* by Brooke-Rose after the film had been shot. In this letter, which we see on the screen, Brooke-Rose corroborates her earlier assertion that '*all* our systems are fictions' by demonstrating point by point how the film itself has constructed a fiction about her. By including this letter in the film, *Bookmark* reveals the tricks of its trade and tacitly admits that it has exploited Brooke-Rose's connection with France in order to construct an image of her. The interaction between the writer and the myth of the writer is staged in such a way that Brooke-Rose is able to confront British perceptions of herself without overt attack. In an irony presumably not lost on the viewer, it is the medium of television assailed in her novels which allows her the freedom to voice her views and the ability to reach the wide audience her novels do not.

The increased receptivity of the British audience of the 1980s to innovative fiction accounts, perhaps, for the fact that Brooke-Rose was able to appear in the more mainstream media of radio and television. But the nature of the British literary establishment is such that an experimental novelist does not rise to fame through radio and television appearances (the way, for instance, Philippe Sollers did in France in the 1980s). If Brooke-Rose is to achieve recognition, it will most likely be through the medium of print and the agency of academic critics.

Critical Reception

Despite the manifold objections to the 'canonization' of fiction, one of which is that it entails 'institutionalization' through critical 'processing', it is still in practice a necessary condition in order for a difficult novel to gain wide and lasting recognition. Brooke-Rose's fiction has been mentioned in several surveys of postmodernism (Hassan 1982; McHale 1987; Nash 1987; Waugh 1984) and contemporary British fiction (Levitt 1987; Massie 1990; R. Hayman 1976; Stevenson 1986; Swinden 1984).[26] Other novelist-critics, including Angus Wilson (1968: 17), B. S. Johnson (1973: 167), David Caute (1971: 116–17), and A. S. Byatt, have recorded a liking for Brooke-Rose's work. She also has entries in the *Oxford Companion to English Literature* (1985), the *Cambridge Guide to Contemporary Fiction in English* (1988), and articles devoted to her in the dictionary *Contemporary Novelists* (Hall 1976), the *Dictionary of Literary Biography* (Levitt 1983), and the *Feminist Companion to Literature in English* (1990). But her work has been the object of some curious omissions as well. Janet Todd fails to include her in the *Dictionary of British Women Writers* (1989), there is no mention of her in Olga Kenyon's *Women Novelists Today: A Survey of English Writing* (1988), nor does she figure in Allison Lee's *Realism and Power: Postmodern British Fiction* (1989). Because she is not explicitly feminist she is left out of recent surveys of feminist fiction by Anne Cranley-Francis (1990), Paulina Palmer (1989), and Patricia Waugh (1989). Furthermore, because the label 'post-modern' has been applied extremely widely and loosely, the number

---

[26] There is a tendency in many of these passing references and brief analyses (Fowler 1977, McHale 1987, Nash 1987, Stevenson 1986, Waugh 1984) to emphasize *Thru*, Brooke-Rose's most difficult novel from the point of view of the average reader, which has undoubtedly had the effect of scaring readers away.

of writers to which it refers is so large that Brooke-Rose is squeezed out of surveys such as the otherwise comprehensive *A Poetics of Postmodernism* by Linda Hutcheon (1988). She has also suffered from critical indifference in the two countries where she lives and publishes. No British-based critic has written an article on her work, and there has been only one such article from France (Lecercle 1992). It has been mainly from elsewhere in Europe and from America that a limited amount of critical attention has been given to Brooke-Rose's work (see the Bibliography).

In Britain contemporary literature is taught in universities less than it is across the Atlantic, which means that critics have less reason to be professionally interested in Brooke-Rose's work. She has, however, been remarked on by several prominent critics, among them Frank Kermode whose praise of *Thru* is quoted on the dust-jacket of that novel (and subsequently reprinted on the jacket of *Amalgamemnon* as well as on the back of the *Omnibus*):

If we are ever to experience in English the serious *practice* of narrative as the French have developed it over the last few years, we shall have to attend to Christine Brooke-Rose. There has been writing in English *about* the subject, and even a small amount of timid pastiche; but Christine Brooke-Rose is the sole practitioner of the real thing.

Though this commendatory description would lead one to suppose that Brooke-Rose's novels would at least be noticed and taken seriously by academic critics, it has the effect also of linking her work once again to the French tradition. To some English readers the hypothetical 'if' might sound ominous rather than hopeful. Her ambivalent position as a writer of novels that question national canons makes their inclusion on the syllabuses of English faculties problematic. This problem is compounded by the fact that English faculties are nearly always separate from the faculties of modern languages which teach Continental and comparative literature. The isolation of English as a discipline reduces the chances that a concept of European literature will be developed in Britain in which Brooke-Rose's fiction might achieve prominence.

Until Carcanet reissued *Out, Such, Between*, and *Thru* in the *Omnibus* edition in 1986, Brooke-Rose's novels had been published and marketed exclusively in Britain, and they had appeared only in hardback. They were thus out of the price-range of much of the younger portion of the audience which might potentially have been interested in them. In a letter to Brooke-Rose in 1979, Raleigh Trevelyan asks 'whom do you regard as your public?' and answers, 'I think it is primarily the academic world, and I also think you would agree with me' (Trevelyan 1979). Her current editor, Michael Schmidt, is adamantly opposed to this view. He describes her audience as readers over 40 who know of her from when she lived in London and worked as a literary journalist (Schmidt 1990). There are signs, however, that both these conceptions are outdated and that Brooke-Rose is beginning to reach a wider, younger sector of the reading public.

Whether or not Christine Brooke-Rose's fiction will eventually be allowed to return from the critical exile to which it has been banished in Britain is a moot point, as is the desirability of her eventual inclusion in the canon. On the one hand, if her novels are to be read and appreciated at all by future generations, they will have to establish at least a marginal place in one of the numerous subgroups that together form the list of canonical texts. On the other hand, the very fragmentation of the canon has led to a situation in which literature can be divided up into so many *de facto* genres. The drawback of this pluralism is that there are a certain number of literary camps, each of which promotes a particular form of literature. If a novelist is not admitted to any of these she is effectively left out in the cold. This is Brooke-Rose's case, but while she laments the fact that she has not received sufficient critical notice, she sees her position itself as a fortunate one:

I have a knack of somehow escaping most would-be canonical networks and labels: I have been called '*nouveau roman* in English' and *nouveau nouveau*. I have been called Postmodern, I have been called Experimental, I have been included in the SF Encyclopedia, I automatically come under Women Writers (British, Contemporary). I sometimes interest the Feminists, but am fairly regularly omitted from the 'canonical' surveys (chapters, articles, books) that come under those or indeed other labels. On the whole I regard this as a good sign. (1991*a*: 4)

The impossibility of placing Brooke-Rose's work in one genre, one national tradition, or one context is disorienting for reader and critic alike, yet this disorientation is precisely what her novels are designed to produce. The placement of a work which accomplishes displacement is not an easy task; it is not surprising that the literary industry should have found Brooke-Rose's fiction difficult to cope with and that it should often have relegated it to the domain of the foreign. This move is not completely unjustified, however, and in the following chapter I shall turn to the question of Brooke-Rose's relation to contemporary literature in France, Britain, and elsewhere in order to asses the extent to which the above-quoted labels provide suitable contexts in which to examine her fiction.

6. Christine Brooke-Rose and Contemporary Fiction

> And then there is the desire nay the absolute need to transgress all the forms of the carefully built model.
>
> (Brooke-Rose 1977*a*: 134)

In Chapter 1 I discussed Brooke-Rose's increasing frustration in the late 1950s and early 1960s with the linear, causal logic of traditional narrative and with the ontological presuppositions of realist character-portrayal. At the same time an intellectual climate was developing in France that was characterized by what Brooke-Rose calls 'interdisciplinary all-inclusiveness', in which 'writers are influenced by and passionately interested in contemporary philosophers and scientists' (1968*c*: 20). Beginning with her experimental fiction of the 1960s, she sought to bring to British fiction this same inter-animation of discourses by radically altering the discourse of the novel.

Brooke-Rose recognized in the French *nouveau roman* a possible means of salvaging the novel from the narrative conventions of realism which had come to define it. But though the *nouveau roman* and its French successors had an undeniable effect on her subsequent fiction, it is not sufficient, for a number of reasons, simply to place her work within the category of contemporary French fiction, or to label it 'the *nouveau roman* in English'. First, there are significant differences between Brooke-Rose's fiction and that of the French writers whose influence she has acknowledged. Secondly, she is British and she publishes in Britain, which means that she will never be considered to be part of any French movement by those who play the largest role in circumscribing and analysing it. To define her work with reference to French fiction alone would therefore be to preclude any significant recognition of her achievements.[1] Finally, her case is not unique. Since the 1960s there have

---

[1] *Xorandor* is the only one of Brooke-Rose's novels to have been translated into French. Unfortunately, the linguistic techniques which would perhaps most appeal to French readers (puns, discursive slips, misquotations) are those most refractory to translation.

been a number of other authors in similarly ambiguous positions who have also suffered at the hands of critics eager to establish a contemporary 'English' canon. It is in the interest of such writers to recognize within British fiction the existence of alternative strains. In Chapter 5 we saw how parallels between Brooke-Rose's writing and the *nouveau roman* have been used by reviewers to marginalize her fiction. This chapter will be devoted to delineating, from the point of view of Brooke-Rose's own conception of fictional discourse, those ways in which her novels differ from the *nouveau roman* and subsequent developments in French fiction. It will also examine the implications of the place her work has come to occupy within British experimental fiction of the 1960s and the suitability of the term 'postmodern' to describe her later fiction. I shall analyse first Brooke-Rose's relation to the fiction of the 1960s in France and Britain, before turning to a discussion of her position with respect to both post–1968 developments in French literature and the field of contemporary experimental literature at large.

The Nouveau Roman

Brooke-Rose engaged with the French *nouveau roman* at a point at which it was undergoing a shift of emphasis from phenomenological realism to narrative and linguistic self-consciousness. But her growing interest in structuralism was assimilated into her fiction of the 1960s more readily than it was into the *nouveau roman*, which had already established its own agenda(s). The seeds of her most characteristic narrative strategies can be traced in the work of the *nouveaux romanciers*, but she has moved away from them in several crucial respects. As we shall see, the relation of her novels to the writing of both Alain Robbe-Grillet and Natalie Sarraute involves a characteristic literalization which both pays tribute to her predecessors and marks her distance from them.

In a review of Michel Butor's *Degrés* and Robert Pinget's *L'Inquisitoire*, Brooke-Rose describes the effect of the *nouveaux romanciers'* rejection of convention in terms of one of her own frequent themes, the defamiliarization experienced while travelling:

by getting away from over-familiar ways of creating a fictional world, they are making us relearn to live each moment for itself so that—as on holiday—it is sufficient for people and things merely to be, without reference to something happening. This 'New Realism' is the only feature its various practitioners have in common, for their methods and results are vastly different. (1966b: 26)

Brooke-Rose here follows Sarraute and Robbe-Grillet in their view of the new fiction as a 'nouveau réalisme' (Robbe-Grillet 1963: 13). Her own growing dissatisfaction with narrative clichés, or what she calls 'signpost language', found an antidote in the resolutely unconventional techniques of these novelists.

The main attraction of the *nouveaux romanciers* for Brooke-Rose was that she saw in their techniques a parallel with the methods of contemporary science. The movement represented for her a successful attempt to redefine the discursive status of the novel in terms of a modern scientific conception of the relation of language to reality. But in fact the novels of her principal influences, Robbe-Grillet and Sarraute, do not for many readers bear out the claims Brooke-Rose made for them. The discrepancy between these novelists' stated aims and her interpretations of their texts provides an indication of the direction her own fiction of the period was taking.

Like Robbe-Grillet (1963: 114–15) and Butor (1960: 7–19), Brooke-Rose conceived of the novel in the early 1960s as research, as a project whose aim it was to probe the possibilities of language in order better to understand the human psyche in its relation both to society and to the non-human world. In 'Dynamic Gradients' she draws an analogy between the developments of science and the work of the *nouveaux romanciers*, whose method she defines as 'an attempt to evolve a language that corresponds structurally to what we know of empirical reality today' (1965a: 92). She describes Robbe-Grillet's novels as enactments of the dissolution implicit in the uncertainty principle of the distinction between perceiving subject and perceived object, for they succeed in rendering geometrical description subjective by presenting it through 'the swerves, blockages and sudden enlargements of the observer's psychological make-up' (93). She also sees a parallel between novelistic and scientific discourse, in that they both construct models of the world based on an absence of empirically verifiable fact.

But it was Sarraute's theoretical pronouncements in the 1950s which convinced Brooke-Rose of the need for a radical break with the conventions of realist fiction. In a recent discussion of her development as a novelist she analyses the influence of Sarraute on her thinking: 'I suppose it was Nathalie Sarraute's *The Age of Suspicion*, and her putting the modern novel in question, which was the first turning point for me, much more so than her novels, for although I like them very much, I can't say there's a direct influence of Nathalie Sarraute on what I write' (1989*e*: 82). Two aspects of Sarraute's collection of essays made a particular impression on Brooke-Rose and were especially significant in the subsequent development of her ideas about the novel: the rejection of conventions of plot, character, and dialogue, and Sarraute's idea that true realism is what is commonly labelled 'formalism', whereas formalism is conventional literature stuck in the rigid forms of an earlier period (Sarraute 1956: 137–46).

The technical innovations of Robbe-Grillet made the most immediately obvious mark on Brooke-Rose's fiction, however. She self-consciously situates *Out* within the bounds of the image the English reading public had of the *nouveau roman* by using the devices of the first-person-absent narrator, temporal ambiguity, camera-like observation of detail, psychological impoverishment, and narrative discontinuity, all of which are characteristic of Robbe-Grillet's early phase. But *Out* also stages the confrontation between Robbe-Grillet's theoretical and his fictional writings. By working out to their logical conclusions the implications of Robbe-Grillet's stance of the 1950s, it reveals the dogmatism latent in too literal a reading of his theories.

Robbe-Grillet's stated goal in the 1950s was to create a world that is neither meaningful nor absurd but simply exists in all its 'solide, évident, inaltérable' quiddity (1955: 88). This is the rationale behind the argument against metaphor in 'Nature, humanisme, tragédie' for which he is perhaps best known. The humanizing complicity of metaphor, its tendency to ascribe meaning to inanimate objects, leads to what he describes as a tragic breach between man on the one hand, and on the other hand the physical world which can never be subsumed completely under his networks of signification (1963: 45–67). Robbe-Grillet sets himself the task of ridding the novel of these systems. Yet with the rise of structuralism in the late 1950s and early 1960s it became increasingly evident that this project assumed the possibility of a transparent language, that of the 'adjectif optique, descriptif, celui qui se contente de mesurer, de situer, de limiter, de définir' (23), which was in fact an illusion.

Out mimics the theoretical claims Robbe-Grillet makes for his novels. It puts into play a fictitious future resembling Robbe-Grillet's unsignifying world; his questioning of causality has led to a revolution, 'the displacement from cause to effect', and a whole new jargon has developed around this 'revolutionary' transformation. The central voice in *Out* practises the 'double mouvement de création et de gommage' (127) which Robbe-Grillet recommends, and it incarnates Robbe-Grillet's ideal narrator who 'invente les choses autour de lui et qui voit les choses qu'il invente' (140).[2]

But the play between mobility and fixity in the novel (see Chapter 2 above) focuses attention on the varying interpretations to which the mind inevitably subjects objects, and at the level of language *Out* implicitly contests Robbe-Grillet's theories of fiction. Though the discursive metaphors employed in *Out* are similar in certain respects to what Jean Ricardou describes as Robbe-Grillet's 'structural metaphors' (1967: 136), Brooke-Rose's novel also demonstrates that the stylistic metaphor whose adjectivity Robbe-Grillet so deplores is an inevitable component of language.

The playful literalization in *Out* of Robbe-Grillet's theoretical claims would seem to suggest that it is a parody.[3] But while *Out* invokes and comments on his novels, it tries in addition to do something more, to place the epistemological breakdown of the narrator in the context of an invented social order which is a reflection on the discursive manipulation operative in our own society. If for Robbe-Grillet language is incompatible with reality, for Brooke-Rose language is 'the material of life' (1976k: 23); the only reality to which we have access is fabricated out of the 'unreliable' material of language.

While Brooke-Rose admits that *Out* was strongly influenced by Robbe-Grillet, she claims that with *Such* she began to move away from the *nouveau roman* and into her own experimental domain (1989e: 83; 1990c: 30) in which she became increasingly concerned with investigating 'the impact of language on the imagination' (1989e: 83). In a sense this brings her work closer to the novels of Sarraute. Brooke-Rose was particularly fascinated in the 1960s by

---

[2] For a more detailed analysis of the allusions in *Out* to Robbe-Grillet's novels, see Birch 1991: 318–29.

[3] Indeed, in a recent study of contemporary fiction Morton Levitt defends Christine Brooke-Rose as a 'modernist survivor' who, in the tradition of Joyce and Woolf, affirms humanist values against the 'de-humanizing' forces of 'post-Modernism', of which Levitt sees Robbe-Grillet as a prime exemplar. He describes *Out* as 'virtually a line-by-line parody of *La Jalousie*' (1987: 58).

Sarraute's technique of using images drawn from the sciences to figure psychic states, and her use in *Such* of astrophysics as a metaphor can be traced back to her reading of Sarraute. In her analysis of *Le Planétarium*, Brooke-Rose describes the 'half-conscious movements and murderous impulses . . . viewed like organisms caught and enlarged in an electron microscope' (1965a: 93/1981: 324) which Sarraute terms 'tropismes'. She notes that the title *Le Planétarium* entails a shift of ontological level, for it

swoops the perspective from submicroscopic to giant-telescopic, our psychic energies being also seen in terms of planets revolving round one another, galaxies receding from one another through the forces of gravitation, electromagnetism and nuclear reactions. (1965a: 93; variation 1981: 324)

Brooke-Rose takes the hint implicit in Sarraute's metaphoric title and literalizes it in *Such*. Sarraute's metaphor of the psyche as a representation of both subatomic particles and a solar system is concretized, and different aspects of the self are brought to life as distinct cosmic bodies/characters whose activities form a coherent if disjointed alternative narrative.[4]

Such extends Sarraute's technique of dramatizing psychic movements. This entails an expansion of the initial conceit to include an extended analogy between verbal communication and distortion. The social surface of the novel is constantly being punctured by chains of linguistic association; as in Sarraute's fiction, words are not received as they are intended. Indeed, the impossibility of smoothing over the discrepancy between supposed intention and effect questions the common view of communication as the transmission of a message.[5] The phrase 'as such' functions like similar phrases in Sarraute's later work to generate a dramatized reflection on the implications of taking language *à la lettre*. The effect is, paradoxically, metaphoric: the character called Something exposes the falsity of expressions such as 'stop prodding me with questions' by taking them literally. Similarly, the expression 'I take your point' is expanded into an enactment of personal relations as an ongoing competition with points lost and won.

[4] Brian McHale has (independently) observed similarities between the two novels (n.d.: 13, 32–3).

[5] Something explains to Someone that he has chosen 'the way of unconsciousness which bends words to breaking point' (24/220) and as noted above, (Chap. 2), words and images are the medium in which Larry's dreaming mind works; their 'internal combustion' fuels his psychological journey (22/218, 51/247).

But Sarraute sees language as a dangerous tool whose nefarious effects can be avoided only if it is deviously manipulated so as to outmanœuvre them and reach beyond the tool itself to the pre-verbal consciousness of the reader (Sarraute 1987: 125). In *Such*, on the other hand, the inability of language to define precisely and unambiguously—its constant tendency to yield associations and alternative interpretations—is the generative power behind the mind's narrative capacity and its ability to come up with creative solutions to abstract problems, both scientific and philosophical. For Brooke-Rose the entire drama of consciousness and identity-formation is tied up in the use and misuse of language. The stuff of pre-conscious reality is language itself; its effects are measured as disruptions of linguistic conventions. In *Such* Larry 'is' both a radio telescope and a solar system: he is both the tool of observation and the object observed. Thus, while Brooke-Rose goes along with Sarraute's rejection of the ontological postulates of realism, she takes this rejection one step further and conflates reality with the tool used to figure it. Commenting on Sarraute's inversion of the distinction between formalism and realism, Brooke-Rose adopts the position that 'formalism *is* realism' because 'form is in itself the reality' (1981: 297).

In contrast to the novels of Robbe-Grillet and Sarraute, those of fellow *nouveau romancier* Claude Simon share with *Out*, *Such*, and *Between* a fascination with the refracting, distorting properties of the psyche manifest in its effects on language. The same logic of combination by association pervades Simon's work. This is a process of juxtaposition, permutation, and repetition of like elements which produces a mosaic of graphic and pictorial images drawn from a number of different discourses. Strangely, Brooke-Rose rarely mentions Simon in her criticism, and there is no evidence of any direct influence of his writing on her work (or vice versa). The relation between the two authors is that of parallel stylistic and technical development as well as a similar conception of the interaction between reality and language.

Thematically as well as structurally, *Between* bears the most striking resemblance to Simon's work. One aspect in particular of Simon's 'formalist' period of the 1970s lends itself to comparison: the attempt to play down chronology in favour of a spatialized construction through the use of recurrent analogies and semantic correspondences organized in the form of what Brooke-Rose calls a 'spiral'. The techniques employed to this end are those which shatter the word, locution, or image into its component parts or the variations it suggests. The semantic tangents generated out of alternative usages of a word, or out of associations with its counterparts in other linguistic systems (be they other natural languages or other professional discourses), provide a means of organizing disparate material in a way that does not follow the logic of temporal sequence or causal relations, but that of metaphor.

In a discussion of the recently completed *Les Corps conducteurs*, Simon argues that since language does not distinguish between 'real' and 'imaginary', 'il m'a donc semblé que supprimer le mot *comme*, c'est-à-dire, en somme, *concrétiser* en quelque sorte la métaphore, c'était peut-être, d'une certaine façon . . . se rapprocher de cet Eden dont il nous sépare' (1972: 91). This penchant for 'concretization', or literalization in Brooke-Rose's terms, indicates a similar intent on Simon's part to use the device of metaphor to question the traditional ontology of fiction which distinguishes between actions accomplished and actions imagined.[6] But because Brooke-Rose's work on language in *Between* operates at the level of smaller textual units, her fusion of the represented with the created is more complete. In Simon's novels the description of a figure in a painting may lead to the memory of a scene between two people, or a play on words may cause the scene to be shifted to an analogous scene, but the various series remain discrete.

Simon's technique is similar in many respects to Pound's ideogrammatic method which influenced Brooke-Rose. Yet as Hélène Cixous points out with reference to *Between*, the difference between Pound's technique and Brooke-Rose's is that whereas Pound juxtaposes, she fuses: 'là où Pound procède par de nouvelles juxtapositions, C. Brooke-Rose pousse plus loin, jusqu'à effacer le parallèlisme, jusqu'à une coalescence' (1968: vii). Discrete series interpenetrate and interact at the level of the sentence in her novels in a way that they do not in either the poetry of Pound or the fiction of Simon. The conflation in *Between* of the real and the constructed through metaphor bears witness to Brooke-Rose's debt to structuralist conceptions of the nature of reality, and her strict subordination of narrative to the logic of linguistic association surpasses even that of the highly metaphoric novels of Simon.

[6] Like Robbe-Grillet, Simon frequently makes use of what Ricardou calls 'structural metaphor'.

The interplay of narrative and principles of organization derived from the structure of language is characteristic of all Brooke-Rose's fiction. The tension between the two can be traced also in the work of Robbe-Grillet, Sarraute, and Simon, and in each case metaphoric techniques are employed to conflate different levels of reality and to threaten the novel's traditional claim to represent the extra-discursive world. What makes Brooke-Rose's novels of the 1960s stand apart from those of the *nouveaux romanciers* is a more thoroughgoing questioning of narrative ontology which bears witness to her increasingly sophisticated conception of the mediatory role of language in experience. For this reason if for no other, the label '*nouveau roman* in English' is inexact and inadequate to describe her novels. The most that can be claimed is that she was keenly aware of the *nouveau roman*, whose accomplishments she admired, but that her conception and use of language sets her off from the writers who had the greatest initial influence on her work.

The British Novel in the 1960s

Despite her gradual drift away from the *nouveau roman*, Brooke-Rose's belief in the novel as a tool for defamiliarizing the known links her more closely to French writers than to the vast majority of her contemporaries in Britain. The 1960s are generally acknowledged to have been a time of branching out for the British novel. Writers such as Angus Wilson, Iris Murdoch, Anthony Burgess, Doris Lessing, and David Storey, who had established reputations in the previous decade, were exploring the formal variety latent in their earlier work. Moreover, the illusion of homogeneity which had dominated the fiction of the 1950s was shattered as novelists as diverse as B. S. Johnson, John Fowles, and Gabriel Josipovici began to be considered significant figures in contemporary fiction. These and other writers increasingly looked to France and America for new ideas as the limitations of the narrative conventions that had evolved out of the nineteenth-century realist novel became glaringly apparent.

Like Brooke-Rose, a number of these writers expressed frustration with what they saw to be the parochialism of British fiction and/or preferred to see their work in the context of a European tradition (Figes cited in Kenyon 1988: 131; Fowles 1974: 32–3; Lessing 1972: 14). But the majority of these writers integrated concepts derived from French and other foreign traditions into the technical conventions of realist and modernist fiction. Furthermore, the categories critics imposed on the burgeoning literary scene tended to emphasize techniques closely associated with traditional realist modes and thus to obscure developments of interest from the point of view of contemporary theories of language and discourse.

From the perspective of the epistemological and ontological uncertainties of the *nouveau roman*, the experiments of the 1960s and the early 1970s would look quite different. But such concepts were not used by those who constructed the critical vocabulary at the time. Instead, writers such as Malcolm Bradbury and David Lodge (whose authority was partly derived from the fact that they also wrote fiction) developed schemata which portrayed the main literary trends in such a way that their own novels were situated at the centre of contemporary fiction. Self-conscious realist novels came to be seen to typify English experiment. In consequence, writers such as Alan Burns, Ann Quin, and Christine Brooke-Rose, who were concerned with the technical problems of language and compositional struc-ture, were thought to have been over-influenced by American and French trends, when in fact this was not generally the case.

In an article published in France in 1967 on recent fiction in Britain, Brooke-Rose cites as the main difference between the situations in the two countries the fact that in Britain there was no sense of a movement equivalent to that of the *nouveau roman*, nor was there any coherent philosophy to account for the experiments that were taking place. As in the article she wrote in 1973 for the *Times Literary Supplement*, the explanation she gives for this is the lack in Britain of a forum for discussion (1967b: 1,243). But she points out that in recent years there had been a considerable amount of writing which drew on English traditions marginal to mainstream fiction. She claims that the experimentation of the 1950s and the early 1960s was dominated by a tendency toward fantasy. There was, she argues, a sharp divide between social-realist fiction on the one hand, and on the other hand novels inspired by science fiction or the absurdist-fantastic tradition stretching back to Lewis Carroll and Edward Lear.

There is indeed a strong line of absurdist fantasy running from Nigel Dennis's *Cards of Identity* (1955) through Andrew Sinclair's *Gog* (1967), Brigid Brophy's *In Transit* (1969), and beyond to more recent neo-Baroque manifestations of the genre. Science fiction played a more significant role in the development of fictional technique, as 'New Wave' science-fiction writers such as J. G. Ballard, Brian Aldiss, and Brooke-Rose's husband Jerzy Pietkiewicz combined generic conventions with experiment in narrative structure. The threat to realism posed by this new development was minimized, however, by the marginal or special status accorded alternative worlds. Malcolm Bradbury acknowledges that 'the British tradition has tended to regard the fantastic as something of an eccentricity or indulgence' (1987: 346). The concepts critics used at the time to characterize British fiction were imported instead from America.

Robert Scholes's contrast between 'fabulation' and 'realism' in his book *The Fabulators* (1967) has served as a touchstone for many critics of the contemporary novel. For Scholes, 'fabulation' is meta-fictional allegory with a strong story-line.[7] British critics who have taken up and revised his schema have therefore assumed that meta-fiction and allegory are the quintessential 'experimental' qualities to be sought and analysed in the works of other novelists. In his influential book *The Novel at the Crossroads* (1971) David Lodge elaborates on Scholes's bipolar schema and develops a paradigm of the choices available to the modern novelist, extending from fabulation at one extreme, through the main line of traditional realism, to the non-fiction novel at the opposite end. With the exception of B. S. Johnson's autobiographical works, the non-fiction novel has flourished mainly in America, and Lodge sees contemporary English fiction as being composed primarily of fabulation, realist fiction, and a fourth category he posits: the 'problematic' novel which 'hesitates' before the choices on offer and takes this hesitation itself as its subject.

For Lodge, 'problematic' novels such as Doris Lessing's *The Golden Notebook* (1962), Julian Mitchell's *The Undiscovered Country*, and John Fowles's *The French Lieutenant's Woman* (1969) are often written by authors of traditional fiction who have become blocked, or for some other reason feel the need to examine the creative process by pausing in mid-career to write a novel about writing novels (1971: 22–4). Rather than constituting a new departure for fiction, the 'problematic' novel is thus likely to stand out in a British author's

---

[7] The British examples he gives are Iris Murdoch and Lawrence Durrell. John Fowles is added in the revised version of the book published in 1979 under the title *Fabulation and Metafiction*.

œuvre as an exception marking a momentary uncertainty or a loss of confidence but not a true change of tack. As either a side-glance at other possibilities or a self-reflexive analysis of technique, the 'problematic' novel is a convenient way of accommodating formal deviations within a basically realist tradition. The pluralism of Lodge's 'aesthetics of compromise' (33) thus denigrates renewed interest in the fantastic by explaining it away as an extreme form of fabulation which is therefore marginal to the novel as a genre unless used as an outlet for the frustrated realist.[8]

Writing from a different perspective, Brooke-Rose distinguishes between the 'anti-novel' in the tradition of Cervantes and Sterne, which is overtly self-reflexive and parodic in its interrogation of the conventions of narrative, and the 'experimental novel', which seeks to extend the possibilities of fiction through the exploitation of new techniques. While the anti-novel may be 'subversive' in that it shows conventional techniques to be outmoded, it is not necessarily innovatory in the way that the experimental novel is. It is no surprise, then, that Lodge's 'problematic' novels are mainly composed of self-reflexive meditation or parody of realist and modernist conventions, but that they rarely exhibit new methods. The fact that *Travelling People* by the supposedly radical author B. S. Johnson can be included in this category along with *I Like It Here* by Kingsley Amis, the exemplary fifties realist, demonstrates that the label does not designate a truly 'experimental' development according to Brooke-Rose's definition.

Likewise, John Fowles is one of the novelists who most often receives the label 'experimental', but though he declares in *The French Lieutenant's Woman* that he is writing in 'the age of Alain Robbe-Grillet and Roland Barthes' (1969: 97), he does not seem to have taken in the rejection of the '*texte lisible*' that their thinking entails. He freely admits that he is unable to write in the manner of the *nouveau roman* (1974: 33), and problems which the *nouveaux romanciers* grappled with through stylistic and narrative strategies, Fowles examines in discursive interpolations much in the style of Thackeray or George Eliot. Similarly, in *The Golden Notebook* Doris Lessing seeks to discover a discourse that will be adequate to the expression of contemporary reality in the same way that *Le Rouge et*

---

[8] It must be noted, however, that in *The Modes of Modern Writing* (1977) Lodge's position shifts somewhat.

le noir or *Anna Karenina* expressed the reality of nineteenth-century France and Russia (1972: 11). Loath to relinquish what they take to be the 'tradition', both Scholes's British 'fabulators' and Lodge's writers of 'problematic' novels recast the contemporary equivalent of the material of the nineteenth-century novel in the trappings of self-conscious frames and other narrative devices that fragment, distort, or comment on it. But by no means do these novelists make the break with plot and character that was accomplished by the *nouveau roman* and by certain authors of the same period in Britain.[9]

In fact, upon closer examination it becomes obvious that even the 'radical' philosophical concepts behind the novels on the extreme edges of Lodge's schema—the 'fabulations' of Iris Murdoch and John Fowles's *The Magus*, and the non-fiction novels of B. S. Johnson—rely heavily on a tradition of existentialist thought associated with realist fiction and a pre-structuralist conception of 'reality' as a domain sealed off from the constitutive processes of language. For both Scholes and Lodge, 'fiction' and 'fantasy' are opposed to 'reality' and 'realism'. The distinction between the two is the central concern of the majority of the novels they examine, be they fabulous, realistic or non-fictional. *The Magus* is a fable in which a young man is taught to distinguish between the real and the constructed and to take responsibility for constructing his own world so as not to be the plaything of others' games. This mistrust of imaginary structures as being somehow false is also evident in Murdoch's fables, though numerous critics have remarked on the problematic relation between her cautionary tales about the dangers of succumbing to the enchantments of a mythic idea or persona, and the form these tales take.[10] B. S. Johnson's rejection of fiction as 'lies' and his insistence in *Albert Angelo* on the need to convey the truth of his experience without recourse to fabulation also reveal a belief in the existence of a pre-discursive reality that, given the proper narrative tools, could be conveyed in its pure state (Johnson 1964: 167–70; 1973: 153–6).

If, on the other hand, the fantastic is understood not as fabulation, but, according to Brooke-Rose's definition, as the perpetuation of a

---

[9] In this they are closer to the overtly self-conscious but stylistically traditional American surfictionists who examine their literary forbears with an ironic and destabilizing eye, but do not relinquish their techniques. See below.

[10] Bradbury 1973: 235–6; Byatt 1979: 24–5, 36; Sage 1979: 70–4; Stevenson 1986: 176.

radical uncertainty as to the ontological status of the events described, the question of the relation between the real and the fictional in the British novel of the 1960s has rather a different history, for this definition challenges the adequacy of conventional realist or even modernist narrative strategies to convey the multiple realities of experience.[11] Based on this definition, the fantastic can be taken to include Brooke-Rose's first two experimental novels, as well as works more obviously influenced by post-war developments in French fiction. These include, for example, Rayner Heppenstall's *The Connecting Door* and Gabriel Josipovici's *The Present*, which would find no place in Lodge's spectrum despite the fact that they are highly innovative. *The Connecting Door* conflates several time-frames in such a way that the same character appears simultaneously at different stages of his life. As in Robbe-Grillet's ludic novels of the 1960s, it is never clear whether certain characters 'actually' exist or whether they are figments of the narrator's imagination. In *The Present*, as in *Such*, two alternative stories are intercalated, and the text is primarily composed of dialogue which gives the illusion of verisimilitude. It gradually becomes clear, however, that the two fictions are mutually incompatible and that either one or the other is being imagined by a woman recovering from a nervous breakdown.

The ambiguous ontological status of characters and events in *Out* and *Such* is characteristic also of a number of novels of the period whose narrators are unreliable. In the fiction of Robbe-Grillet, Sarraute, Beckett, and Marguerite Duras questions of 'sanity' and 'insanity' are generally considered to be of secondary importance when applied to 'characters', the main aim being to explore the concept of subjectivity. The British novel was less willing to relinquish the mimetic assumption; as in *Out* and *Such*, dissection of the Cartesian subject was often psychologically oriented. Spurred by the writings of R. D. Laing and other advocates of alternative psychiatry, many novelists of the 1960s and 1970s couched an exploration of 'inner space' in terms of mental breakdown, using the psycho-narrative 'tropes' of schizophrenia and amnesia. Lessing's *Briefing for a Descent into Hell* (1971), Andrew Sinclair's *Gog*, and Figes' *Nelly's Version* (1977) all depict the mind of an amnesiac

---

[11] Brooke-Rose develops her conception of the fantastic out of Todorov's theory of genres (see Brooke-Rose 1981: 62–71). Patrick Parrinder (1987: 109–14) has also proposed the category of the fantastic as one more germane to British fiction than those currently in use.

narrator. Contemporary 'schizologue' novels include Jennifer Dawson's *The Ha-Ha* (1961), David Storey's *Radcliffe* (1963), Peter Everett's *Negatives* (1964), and, perhaps most notably, the fiction of Ann Quin.

Brooke-Rose and Quin stand out from the majority of novelists who use insanity to explore human experience as writers with a particular sensitivity to the linguistic and discursive variation to which thought is subject. Quin's first novel *Berg* has much in common with *Out*. It was published the same year, it is narrated from the point of view of a man of doubtful mental stability, and fantasy is not clearly differentiated from actual events.[12] As in *Out*, abrupt shifts in style indicate changes in mental state, and fantasized scenes are conveyed in lyrical associative passages which stand out from the more conventional sections of the text. In both *Three* (1966) and *Passages* (1969), components of the fragmented psyche are externalized as separate characters (a device employed also in *Such*), narrative is sparse, and composition is governed by a contrapuntal structure which juxtaposes different discursive modes (dialogue, stream-of-consciousness in free verse, journals, 'quotations' from the television, descriptions of dreams, and so on). Philip Stevick notes that on the micro-textual level the organization of elements in Quin's fiction reflects sensory experience and the associations it conjures up rather than an analytic or a narrative principle (1989: 237). As in Brooke-Rose's novels, syntactic structure becomes the primary mechanism for conveying this logic.

In the late 1960s and early 1970s the fiction of alternative worlds—futuristic, hallucinated, or fantastic—gave way in the writing of novelists such as Ann Quin, Alan Burns, and J. G. Ballard to discursive effects frequently described as 'surreal'.[13] There was a shift from 'un avenir imaginé qui est un commentaire indirect sur le présent' (Brooke-Rose 1967*b*: 119)—this being the description Brooke-Rose gives of the fantasies of the previous years—to a more

---

[12] Quin suffered much the same fate in the hands of the publishing industry as Brooke-Rose: her fiction was immediately assimilated to the *nouveau roman* without being read for what made it unique. Brooke-Rose observes in her review of *Berg* that: 'The book is said by the publisher to have been influenced by the *nouveau roman*, but apart from the dialogue running Sarraute-like without breaks or quotes to distinguish it from narrative, and plenty of interleaved memory-flashes to childhood and to Berg's mother talking, I found little relationship' (1964*d*: 802).

[13] Charles Sugnet (1981) is one of the few critics to have recognized this stream in post-war British fiction.

direct involvement with the codes and figures of popular culture. As in the *nouveau roman*, increasing concern with composition and the attempt to move away from the causal logic of linear narrative toward alternative principles of patterning was evident in the work of these writers. This was accompanied by a tendency to conflate language with reality, truth with fiction.

Brooke-Rose traces the legacy of earlier twentieth-century literary movements in contemporary British fiction, lamenting the failure of novelists to capitalize on the rediscovery by Eliot and Pound of 'spiral' composition. Yet in the years just after she spotted this lack, Nicholas Mosley's *Impossible Object* (1968) and J. G. Ballard's *Atrocity Exhibition* (1969) both adopted repetition as a principle of formal patterning by combining thematic elements, situations, and symbols to weave a web of resonances and variations. Language and narrative technique remain largely conventional in these novels, however, and it is the later fiction of Alan Burns which goes furthest in exploring non-narrative principles of organization.

Using William Burroughs's cut-up method—which Burns claims to have discovered independently (1981: 166)—to remove the linear logic of narrative from his work, he experimented with different types of juxtaposition. Burns effectively rids his prose of order altogether in *Babel* (1969) where he applies the cut-up method to newspaper jargon and, as in *Between*, effects mid-sentence switches of context. In both novels causality is severely undermined by the seemingly arbitrary but subtly ironic combination of units of text, and the question of 'truth' versus 'fiction' becomes inapplicable as documentary material is turned back on itself and 'falsified'.[14] In *Dreamerika!*, Burns voids the story of the element of suspense by choosing the Kennedy family as his material. As with epic and fable, the familiarity of the 'plot' shifts emphasis from the tale itself to its telling. But because the novel is composed of news copy, the author's presence is only evident in the irony of the juxtapositions he contrives. The 'message' of *Dreamerika!* is entirely encoded in the relations between elements, and in this sense it is the ultimate 'structuralist' novel, with the minimum of narrative 'fabulation'. There is an obvious parallel between this technique and those employed by Brooke-Rose during the same period.

---

[14] This novel is a good example of the fact that Scholes's spectrum, ranging from the non-fictional to fabulation, is itself slightly 'problematic' in that many non-fiction or 'documentary' novels exhibit elements of allegorical fabulation.

Brooke-Rose's novels portray a reality which is itself fictional through and through; the everyday is rendered in her writing of the 1960s as a complex mythology of consumer-age fables structured according to associative principles. For her, as well as for a handful of other British writers, the break with conventions of realism was definitive. Their fiction was seen at the time as both un-English and part of a general experimentation with altered states subsequently dismissed as a fad of the sixties generation. Like Brooke-Rose, Alan Burns claims to have written his first experimental novel in a trance-like state (cited in Madden 1983: 189), and Ann Quin made extensive use of drugs to help her write (1972: 8). But whatever the sources of inspiration of these three writers, the 'surreal' quality of the resultant fiction and their innovative uses of the discourses of popular culture are some of the most interesting but least recognized characteristics of post-war British fiction.

In the foregoing analysis of Brooke-Rose's place in relation to French and British fiction of the 1960s, two features of her work stand out: the metaphoric 'literalizations' whereby she conflates language with reality, and the 'synchronic' poetic structures achieved through the use of metaphor as a principle of composition. The role of the individual in society is central to each of her novels of this period, but she treats this typically English subject in discursive terms, an approach conditioned by her interest in the *nouveau roman* and structural linguistics. The fact that the variety of influences on her work was not recognized by contemporary critics testifies to the narrowness of their view of 'English' fiction. Like her early novels, her experimental work of the 1960s did not conform sufficiently to native categories. Whereas her early fiction was similar enough to contemporary mainstream fiction to be judged according to its standards, her later work was expelled from the English tradition altogether, though it exhibits notable divergences from the *nouveau roman* to which it was invariably compared.

The Generation of '68

Christine Brooke-Rose lived and worked in Paris from 1968 till 1988, and it is therefore not surprising that her writing should have been suffused with the debates in which literary studies were currently involved. Because of this it would be tempting to claim that the novels she wrote during that time are more closely allied with the contemporary French novel than with its British counterpart, just as reviewers had done during the previous decade and continued to do for a number of years. But this claim too is problematic. As we have seen, the ideas about fiction put forward by certain French writers in the late 1950s had as much impact, if not more, on Brooke-Rose's work as the novels these writers wrote. The same is true to an even greater extent with post-1968 movements in French literature. Experimental French fiction has gone in several different directions since the late 1960s, but in nearly all cases it has been defined by its relation to post-structuralist theories of writing and language. Brooke-Rose's post-1968 novels are subversive of the rigorous formulations of theory, but their awareness of theoretical constructs invites comparison with several recent strains of fiction inspired by what can be loosely termed 'post-structuralist thinking'.

When Brooke-Rose arrived in Paris in late 1968 the proliferation of theory which France had witnessed in the 1960s had recently gained impetus from the student demonstrations of May. The highly charged intellectual atmosphere left discernible marks of two sorts on the novels she wrote over the next fifteen years. First, the radicalism of the *Tel Quel* school and the work of French 'feminists'[15] led her to radicalize the formal and linguistic experimentation she had begun while still in London. Secondly, this same radicalism led her to question the authority and the systematicity of these theories themselves. Her self-reflexivity therefore involved an element of dialectic which was not always evident in what has been labelled the *nouveau nouveau roman*.

By her own admission, Brooke-Rose's awareness of literary theory made her fiction more complex: 'Theory has released an immense hidden strength in me, but it has also made writing more and more difficult, because more and more demanding' (1991a: 13). Yet when she speaks of 'theory', she is speaking of a body of knowledge she assimilated and manipulated in her capacity as a professional critic, not an activity she herself engaged in to any great extent.[16] The

[15] The word 'feminist' is here in inverted commas because many members of the movement in the 1970s known in Anglo-American circles as 'French feminism' did not consider themselves feminists. 'Gender-conscious' would perhaps be a better term, but the critical discourse which has arisen out of this movement generally retains the word 'feminist' in some form.

[16] She writes: 'I'm a good critic. But I have never considered myself a theorist, not, at any rate, in the sense of "having" a theory or theories I would defend against all comers or revise and accommodate, as a fulltime job and work of a lifetime' (1991a: 26).

theories she invokes and deploys in her writing have always been in some sense foreign to her. This foreignness is felt in works such as *Thru* and *Amalgamemnon* as a distancing, a self-conscious mimicry of modes of writing and ways of articulating problems to which Brooke-Rose the intellectual nevertheless fully subscribed. Whereas novelists such as Philippe Sollers or Hélène Cixous could appropriate the concepts of Lacan or Derrida and integrate them seamlessly into their own thought, theory in Brooke-Rose's fiction is always associated with a pose or stand. It has what Bakhtin would call a different 'orientation' with respect to the work of which it is part.

Brooke-Rose notes that many of her French contemporaries are often lacking in humour (1976*k*: 8; 1991*a*: 267; cf. 1968*a*: 18; 1977*c*: vii). Humour in the Freudian sense of a joke as a frustrated expectation is the primary effect of Brooke-Rose's efforts to 'poke fun at' (1976*k*: 11) theories and discourses.[17] She records an admiration for OuLiPo[18] members Raymond Queneau and Georges Perec, who are among the few French writers to mix the serious and the comic (1990*e*: 29), but it is with Maurice Roche that she most identifies, because he combines anti-realist textual principles with a comic vision (1981: 338). Though her fiction evolved in parallel with *Tel Quel*, 'feminism', and OuLiPo, it bears the greatest resemblance to works by Roche and Michel Butor who, like Brooke-Rose, refuse to be associated with any group. Her active efforts to distance herself from dogmas, credos, and common stands can perhaps help explain this fact.

Alain Robbe-Grillet opens *Pour un nouveau roman* with the explicit statement: 'Je ne suis pas un théoricien du roman' (1963: 7), and I argued above that the discrepancy between his 'theories' of the novel and his novels themselves is one of the most striking and revealing features of his *œuvre*. The members of the *Tel Quel* group, on the other hand, are undeniably theorists: in addition to the collective volume *Théorie d'ensemble* (1968), they have all published numerous

---

[17] She sees this as characteristic of the English-language literature in which she recognizes her sources: 'This is . . . what I like about both Pound and Beckett so much, this high seriousness and humour in both; and I think this is English and not French' (1976*k*: 11).

[18] 'OuLiPo' is short for 'Ouvroir de Littérature Potentielle', a group founded by writer Raymond Queneau and mathematician François le Lionnais in 1960, with the aim of bringing together mathematics and literature in order to invent new formal strategies which would broaden the scope of literary experiment.

articles in the journal *Tel Quel* itself conceptualizing the nature and role of the type of literary practice they advocate, alongside excerpts from their fictional work. In many respects the fiction of the *Tel Quel* school, and especially that of its leading member Philippe Sollers, provides a more apt term of comparison for much of Brooke-Rose's fiction than the *nouveau roman*. The similarities between her work and that of Sollers include the flagrant but unattributed borrowings from other texts (or what Kristeva (1969: 271) calls '*prélèvements*'), formalized structure, and a consciousness of language as an event or a character rather than a means of relating events external to it. But to claim that her novels are '*Tel Quel* in English' is even more misguided than the same claim made in relation to the *nouveau roman*, for the conceptual underpinnings of her writing are at variance with those of *Tel Quel* in a number of ways.

When in 1968 Christine Brooke-Rose began teaching American literature at the recently created Université de Paris VIII at Vincennes, *Tel Quel* was leading a literary guerrilla attack on established institutions, advocating revolutionary textual practices derived from an amalgam of Marx, Nietzsche, and Freud. Sollers' well-known dictum: 'Qui n'écrit pas est écrit' (1968: 242) encapsulates much of the *Tel Quel* ideology. Working with the Lacanian-Marxian theories of Althusser, the group developed an extended multi-layered analogy between the relation of production to product, of the unconscious to consciousness, and of the act of writing to the text. The main idea behind much of their fiction was that by actively privileging the unconscious forces of textual production they could liberate language from the linguistic clichés of bourgeois society, and that this subversion of the language of the ruling classes would undermine their power to control people's minds.

Tel Quel advocated a 'théorie tirée de la pratique textuelle' (*Tel Quel* 1968: 3), and contemporary pronouncements by Sollers imply that scriptural practice generates theory spontaneously: 'la théorie de l'écriture textuelle se fait dans la pratique de cette écriture' (1968: 10). Celia Britton points out that the 'cost' of *Tel Quel*'s concept of the practice of theory is a loss of 'the specificity of theoretical, as distinct from scriptural (or textual) practice' (1989: 92). One could even argue that the novels produced by members of the group were by-products of *Tel Quel* as a phenomenon, interesting only in light of the theoretical and critical work which is indispensable to an appreciation of them.

It cannot be denied that Brooke-Rose's writing was influenced by this movement, but her work is distinguished from that of *Tel Quel* by its lack of any programmatic aim. From Brooke-Rose's point of view, the *Tel Quel* writers failed to recognize that systematic theories are by nature dogmatic and constantly in need of criticism. A feedback loop was established between the theoretical and novelistic writing of the group, which became, as the metaphor suggests, a self-regulating device which was autotelic and hermetic. Despite its self-consciously marginal position and its iconoclastic, anti-academic rhetoric, *Tel Quel* was not in any real sense excluded from the academy. The journal was dependent on and curiously mimetic of the university system, and this system provided the mechanism whereby it hoped eventually to achieve its ends. The structure of the *Tel Quel* organization was an imitation in miniature of the university apparatus: seminar-like weekly meetings with students, a journal and an imprint with a prestigious publisher, and an audience composed largely of academic critics, students, and those who ran similar journals. From this perspective *Tel Quel*'s 'radical' stance is somewhat diminished.

Indeed, Brooke-Rose accuses *Tel Quel* of a tendency toward self-indulgence which led in the end to individualism and an apolitical aestheticism (1977c: vii). Her own relation to literary theory, to the literary tradition, and to literary institutions is quite different. While in Paris she was self-consciously positioned both within and without the academy. There is thus an internal division in her *œuvre*, but an interanimation as well. It is noteworthy that the journal she founded at Vincennes is called *Théorie, littérature, enseignement (TLE)*, for these are the three areas in which she was implicated: the theory of literature, the writing of literature, and the criticism and teaching of literature. This tripartite structure poses a challenge to the neat duality of academic *versus* subversive which underlies *Tel Quel*'s proclaimed literary enterprise.

Her position is basically that of a sceptic: she admits the need for theories but is prone to question them. For Brooke-Rose, fiction and criticism alike are testing-grounds for literary theory, stages on which it is continually destroyed and reconstituted along new lines; but if criticism is the use of theoretical language, art is the breaking of its rules:

the novelist can often throw an aura of doubt or humour or particular perception upon theory . . . [The novelist is] aware of the fundamental inseparability of elements that critics and teachers have to separate, even rejoice in separating, pin-pointing, for the purpose of this or that type of analysis, though some try to refound them into large universal systems which the novelist knows can only hold in a precarious suspension of disbelief. (1991a: ix)

Her position as a novelist gives her a heightened awareness of the fictional aspects of theory which the critic is able to overlook.

These domains cannot but infect one another, however, and whereas *Tel Quel*'s theoretical and critical writings dominated their fiction, in Brooke-Rose's case the interaction between the two has resulted in a certain amount of ludic manipulation of critical convention, significant form, and other typically literary devices in her criticism which often have parallels with her novels of the same period. In her most recent collection of essays, *Stories, Theories and Things*, she foregrounds the relation between the two roles she plays as a writer: 'The book . . . is in fact about this connection, about how the critic and teacher reads also as writer and how the novelist writes also as theorist' (1991a: ix). The first three articles in the book together elaborate this concept. The first, from which the collection takes its title, is an updated version of 'Self-Confrontation and the Writer'. Brooke-Rose here reflects on the role of theory in her writing:

Is theory for me, then, simply the Mentor, the Law-Giver and Forbidder . . . the lure of constraints and difficulties all artists need, if only to break the rules? But then, so is grammar. So are the conventions of whatever world one ventures into. Perhaps then, I merely need more constraints than those who scoff at theory and do (they think) without. (15)

Her will to 'break the rules' of theory is apparent in *Amalgamemnon*, which originated with the desire to show up the inadequacies of Genette's typology of narrative (see Chapter 3 above). In the second article, 'Whatever Happened to Narratology?', she shows that the history of narratology is itself narrative in form and furthermore, that: 'The story of narratology became as self-reflexive as a "postmodern" novel' (27), which is the main theme of *Thru*. In the third article, 'Id Is, Is Id?', she demonstrates that any statement based on the copula is necessarily dogmatic, and that the failure to recognize the verb 'to be' as a trope leads to a dangerous faith in theoretical systems as representations of the truth (34–7), an idea obliquely treated in *Between*. Mapped on to the post-structuralist paradigms shared by *Tel Quel* and *Thru*, theory for Brooke-Rose represents a *langue* or discursive competence, the writing of fiction is the unconscious or 'other scene' which disrupts and questions this relationship, and teaching and criticism are the *parole*, or performance.

Brooke-Rose sees fiction as a tool for exploring the gaps and inconsistencies she perceives in literary theory. She draws her inspiration from the fact that theory does not accomplish on its own terms what it sets out to accomplish. This distinguishes her writing from that of *Tel Quel* which, despite energetic attempts by the group to distance itself from academic discourse, is 'academic' in the sense that it was often produced according to pre-established theoretical formulae.

The mutual permeability of *Tel Quel*'s theoretical and fictional writing is evident to an even greater extent in the writing of many French 'feminists', but because it is in the nature of their project to question discursive categories such as these, the status of theory in their texts is very different. Hélène Cixous and Monique Wittig stand out as the best-known 'feminist' writers of both 'theory' and 'fiction' whose work dismantles these divisions. Texts such as Wittig's *Le Corps lesbien* and 'Sorties' by Cixous mix autobiography, myth, and conceptual discourse in such a way as to defy generic classifications. Yet often their writing is reduced by others to paradoxical theoretical pronouncements about the evils of theorization. Brooke-Rose has been able to avoid reductive readings of her work by retaining the traditional distinction between the use and analysis of theory which she practises in her critical writings, and the subversive parody of theory which she practises in her novels. At the same time, this means that she rejects the discursive aesthetic that reigns among 'feminists'. To define her fiction as *écriture féminine* or feminist writing would represent a serious misnomer; but to deny any links between her writing and that of French 'feminists' would be an equally grievous fault, for if they use different methods, they do in certain cases share the same concerns.[19] In Chapter 3 I analysed the link in *Between*, *Thru*, and

[19] The writing dubbed *écriture féminine* and linked most often with Hélène Cixous is generally seen as a means of 'writing the (female) body', of writing in such a way as to mime female sexuality. The devices used to achieve this end vary widely, however, from the lushness of Cixous's own prose to the spareness of the fiction of Marguerite Duras.

Amalgamemnon between the discursive position of women and the novelistic technique of parodic appropriation of another's discourse. It is not surprising that this tactic is manifest also in much of the gender-conscious writing of the period in France.

Hélène Cixous became interested in Brooke-Rose's writing in the late 1960s. She reviewed both *Such* and *Between* in *Le Monde*, and Brooke-Rose went to Paris in 1968 on Cixous's invitation. The most active producer of *écriture féminine* was thus also an enabling force behind Brooke-Rose's post-1968 career. But in terms of their activities within Vincennes, the two writers took very different paths. While Brooke-Rose benefited from and contributed to the changes taking place in French education in the late 1960s and early 1970s, she did not play the same role in the founding of radical institutions.[20] The journal she did found was not ideologically oriented, and though she rose quickly through the ranks of the academic system, she had little taste for organized groups with a common project.

There are, however, aspects of her writing which encourage comparison with certain examples of Cixous's fiction. The appropriation and reformulation of pre-existing texts is one of the main techniques employed by Cixous who sees it as a typically female approach to language use: 'Voler est geste de femme. Voler dans la langue, la faire voler' (1975: 178). As the polysemy of the word '*voler*' in this quotation indicates, Cixous's writing is 'poetic': plays on words abound, syntax is stretched and altered, links are associative rather than causal, and the tone is lyrical. This 'poetic' quality, a high degree of allusiveness, and an orientation toward the future are features it shares with Brooke-Rose's fiction. Both Cixous and Brooke-Rose see fiction as a 'poetic' manipulation of the discourses in which they are implicated professionally, but whereas Cixous's novels constitute a response in a 'feminine' voice to male discourse, Brooke-Rose's fiction interrogates this discourse by engaging directly with it. Cixous relieves the concepts of male thinkers of the androcentrism and the theoretical rigour by which they are constrained and allows them to swim freely in a flowing, 'feminine' language. Brooke-Rose, on the other hand, turns such

---

[20] The Psychanalyse et Politique group, started at Vincennes and led for a time by Hélène Cixous, was linked to the 'feminist' movement of the 1970s, though a number of women—Monique Wittig among them—broke with the group and established their own organizations.

concepts back on themselves in those cases where they are blind to their own systematicity and to the ancient narratives which subtend them.

Monique Wittig is the other major novelist to have emerged from the French 'feminist' movement, and whatever their differences, she and Cixous can be seen to be working with many of the same assumptions about the relation of language and gender. Like Brooke-Rose and Cixous, Wittig uses intertextuality in a specifically feminine way. Her tactic of discursive guerrilla warfare in *Les Guerillères* (1969) may be likened to Brooke-Rose's strategy of subversive mimesis in *Thru* and *Amalgamemnon*, and her use of the *Divine Comedy* in *Virgile, non* (1981) is in many respects similar to Brooke-Rose's use of the *Histories* in *Amalgamemnon*. But if Brooke-Rose works by means of parody and subtle defamiliarization to mock sexist bias, Wittig's novels are discursively separatist. Brooke-Rose stages a struggle against masculinist ideology but does not ever endorse the possibility of either an alternative social order or a specifically feminine or feminist form of discourse.

But the fact that her view is less radical than that of Wittig and her style less ebulliently celebratory of femininity than that of Cixous does not mean that it is less efficacious in terms of the battle against sexism. Many writers have commented on the idealized abstraction of the French 'feminists' and their distance from the social issues which face real women (Cameron 1985: 132; Moi 1985: 123,171; Spivak 1988: 140).[21]

Brooke-Rose rejects the essentialism of the most pessimistic form of 'feminism', which consists in the belief that woman is man's unconscious and that she can thus never articulate herself in language. But she also rejects the most optimistic scenario according to which there might be a distinctly female form of language-use free from the hidden biases and hierarchies of the 'patriarchal' language we are obliged for the time being to use. She takes the middle road, using her historically constructed position of 'otherness' as a point of leverage from which to question the suppositions of male-dominated discourses.

---

[21] Wittig confronts this problem in *Virgile, non*, which implicitly criticizes the idealism of much of the 'feminist' writing of the 1970s. It suggests that the most urgent task is finding a means of dealing with society on its own terms rather than simply rejecting it. This is the terrain on which Brooke-Rose had been working since *Between*.

In the 1960s and 1970s the OuLiPo group held in common with the *nouveau roman, Tel Quel,* and the French 'feminists' the conviction that to change language is to change our conception of the world, yet their ludic manipulation of arbitrary constraints on writing distances their project from the more directly political aims of these two groups and encourages parallels with independent experimental writers such as Michel Butor and Maurice Roche.

OuLiPo is best known for applying the formal principles of mathematics and logic to literature. The group's preoccupation with linguistic games is evident in the novels of members such as Raymond Queneau, Georges Perec, Jacques Roubaud, Italo Calvino, and Harry Mathews. The principle strategy of OuLiPo is to subject literary texts (either pre-existing texts or those of their own invention) to arbitrary but systematic manipulations as a means of artificially inducing creativity by consciously creating the chance juxtapositions and associations which are creativity's raw material. Like Brooke-Rose, they see formal play as a means of combating dogma and the imposition of arbitrary constraints as an oblique way of dealing with the problem of order and systematicity.

Of all the Oulipian novelists, George Perec has taken the formal manipulation of language the furthest. Unlike Queneau, Roubaud, and Mathews, who structure their fiction primarily according to mathematical principles, Perec imposes linguistic rules on his prose. He is famous for, among other things, his lipogrammatic novel *La Disparition* (1969), which omits the letter *e*. Brooke-Rose writes of this novel that the technique employed 'plunges the reader into a strange duality, forcing him both to believe and not to believe what he is reading' (1991*a*: 220). This ontological ambiguity is produced also by *Between* and *Amalgamemnon* which are variations on the lipogram, their common target being the ontological stability implied by the word 'is'. Brooke-Rose attacks the present indicative of the copula from two angles: first in *Between* she expunges the verb, and then in *Amalgamemnon* she banishes the mood. *Between* is thus a lipogram in 'to be', while *Amalgamemnon* is what Jean-Jacques Lecercle terms a 'syntactic lipogram' (1991: 95; 1992: 4).[22]

But in addition to rejecting the verb 'to be', *Between* also rejects the structure of traditional narrative. Perec fabulates stories out of a

[22] Perec in fact makes an oblique reference to *Between* in a 1973 article: 'une romancière anglaise contemporaine s'est . . . interdit tout recours aux diverses formes et dérivés de "to be" ' (1973: 92).

linguistic or structural given which accounts for the technique which initiated it. Brooke-Rose's method in her novels of the 1960s differs from this type of 'fabulation'. The absence of the verb 'to be' in *Between* is motivated by principles integral to the novel's paratactic symbolic and structural organization (the themes and structures of constant mobility, loss of identity in language, and so on), just as the absence of the present indicative in *Amalgamemnon* is motivated by a desire to explore the unrealized potential of literature. In both cases the adherence to strict formal laws goes hand in hand with a transgression of the laws of traditional narrative and the elaboration of new, non-causal narrative modes. *Amalgamemnon* is in this sense a paradigm of 'potential literature'. In his discussion of this novel Jean-Jacques Lecercle remarks that 'le lipogramme syntactique est en réalité un lipogramme pragmatique' (1992: 5), for what is excised is the realization of events. The concept of potentiality is enacted in the novel's tense structure, which mimes not only the ontological status of fiction, but also the position of *Amalgamemnon* within literary discourse: it performs what has not yet been done in the mode of the not-yet-done.

The multiple narratives in Perec's *La Disparition* follow what is described in the novel as 'la tradition du plus strict roman' (1969: 208), and in terms of narrative conventions, most of the fiction produced by OuLiPo members is relatively conservative. The innovation associated with these texts is often evident only at the level of their genesis—algorithms for composition and rules for structuring narrative which would not be evident to the casual reader. Their activity is 'play', but play which consists in the manipulation of the rules of the game more than it does the invention of new moves.

In the case of writers such as Michel Butor and Maurice Roche, however, fictional convention is often dispensed with altogether as the causal links of linear narrative are banished in favour of structures which evoke simultaneity, polyphony, and arbitrary order. In their texts of the 1960s and 1970s both authors also replace characterization with caricature of social and discursive conventions. Like Brooke-Rose, these authors portray subjectivity as a process of structuring, and meaning (or at least semantic interaction) is generated in their work through parody and incongruous juxtaposition.

Michel Butor is often associated with the *nouveau roman*, but this label cannot be applied with any accuracy to the texts he has published since 1960, none of which he calls 'novels'. Starting with *Mobile* (1962), the narrative voice is relinquished in favour of a formal organization miming the object of representation. In *Mobile* Butor does with the discourses of popular culture what Brooke-Rose does with specialized discourses. He claims that: 'La citation la plus litérale est déjà dans une certain mesure une parodie' (1968:18), and in *Mobile* he demonstrates the truth of this statement by arranging quotations so as to highlight the ironies of the myths of American culture and American history in much the same way as Brooke-Rose manipulates public texts in *Between* and Herodotus's *Histories* in *Amalgamemnon*. But if Butor's task is critical, it is also mimetic. His object is 'the world'; he sees language as a tool for grasping that world, not as an object to be studied in its own right (1967: 240–1). Brooke-Rose's focus is more firmly fixed on the discourses operative within language. Whereas he puts linguistic systems into play and uses them to represent the world, she concentrates her efforts on dismantling the systems themselves.

In this her *œuvre* is closer to that of Maurice Roche, who since the mid-1960s has been writing highly unconventional fiction which pushes language, typography, and imagery to extremes not found in the work of any of the writers so far discussed. Brooke-Rose describes her discovery of Roche when she came to Paris as an 'éblouissement' (1976*k*: 15), for up till that time she had been unaware that there were any French writers who shared her explosive sense of humour.[23]

Butor and Roche both exploit the visual characteristic of print by employing a variety of typefaces. But of the two, Roche takes this device the furthest, combining a dazzling variety of symbolic codes, natural languages, typographic acrobatics, and page-designs to create what is described in *Circus* as a 'stéréographie asémique aux développements absents, passant à présent pour FICTION THEORIQUE à venir' (1972: 3).[24] In this tongue-in-cheek definition, the implicit negation of meaning, causal logic, unity of voice, and actualization in the present indicate that Roche's concerns are similar to those of

---

[23] Roche's appreciation of the similarity between their work is indicated in his inscription in her copy of *Compact*, which describes the novel as 'une loterie de pronoms . . . en attendant de perdre le verbe être' (cited in Brooke-Rose 1981: 336–7).

[24] Like Brooke-Rose, Roche 'pokes fun at' the concept of theory by punning here on the word 'théorique': his novels are theoretical mainly in the sense that their fictions exist 'in theory' rather than in reality.

Thru, and Brooke-Rose's fiction in general. But the principal quality which binds the two authors is the irreverent and often parodic attitude which prevents them from becoming dogmatically fixated on the theories they play with and which makes the establishment or implementation of fixed systems impossible in their work.[25]

Christine Brooke-Rose has never allied herself with literary movements, nor has she been part of any group. The literary 'scene' in Paris in the 1960s and the 1970s was dominated by such groups, however, chief among them *Tel Quel*, a variety of 'feminist' circles, and OuLiPo. It was a period of polarization and intense in-fighting, and ideological or theoretical stands were difficult to avoid if one was to participate in current debates. Even a non-ideological group such as OuLiPo defined its territory, declared the orthodoxies and heresies of the procedures it used. Yet there were a few isolated figures who kept apart from collective declarations and who led fiction in directions also being taken by Brooke-Rose. It is with one such writer, Maurice Roche, that Brooke-Rose's writing of the period has most in common.

International Postmodernism

The single most significant critical concept to have emerged over the last two decades within the Anglo-American literary world is that of international postmodernism. Because it crosses national boundaries which have for so long divided up literature to the detriment of cross-cultural writers, the advent of this category within English-language criticism would seem to represent the ideal solution to the problem of placing a writer such as Christine Brooke-Rose. But Brooke-Rose's relationship with and attitude toward postmodernism have been uneasy, and from her point of view the term has a number of disadvantages. Its main difficulty—and its strength—is the fact that it means something different for everyone who uses it. Postmodernism has been characterized as heterogeneous, parodic, anti-totalizing, anti-hierarchical, self-conscious, and so on, but these descriptions are so vague that nearly every cultural practice past or

---

[25] As mentioned in Chap. 3 above, certain sections of *Compact* are narrated in the future, producing an effect similar to that of *Amalgamemnon*.

present can be made to have an air of the postmodern about it. This vagueness allows individual critics to define postmodernist fiction each according to his or her specific needs. For Brian McHale (1987) it involves an 'ontological flicker', for Linda Hutcheon (1988) it is 'historiographic metafiction', for Alan Wilde (1981) it is a specific kind of irony, and so on. Christine Brooke-Rose is understandably hesitant to condone the use of the concept, for it does not always establish classifications relevant to her own work. According to McHale's definition, her fiction alternates between modernism and postmodernism (n.d.: 5), according to Hutcheon's definition, a number of her experimental novels would not be considered postmodernist at all but her realist novel *The Dear Deceit* would qualify, while all her novels up to and including *Thru* would fall into Wilde's category of modernist 'disjunctive irony', and only with *Amalgamemnon* could she be seen to be venturing into the postmodernist territory of Wilde's 'suspensive irony'. Despite the fact that it is not generally defined in geographical terms, the label 'postmodernism' would appear to work against a novelist as unique and difficult to classify as Brooke-Rose.[26]

There are, however, certain advantages to being included in a category such as this, not least of which is that one receives treatment in the numerous books on the topic. At its best, postmodernism is a concept which enables us to reject the view of literature as so many national trees, each with its own main trunk and subsidiary branches, allowing us instead to see it as a network of overlapping groupings corresponding to areas of interest—technical, ideological, thematic, and so on. We can then talk about the tendency toward ludic manipulation of language in the work of some writers, gender-consciousness in the work of others, the recent trend in science fiction toward the use of metafictional techniques, as well as developments specific to a given culture, as so many 'postmodernisms' which together comprise a loose coalition. According to this view of postmodernism, each individual writer could be seen as having a stake in a number of different postmodernist enterprises.

---

[26] She complains that the term is a period term 'completely lacking in content', and jokingly refers to it as 'most-modernism' (1981: 345). When she does use the word 'postmodernism', it is generally placed in inverted commas or otherwise distanced from her own critical vocabulary. In an analysis of Lodge's (1977) discussion of postmodernism she demonstrates that none of the typically postmodernist devices Lodge lists is truly new (1981: 354–63), further justifying her mistrust of the word.

Only if it is understood in this way will the concept of postmodernism benefit a writer such as Christine Brooke-Rose, and it is therefore in this way that I shall employ it. Brooke-Rose's fiction can be potentially allied with four such postmodernisms: American 'surfiction', feminist or gender-conscious postmodernism, 'cybernetic interface fiction', and British postmodernist fiction.

The term 'surfiction' was coined in 1975 by the novelist and critic Raymond Federman to cover a wide range of fiction from the *nouveau roman* and *Tel Quel* to the work of Julio Cortázar and John Barth. Federman came to America from France in 1947, but he retained close ties with French intellectuals, including the *Tel Quel* group and Maurice Roche. His definition of surfiction is clearly indebted to the theories of fiction developed in France in the 1960s: 'the only fiction that still means something today is that kind of fiction that tries to explore the possibilities of fiction . . . This I call SURFICTION. However, not because it imitates reality, but because it exposes the fictionality of reality' (1975: 7).[27] Federman's desire to explore the possibilities of fiction bears an obvious likeness to Brooke-Rose's project, and the methods he proposes to achieve this end—non-linear form, typographic innovation, 'disordered' structures requiring reader participation in the generation of meaning—recall those employed by Brooke-Rose in *Thru*. But the majority of surfiction practised in the United States is not as extreme as Federman's characterization of the movement would lead one to believe. Typical surfictionist techniques include the transgression of narrative ontology, Roussellian linguistic procedures, and the discursive heterogeneity of 'montage'. It is therefore Brooke-Rose's two most recent novels which have the most in common with American surfiction. *Verbivore* displays discursive heterogeneity and *Textermination* transgresses the ontology of the fictional character; both contain metalepses, and their common aim is unquestionably to expose the fictionality of 'reality'.

But though the anti-mimetic impulse evident in her novels was strong among the American surfictionists, Brooke-Rose remarks that

---

[27] Like 'postmodernism', the word 'surfiction' has undergone a considerable amount of slippage between critics. For Mas'ud Zavarzadeh surfiction is more directly engaged with the real world than meta-fiction (1976: 40), whereas for Patricia Waugh the opposite is true (1984: 14); for Hutcheon it is the most hermetic and reflexive form of late modernism (1988: 52). Brooke-Rose does not define the term, but uses it loosely with reference to Federman's and Zavarzadeh's definitions.

'the same mimetic crisis has on the whole found different solutions in England and especially America, that is, through a change of "content" only' (1981: 338). Most of the American representatives of surfiction were far less willing than Federman to relinquish conventional modes of discourse on the micro-textual level. They often abandoned traditional narrative convention only to adopt other available modes—colloquial monologue, essay-like digressions, letters, unnarrated dialogue, pastiche of newspaper jargon, and so on. Brooke-Rose points out that stylistic innovation in surfiction is mainly limited to parody, and that what is parody on the thematic level is only stylization on the technical level (1981: 371).[28] She observes that this device frequently functions as a substitute for the genuine renovation of language she admires in much contemporary French experiment:

One often has the impression that the famous renewal in some American postmodernism is achieved entirely through anti-illusionist devices, self-reflexive 'strategies' and topoi, by now pretty fatigued, rather than through language itself finding and forming a renewed and renewing content. (1991a: 217)

This is undoubtedly due partially to the fact that these writers have no ideological bone to pick with the texts and styles they parody. In the Quartet, Brooke-Rose confronts fiction with the non-literary in an explicit attempt to vindicate novelistic discourse. Likewise, her parodic effects in *Thru* and *Amalgamemnon* are critical precisely because they seek to uncover the groundlessness of faith in the truth of theoretical discourse. This critical stance is a characteristic her work shares with certain contemporary feminist novelists who use their ambiguous status within the tradition to question the authority of non-fictional discourses.

At a round-table discussion in 1982 on the 'American New Novel', John Hawkes was asked about the role of women in the emerging postmodernist tradition. He replied that while there were 'as many if not more current works of American fiction written by women as by men', he could not 'think of any American woman writer working beyond the realistic tradition', with the exception of his own former student Marilynne Robinson (1982: 200–1). Hawkes's ignorance of experimental fiction by women can perhaps be explained in part by

[28] She later modifies her view and redefines these texts as dialogic discourse or hidden polemic which merely give the illusion of parody (1991a: 202).

the fact that, as Brooke-Rose maintains, women 'still shrink from declaring all over the place how revolutionary they are' (1991a: 262). While this is manifestly not the case with feminist writers, the only self-consciously experimental movements in which women play a significant role do appear to be certain offshoots of feminism. Though Brooke-Rose does not consistently write from a feminist position, it is possible to discern a body of 'feminist postmodernist' fiction in which *Amalgamemnon* at least might find a place.

The conjunction of the terms 'feminism' and 'postmodernism' has not been without its frictions, and perhaps it is appropriate that Brooke-Rose's novel should fit only into a category such as this which is inherently problematic. Feminist critics confront the problem of integration with male postmodernism in a number of ways. Like Cixous and Kristeva, Rachel Blau DuPlessis advocates bringing together the avant-garde and the feminine in an effort self-consciously to appropriate experimental style for women. In the influential essay 'For the Etruscans', DuPlessis recognizes that what she defines as the 'female aesthetic' is close to that of postmodernism (1981: 286), but she adds that 'women reject this position as soon as it becomes politically quietistic or shows ancient gender values' (287). Patricia Waugh is wary of such an allegiance for just this reason; she sees emerging in contemporary writing by women a relational concept of subjectivity which complements postmodernism rather than joining it (1989: 13). Similarly, Susan Suleiman claims that 'if women are to be part of an avant-garde movement, they will do well to found it themselves' (1990: 32), but she points out that there are many substantive differences among feminists and many similarities between male avant-garde writers and their female counterparts. In consequence, women avant-garde writers—Suleiman gives Brooke-Rose and Angela Carter as examples (237, n. 17)—have a 'double allegiance' (162). For her part, Christine Brooke-Rose 'wholly concur[s]' (1991a: 225) with Marianne DeKoven's similar argument that 'it behoves us . . . to establish ourselves as an "ambiguously nonhegemonic group" *in relation to male avant-garde hegemony*, simultaneously within it and subversive of it' (DeKoven 1989: 97, italics in the original).

From this point of view it is in the interest of women to acknowledge the difficulty of their position, the fact that as writers they are necessarily defined relationally, and that they are obliged to speak in an idiom fashioned mainly by men. Those few writers who do this are, in Brooke-Rose's words, like 'the sea between two continents' (1991a: 264). This is clearly where she herself lies, and as we have seen, it is a position which allows her to have a critical and humorous angle on the world.[29] The feminist writing which has the most bearing on Brooke-Rose's fiction is that which also takes advantage of the ambiguity of women's status and their link with fictional modes in order to question the validity of hegemonic discourses. Critics have recognized parody as a typically feminine fictional strategy (Gilbert and Gubar 1979: 80; Suleiman 1990: 142), and as we have seen, it is the common denominator of Brooke-Rose's fiction and French 'feminist' writing. Postmodernist parody by women takes two typical forms: the appropriation of cultural myths, as, for example, in the fiction of Angela Carter, and the creative plagiarism of actual texts of the past, as in that of Kathy Acker. The voice of Cassandra has also proved a convenient means for certain women of exploring the gender-coded discursive roles that have been encoded in our heritage. Like *Amalgamemnon*, Ursule Molinaro's *The Autobiography of Cassandra, Princess and Prophetess of Troy* (1981) and Christa Wolf's *Kassandra* (1983) both use the first person to vindicate the role of a figure who is condemned in Western culture to be considered a prophet of doom. The act of rewriting history and debunking myth is seen by both writers to be intimately linked with the unheeded and unrecorded voices of women. Though Mira in *Amalgamemnon* assumes the Cassandra role reluctantly, she recognizes that it is one of the only discursive positions available to women who want to expose the fictionality of the discourses of knowledge. If 'feminist postmodernism' is understood as writing which examines the question of fact versus fiction from a gender-conscious position, then *Amalgamemnon* undoubtedly falls within its domain.

The spate of recent science fiction by women has prompted one writer to speculate that this might be the ideal contemporary women's form (Florence 1990). Yet, unlike most feminist instances of the genre, Brooke-Rose's only true science-fiction novels, *Xorandor* and *Verbivore*, do not offer a critique of patriarchal society from the standpoint of a (feminist) alternative world. There has been

[29] She points out that postmodernism is generally associated with humour, and that humour (as opposed to wit) requires a capacity for independent judgement which women have, for cultural reasons, been inhibited from developing: 'the different "view" of the world needed for high comedy, and apparently not acquired by women, might, however, also explain the lack of success (broadly speaking) of women in "postmodern" experiment, where outrageous humour is one of the chief ingredients on the male side' (1991a: 274).

a notable convergence, however, between recent science fiction and more 'mainstream' postmodernism, as Brooke-Rose herself recognizes (1981: 102; 1991a: 175). Teresa Ebert terms the fiction produced at this nexus 'metascience fiction' (1980: 92). She remarks that since the Second World War technology has come to play a secondary role in much science fiction, whereas in non-science fiction its role has increased. This has resulted in a blurring of boundaries between the two categories (95) which accounts, perhaps, for the ambiguous position of Brooke-Rose's fiction *vis-à-vis* science fiction in the traditional sense.

The issues addressed in *Xorandor* and *Verbivore*—the role of the novel in an ever-more technological society and the nature of the discourses through which we communicate—are related to only a limited domain of science, namely those advances in technology which involve cybernetic-controlled information systems. For this reason the term 'cybernetic interface fiction' coined by Brian McHale provides a more accurate way of describing them. Cybernetic interface fiction, of which Brooke-Rose's Quartet is given as an example, is that form of postmodern narrative which emerges at the convergence of cybernetic technology and the humanities (n.d.: 25).

Artificial intelligence provides a way of joining these two domains. In many respects Brooke-Rose's fiction resembles the new 'emergent' artificial intelligence which Sherry Turkle describes as breaking away from rule-governed models of information-processing. This new generation of computers consists of machines in which there is 'no distinction between processors and the information they process' (1988: 248). It is at this point that artificial intelligence becomes a matter of 'making' something rather than 'passing' something (255), or, in discursive terms, of telling, as the creature Xorandor does, rather than simply conveying facts. A positive orientation toward cybernetics is manifest also in novels such as Joseph McElroy's *Plus* (1977). McElroy's disembodied brain is, like the thinking stone in *Xorandor*, a being which is coextensive with its language. By dividing the mind from its habitual environment, *Plus* explores the linguistic and cognitive consequences of information technology in a way that is 'poetic' in Brooke-Rose's sense (Brooke-Rose 1981: 273).

In a similar vein, Brian McHale points to the parallels between *Verbivore* and the recent wave of 'cyberpunk' fiction, including William Gibson's *Neuromancer* (1984) and Bruce Sterling's *Islands in the Net* (1988), which use hypothetical developments in science to generate solutions to narrative problems such as point of view and the circulation of information (McHale n.d.: 37). The symbiotic relation between science and fiction in both cybernetic interface fiction and cyberpunk fiction indicates a move away from the technophobia of some earlier writers, and it is within this more recent development that Brooke-Rose's own science-fiction novels *Xorandor* and *Verbivore* can be situated.

Even in science-fiction terms, *Xorandor* and *Verbivore* adhere to specifically British norms,[30] and British postmodernism, though not well-defined as a category, is a potential label which could be applied to Brooke-Rose's novels. There are two features prominent in recent British fiction which could be qualified as postmodern, and which also play a major role in Brooke-Rose's Intercom Quartet: inter- and hetero-textuality on the one hand, and a persistent tendency toward the fantastic in its various guises (science fiction, Gothic, magic realism, and so on) on the other.[31] Technically, however, British fiction in the last two decades has been reluctant to relinquish the conventions of realism and has been content instead to stretch them. Patricia Waugh observes that in British metafiction the problem of representation 'tends to be explored thematically, or through macro-structures like plot and narrative voice'. She goes on to add that: 'The sign as sign is still, to a large extent, self-effacing in such fiction' (1984: 57). Even a novel such as Alasdair Gray's *Lanark* (1981), which combines fantastic elements with self-conscious intertextuality, including, like *Thru*, an index of its literary borrowings, exhibits a high degree of conformity to the genres—naturalism, science fiction, the *Bildungsroman*—on which it draws.[32]

---

[30] Christopher Priest identifies as the quintessentially British science-fiction type the 'British disaster novel', to which both Brooke-Rose's science-fiction novels nominally conform: 'the *status quo* is overturned by some hitherto unanticipated development . . . and the story follows a small group of ordinary people as they confront the upheaval' (1979: 195).

[31] Patrick Parrinder notes that British novelists do not have a high profile in the international canon of postmodernism, and he proposes the category of the reflexive fantastic to accommodate their writing (1987: 113). I advocated a similar concept in relation to British fiction of the 1960s, but on the grounds outlined above, I shall retain the admittedly deficient term 'postmodernism' for the purposes of the present discussion.

[32] Similarly, David Lodge's *Small World* thematizes theories of structuralism and poststructuralism, but unlike *Thru*, it conforms in other respects to the genre of the post-war British university novel as characterized by Ian Carter (1990), for whom it is the most innovative example. It is significant that Carter does not mention *Thru* in his study of a form which he demonstrates to be on the whole both formally and politically conservative.

The strength of such writers' grounding in realism is due to the fact that, like Lodge's 'problematic novelists', they do not often challenge the common-sense conception of reality. For Allan Massie this is the quintessential paradox of contemporary British fiction: 'the concept of character has been challenged by physiological and psychological advances and theories; yet perception of "real" character remains central to the way we try to understand the world' (1990: 71). In other words, contemporary British novelists have, for the most part, little interest in changing our perceptions, though they are vaguely aware that these are in some sense inadequate.

Richard Todd sees British postmodernism's distinguishing feature as a self-consciousness of literary heritage dramatized in novels by authors such as Iris Murdoch, Anthony Burgess, and Julian Barnes, in which literary works of the past play the role of talisman. In Brooke-Rose's terms these novels could be classified as 'palimpsest literary histories'. A variation on this type of intertextuality is the confrontation of narrative with other discursive modes. This heterotextuality can be seen as an aspect of the return to eighteenth-century devices which has characterized British fiction since the war. In its 'postmodernist' guise the trend is manifest in the use of documentary modes and 'found texts'. A forerunner of this trend is Burns's *Dreamerika!* discussed above; other examples include the documentary collage in Golding's *Rites of Passage* (1980), Fowles's *A Maggot* (1985), as well as the self-conscious autobiographical picaresque modes of Angela Carter's *Nights at the Circus* and Salman Rushdie's *Midnight's Children* (1981). Another technique evident in recent British fantasy and magic realism is the literalization of metaphor. In *Midnight's Children*, for example, Saleem Sanai is able to 'sniff out the truth' by actually smelling emotions and moral qualities, and in the afterworld of *Lanark* the saying 'time is money' has generated credit cards through which people draw on their future.

With respect to these characterizations, Brooke-Rose's fiction manifests the attributes of British postmodernist fiction in magnified form. In her work the literalization of metaphor is generalized and used as a structural principle, magic realism is combined in *Textermination* with palimpsest literary history, and in *Verbivore* with documentary materials such as letters and journals. Yet if most contemporary British fiction clings to realist models, Brooke-Rose has clung to experiment. Though her most recent work follows that of her compatriots in its use of genre, she still shies away from their common-sense view of reality.

The theories and practice of literature which have held sway in France since the 1960s had the effect of enabling Christine Brooke-Rose to break with realism and to conceptualize what she was trying to do in her fiction. Yet while her critical writing provides an intellectual context for her novels and to some extent defines the intertextual matrix on which she draws, it is not prescriptive in the way that theory and criticism are for certain of the French writers of the period, nor did it lead her to adopt a method or credo. With her last three novels she has returned to the fold, so to speak, of British fiction, but the 'fold' to which she has returned is a composite of styles and approaches, and the term 'English', or even 'British' is often inadequate to describe many of its members. Furthermore, it would be false to say that in moving away from what were seen as 'French' modes Brooke-Rose has abandoned one tradition for another. The ideologically polarized and group-oriented literary atmosphere of France in the 1960s and 1970s has since given way to a more eclectic and individually minded set of writers who have little sense of common cause or method. As an increasing number of writers are like Brooke-Rose in that they resist placing and labelling, new ways of accommodating their fiction within intelligible frameworks must be sought. It is for this reason that the polymorphous concept of 'postmodernism' has proved useful to many critics. As we have seen, it is the novels of Brooke-Rose's Intercom Quartet which fit best within the various sub-categories of postmodernism. We may hope that this concept will provide Brooke-Rose's Quartet with a means of entry into the critical canon, and that those readers who are introduced in this way to her more recent fiction will explore her œuvre further and learn to appreciate her earlier, less easily classifiable novels on their own terms.

Conclusion

Christine Brooke-Rose's fiction is written with the object of stretching people's mental horizons and questioning the conceptual language in which they think. Because conventional categories are often inappropriate or inadequate in discussing her novels, it is no surprise that as recently as 1990 she alleged that 'critics have not found a critical language to talk about my books' (1990e: 21). This study has been an attempt to find such a language. Through concepts such as the discursive metaphor, *mimétisme*, and the process of 'ex-tradition', I have developed a means of reading and placing Brooke-Rose's work which is, I hope, neither reductive nor exclusive.

Brooke-Rose has consistently maintained the position of the outsider, and her novels re-map the cultural terrain by inventing hybrid discursive spaces. Her early novels manifest a growing dissatisfaction with the conventions of realism which led her in the 1960s to begin to manipulate the discourses of specialized knowledge. In *Between*, *Thru*, and *Amalgamemnon* she employs parody to mount ever-more direct attacks on discursive systems which arrogate themselves to positions of authority by excluding what they designate as unauthoritative 'feminine' modes of language-use. This criticism paved the way for a vindication of the novel in the Intercom Quartet as a mode of knowledge and a means of communication which, contrary to popular belief, is highly compatible with advances in information technology.

Given the originality and cultural heterogeneity of Brooke-Rose's writing, placing her as a novelist is problematic. The concept of the national tradition most commonly invoked to this end has worked against her, leading to her ostracism from the domain of English letters. French literary and cultural theory, the *nouveau roman*, and experimental movements in France in the 1960s and 1970s stimulated her and pushed her to extend her experimentation, but she never allowed herself to be assimilated to any of these movements. Her work does invite comparison, however, with several figures who have also kept aloof from groups and schools, Alan Burns and Maurice Roche in particular, and it can read in terms of 'postmodernism', provided this is understood as a range of strategies available to the novelist, not as a movement.

As with a growing number of cross-cultural writers, Brooke-Rose's position astride boundaries and the tendency of her writing to dislocate them mean that her novels can only be productively read *through* various cultural and literary contexts. This approach emulates that of the novels themselves, whose common feature is their technique of passing language and experience through the lenses of different discourses. An awareness of systems of thought as constructs or fictions is shown in her writing to be the key to defending against their dogmatic tendencies. Yet Brooke-Rose's project is not limited to laying bare the devices of conceptual language. The true accomplishment of her fiction is to take the jargons of the various languages in which we live and work, and to bring them beyond the realm of the instrumental, to make of them what she calls 'a kind of poetry'. By fusing the discourses of knowledge, her novels push to their limits state-of-the-art linguistic systems in a number of fields; in so doing they perform highly unusual cognitive moves which stimulate the imagination and dazzle the mind.

To read Brooke-Rose's novels is to be confronted with a variety of conceptual fields and a network of intertextual allusions that extends far beyond the institutionalized canon of English literature. Because her *œuvre* touches on so many intellectual trends, social phenomena, and literary domains, even a multi-faceted treatment such as I have provided is not adequate to circumscribe it. But perhaps this is just as well. Circumscription is precisely what her fiction strives to avoid. I hope instead to have laid the groundwork for further research in the multiple directions Christine Brooke-Rose's writing indicates to imaginative readers in search of the novel.

Appendix: A Chronology of Christine Brooke-Rose

1923	16 Jan. born in Geneva to Evelyn Blanche Brooke (Swiss of American descent) and Alfred Northbrook Rose (English).
1928–36	Educated in London and Brussels.
1936	Moved to England. Attended school in Folkestone.
1941–5	Worked as an Information Officer in the WAAF at Bletchley Park reading decoded German messages.
1948	Married Jerzy Pietrkiewicz.
1946–9	Studied English and Philology at Somerville College, Oxford.
1950–4	Worked for a Ph.D in Medieval French and English Literature at University College, London.
1956–68	Worked as a literary journalist in London.
1957	*The Languages of Love.*
1958	*A Grammar of Metaphor.*
1959	*The Sycamore Tree.*
1960	*The Dear Deceit.*
1961	*The Middlemen.*
1962–3	Suffered a severe illness; was hospitalized for several months.
1964	*Out.* Travelling Prize of the Society of Authors.
1966	*Such.* James Tait Black Memorial Prize.
1968	*Between.*
1968	Left her husband and moved to Paris.
1968–88	Taught American Literature and Literary Theory at the Université de Paris VIII at Vincennes (later Saint Denis), first as *Maître de Conférences*, then as Professor.
1970	*Go when You See the Green Man Walking.*
1971	*A ZBC of Ezra Pound.*
1974	Held a Guest Chair at SUNY-Buffalo.
1975	*Thru.*
1976	*A Structural Analysis of Pound's* Usura Canto.
1976	Guest Chair at New York University.
1979	Guest Chair at the Hebrew University of Jerusalem.
1980	Guest Chair at Brandeis Univeristy.
1981	*A Rhetoric of the Unreal.*
1984	*Amalgamemnon.*
1986	*Xorandor.*
1988	Retired, moved to Provence.

Bibliography

I. BY CHRISTINE BROOKE-ROSE

Novels

The Languages of Love (London: Secker and Warburg, 1957). Swedish tr., *Karlekens Språk*, Hillevi Blomberg (tr.) (Stockholm: Sven-Erik Berghs Bokförlag, 1958).

The Sycamore Tree (London: Secker and Warburg, 1958; New York: Doubleday, 1959).

The Dear Deceit (London: Secker and Warburg; 1960; New York: Doubleday, 1961).

The Middlemen: A Satire (London: Secker and Warburg, 1961).

Out (London: Michael Joseph, 1964).

Such (London: Michael Joseph, 1966).

Between (London: Michael Joseph, 1968). Italian tr.,*Tra*, Massimo Ferretti (tr.) (Milan: Feltrinelli, 1971).

Thru (London: Hamish Hamilton, 1975).

Amalgamemnon (Manchester: Carcanet, 1984).

Xorandor (Manchester: Carcanet, 1986; pbk. edn. London: Paladin-Grafton, and New York: Avon, 1987). French tr., *Xorandor*, Bernard Hoepffner (tr.) (Grenoble: Cent Pages, 1990).

The Christine Brooke-Rose Omnibus (Manchester: Carcanet, 1986); contains *Out, Such, Between*, and *Thru*.

Verbivore (Manchester: Carcanet, 1990).

Textermination (Manchester: Carcanet, 1991).

Short Fiction

Go When You See the Green Man Walking (London: Michael Joseph, 1970). French tr. of 'The Foot', *Le Membre fantôme*. Bernard Hoepffner (tr.) (Grenoble: Cent Pages, 1990).

Poetry

Gold: A Poem (Aldington: The Hand and Flower Press, 1954).

'The Five Senses', *Whidow* 9 (1956), 20–1.

'Once Upon a Time', *Truth* (27 Apr. 1956), 479.

'The Lunatic Fringe', *Times Literary Supplement* (17 Aug. 1956), A xxxvii.

'Responses', *Truth* (18 Oct. 1957), 1,196.

'Mourning', *Truth* (6 Dec. 1957), 1,386.

'The World A Catechumen', *Botteghe Oscure* 19 (1958), 123–33.
'The Isle of Reil', *Botteghe Oscure* 21 (1958), 101–5.
'To My Mother, Taking the Veil', *London Magazine* (Apr. 1959), 49.
'Today the Acupuncturist', *Times Literary Supplement* (25 Jan. 1963), 61.

Criticism, Commentary, and Reviews Cited

1947. 'La syntaxe et le symbolisme dans la poésie de Hopkins', *Europe*, NS 25/17, 30–9.
1955*a*. [C. F. E. B. Pietrkiewicz], The Use of Metaphor in Some Old French and Middle English Lyrics and Romances, Ph.D thesis, University of London.
1955*b*. 'The Voice of Eternity', *Times Literary Supplement* (17 June), 325–6.
1955*c*. 'The Mickiewicz Centenary', *Tablet* (26 Nov.), 527.
1958*a*. *A Grammar of Metaphor* (London: Secker and Warburg; repr. Mercury Books, 1965).
1958*b*. 'Samuel Beckett and the Anti-Novel', *London Magazine* (Dec.), 38–46.
1959*a*. 'Mood of the Month—XI', *London Magazine* (Sept.), 45–50.
1959*b*. 'The Critic's Eye', *Times Literary Supplement* (20 Mar.), 160.
1959*c*. 'Return from Avilion', *Times Literary Supplement* (25 Dec.), 755.
1960*a*. 'Southey Ends His Song', *Times Literary Supplement* (1 Apr.), 208.
1960*b*. 'His Name in the Record', *Times Literary Supplement* (10 June), 368.
1960*c*. 'Feeding Mind', *Times Literary Supplement* (1 July), 417.
1961*a*. 'Ezra Pound: Piers Plowman in the Modern Waste Land', *Review of English Literature* 2/2, 74–88. Also in Noel Stock (ed.), *Ezra Pound: Perspectives* (Chicago: Regnery), 154–76.
1961*b*. 'The Vanishing Author', *Observer* (12 Feb.), 26.
1961*c*. 'The American Literary Scene: Writers in Search of Community', *Observer* (30 Apr.), 28.
1961*d*. 'Anatomy of Originophobia', *Times Literary Supplement* (19 May), 308.
1961*e*. 'Buzzards, Bloody Owls and One Hawk', *London Magazine* (Sept.), 76–80.
1963. 'Notes on the Metre of Auden's "The Age of Anxiety" ', *Essays in Criticism* 3/3, 253–64.
1964*a*. 'L'Imagination baroque de Robbe-Grillet', *Revue des Lettres Modernes* 94–5, 129–52. Also in *Modern Fiction Studies* 11/4 (1965–6) as 'The Baroque Imagination of Robbe-Grillet'.
1964*b*. 'Lady Precious Stream', *London Magazine* (May), 93–6.
1964*c*. 'Where Have All the Lovers Gone?', *London Magazine* (June), 80–6.

1964*d*. 'Out of the Past' (review of *The Day the Call Came* by Thomas Hinde, *Berg* by Ann Quin, *The Deep Freeze Girls* by Eva Defago, and *Smoke Island* by Antony Trew), *Spectator* (12 June), 802.

1965*a*. 'Dynamic Gradients', *London Magazine* (NS Dec.), 89–96.

1966*a*. 'How Far de Lonh?', *Times Literary Supplement* (14 Apr.), 326.

1966*b*. 'Making it New', (review of *The Inquisitory* by Robert Pinget and *Degrees* by Michel Butor), *Observer* (2 Oct.), 26.

1967*a*. 'Metaphor in *Paradise Lost*: A Grammatical Analysis', in R. Emma and J. T. Shawcross (eds.), *Language and Style in Milton: A Symposium in Honour of the Tercentenary of* Paradise Lost (New York: Ungar), 252–303.

1967*b*. 'Lettres d'Angleterre', *Nouvelle Revue Française* (June), 1,241–9 (July), 116–25. Also in *Langues Modernes* (Mar., Apr. 1969), 158–68 as 'Le Roman experimental en Angleterre'.

1967*c*. 'Lay by me Aurelie', in Eva Hesse (ed.), *New Approaches to Ezra Pound* (London: Faber and Faber), 242–69. German tr. in Eva Hesse (ed.), *22 Versuche über einen Dichter* (Athanäum Verlag), 304–31.

1968*a*. 'French Fiction: The Long Revolution', *The Times* (3 Aug.), 18.

1968*b*. 'La Dévaluation du livre', *Le Monde* (24 Jan., Supp. to No. 7,163).

1968*c*. 'Claude Lévi-Strauss: A New Multi-Dimensional Way of Thinking' (review of *Structural Anthropology* by Claude Lévi-Strauss), *The Times* (2 Mar.), 20.

1971. *A ZBC of Ezra Pound* (London: Faber and Faber). Contains a revised version of 1967*c*.

1973*a*. 'Ezra Pound', *Littérature de notre temps* (Paris: Casterman).

1973*b*. 'Viewpoint', *Times Literary Supplement* (1 June), 614.

1976*a*. *A Structural Analysis of Pound's Usura Canto: Jakobson's Method Extended and Applied to Free Verse* (The Hague: Mouton).

1976*b*. 'An Excerpt from the Novel *Thru*: Author's Note', *New Directions* 33, 144.

1976*c*. 'Historical Genres / Theoretical Genres: A Discussion of Todorov on the Fantastic', *New Literary History* 8/1, 145–58.

1976*d*. 'The Squirm of the True I: An Essay in Non-Methodology', *Poetics and Theory of Literature* 1/2, 265–94.

1976*e*. 'The Squirm of the True II: The Long Glasses', *Poetics and Theory of Literature* 1/3, 513–46.

1976*f*. 'Paris Letter: Dramatics', *Spectator* (28 Feb.), 25.

1976*g*. 'Letter from Paris: Ganging Up', *Spectator* (27 Mar.), 26.

1976*h*. 'Letter from Paris: Tricolore Tape', *Spectator* (22 May), 26.

1976*i*. 'Letter from Paris: Le Pop', *Spectator* (12 June), 26.

1976*j*. 'Letter from Paris: All the City's a Stage', *Spectator* (24 July), 25.

1977*a*. 'Self-Confrontation and the Writer', *New Literary History* 9/1, 129–36.

1977*b*. 'The Squirm of the True III: Surface Structure in Narrative', *Poetics and Theory of Literature* 2/3, 517–62.

1977c. 'Imitations Are Proof of New Writing's Power', *The Times* (31 May), vii.

1978. 'Transgressions: An Essay-say on the Novel Novel Novel', *Contemporary Literature* 19/3, 378–407.

1980a. 'The Readerhood of Man', in Susan R. Suleiman and Inge Crosman (eds.), *The Reader in the Text: Essays in Audience and Interpretation* (Princeton, NJ: Princeton UP), 120–48.

1980b. 'Round and Round the Jakobson Diagram: A Survey', *Hebrew University Studies in Literature* 8/2, 153–82. French tr. in *Théorie, littérature, enseignement* 1 (1981).

1980c. 'Where Do We Go From Here?', *Granta* 3, 161–88.

1980d. 'The Evil Ring: Realism and the Marvelous', *Poetics Today* 1/4, 67–90.

1981. *A Rhetoric of the Unreal: Studies in Narrative and Structure, Especially of the Fantastic* (Cambridge: Cambridge UP). Includes revised versions of 1964a, 1976c, 1976d, 1976e, 1977b, 1978, 1980a, 1980b, 1980c, 1980d, and 1982.

1982. 'Eximplosions', *Genre* 14/1, 9–21.

1983a. 'Théorie des genres: la science-fiction', in Alain Bony (ed.), *Poétique(s): Domaine anglais* (Lyon: Presses Universitaires de Lyon), 251–62. Also in *Théorie, littérature, enseignement* 2 (1982).

1984a. 'Fiction, figment, feindre', *Fabula* 3, 121–32.

1985a. 'Woman as a Semiotic Object', *Poetics Today* 6/1, 9–20. Also in Susan Rubin Suleiman (ed.), *The Female Body in Western Culture* (Cambridge, Mass.: Harvard UP), 1986.

1985b. 'Palimpsestes en paragrammes: une "phrase narrative" bien cachée', *Caliban: L'Esthétique de la science-fiction* 22, 87–99. Revised version of ch. 10 of 1981.

1985c. 'Illusions of Parody', *Amerikastudien/American Studies* 30/2, 225–33. Also in *Théorie, littérature, enseignement* 4 as 'Chimères de parodie'.

1986a. 'The Dissolution of Character in the Novel', in Thomas C. Heller, et al. (eds.), *Reconstructing Individualism: Autonomy, Individuality and the Self in Western Thought* (Stanford, Calif.: Stanford UP). 184–96.

1986b. 'Ill Logics of Irony', in Lee Clark Mitchell (ed.), *New Essays on The Red Badge of Courage* (Cambridge: Cambridge UP), 129–46.

1986c. 'Un poème sur tout', *Quinzaine littéraire* 16–31 (May), 5–6.

1986d. 'Problématique de la réception', *Revue française des études américaines* (Nov.), 393–8.

1987a. 'Id is, is Id?', in Shlomith Rimmon-Kenan (ed.), *Discourse in Psychoanalysis and Literature* (London and New York: Methuen), 19–37.

1987b. 'Cheng Ming Chi'i'd', *PN Review* 13/5, 29–37.

1987c. 'A for But: "The Custom House" in Hawthorne's *The Scarlet Letter*', *Word and Image* 3/2, 143–55.

1988a. 'Ill Wit and Good Humour: Women's Comedy and the Canon', *Comparative Criticism* 10, 121–38.

1988b. 'Ill Locutions', *Review of Contemporary Fiction* 8/3, 67–81. Also in *Théorie, littérature, ensignement* 6 (1988) as 'La controverse sur le discours indirect libre: Ann Banfield v. les littéraires', and in Nash 1990.

1989a. 'Illiterations', in Ellen G. Friedman and Miriam Fuchs (eds.), *Breaking the Sequence: Women's Experimental Fiction* (Princeton NJ: Princeton UP), 55–71.

1989b. 'Ill Wit and Sick Tragedy: *Jude the Obscure*', in Lance St John Butler (ed.), *Alternative Hardy* (Basingstoke: Macmillan), 26–48.

1989c. 'Stories, Theories and Things', *New Literary History* 21/1, 121–31.

1989d. 'Illicitations', *Review of Contemporary Fiction* 9/3, 101–9.

1990a. 'Diary', *London Review of Books* (10 May), 25.

1991a. *Stories, Theories and Things*, (Cambridge: Cambridge UP), Includes revised versions of 1963, 1984a, 1985a, 1985c, 1986a, 1986b, 1987a, 1987b, 1987c, 1988a, 1988b, 1989b, 1989c, 1990a, and 1991b.

1991b. 'Whatever Happened to Narratology?', *Poetics Today* 11/2, 283–93.

1992. 'Palimpsest History', in Umberto Eco, Richard Rorty, Jonathan Culler, and Christine Brooke-Rose; Stefan Collini (ed.), *Interpretation and Over-Interpretation* (Cambridge: Cambridge UP), 125–38. Expanded version of 1990a.

Translations

1959d. *Children of Chaos*, by Juan Goytisoto (London: MacGibbon and Kee).

1960d. *Fertility and Survival: Population Problems from Malthus to Mao Tse Tung*, by Alfred Sauvy (New York: Criterion Books, and London: Chatto and Windus, 1961).

1968d. *In the Labyrinth*, by Alain Robbe-Grillet (London: Calder and Boyars).

Interviews

1964e. 'Out's Out—It's In to be Anti', with Myrna Blumberg, *Guardian* (7 Nov.), 6.

1965b. 'Writer Out on a Limb', with 'Boswell', *Scotsman* (17 Apr.), 3.

1970. 'A Novel Theory', with John Hall, *Guardian* (16 Nov.), 9.

1976k. 'An Interview with Christine Brooke-Rose', with David Hayman and Keith Cohen, *Contemporary Literature* 17/1, 1–23. (Recorded in 1974.)

1984b. With Sue Macgregor, *Woman's Hour*, BBC Radio 4, London, 25 Sept.

1987d. With Ian Hamilton, *Bookmark*, 'Programme 16: The Yorkshire Ripper, Melvyn Bragg, Christine Brooke-Rose', BBC 2, London, 7 May. (Filmed in 1986.)

1988c.   Personal interview, 20 Jan.
1989e.   'A Conversation with Christine Brooke-Rose', with Ellen G. Friedman and Miriam Fuchs, *Review of Contemporary Fiction* 9/3, 81–90.
1990b.   'Global Wordcrunching', with Jenny Turner, *City Limits* (22–9 Mar.), 91. (Interview-Review.)
1990c.   'Christine Brooke-Rose in Conversation', with Nicholas Tredell, *P.N. Review* (Sept./Oct.), 29–35.
1990d.   'News of the Day Programme Four: Lorna Sage Talks to Christine Brooke-Rose', University of East Anglia Video Archive (9 Jan.).
1990e.   'Reclaim the Brain', with Jenny Turner, *Edinburgh Review* 84, 19–32.
1990f.   Personal interview, 6 Dec.

Published Letters and Unpublished Letters Cited

1979.   To Raleigh Trevelyan, 16 Mar. (Hamish Hamilton Archives, Bristol University Library, Bristol).
1983b.   To Michael Schmidt, in Mark Fisher (ed.), *Letters to an Editor* (Manchester: Carcanet, 1989), 209–10.
1984c.   To Michael Schmidt, ibid. 220–1.
1985d.   To Michael Schmidt, 1 Sept. (Manchester: Carcanet Press).

II.   CRITICISM OF BROOKE-ROSE'S FICTION

BERRESSEM, HANJO (1989), '*Thru* the Looking Glass: A Journey into the Universe of Discourse', *Review of Contemporary Fiction* 9/3, 128–33.
BIRCH, SARAH (1991), 'Christine Brooke-Rose and Post-War Writing in France', D.Phil. thesis, Oxford University.
BYATT, A. S. (1987), 'Programme 16: The Yorkshire Ripper, Melvyn Bragg, Christine Brooke-Rose', *Bookmark*, 7 May (BBC 2: London).
The Cambridge Guide to Literature in English (1988), Ian Ousby (ed.) (Cambridge and New York: Cambridge UP), 128–9.
CASERIO, ROBERT L. (1988), 'Mobility and Masochism: Christine Brooke-Rose and J. G. Ballard', *Novel* (Winter/Spring), 292–310.
DEL SAPIO, MARIA (1988), 'Le Maccine Della Scrittura: *Between* e *Amalgamemnon* di Christine Brooke-Rose', paper presented at the Eleventh Convegno Nazionale dell'Anglistica Italiana, University of Bergamo, 24–5 Oct.
——(n.d.) '*Between* the Frontiers: Polyglottism and Female Definitions of Self', unpublished essay.
DEL SAPIO GARBERO, MARIA (1991), *L'Assenza e la voce: Scena e intreccio della scrittura in Christina Rossetti, May Sinclair e Christine Brooke-Rose* (Naples: Liguori).

DICK, KAY (1973), 'Christine Brooke-Rose', *Littérature de notre temps* (Paris: Casterman).

The Feminist Companion to Literature in English: Women Writers from the Middle Ages to the Present (1990), Virginia Blain, Patricia Clements, and Isobel Grundy (eds.) (London: B. T. Batsford), 143.

FRIEDMAN, ELLEN G. (1987), 'Christine Brooke-Rose's *Xorandor*: Feminine Narrative, Science Fiction and the Science of Fiction', unpublished paper given at the 1987 MLA Conference.

——(1988), 'Utterly Other Discourses: The Anticanon of Experimental Women Writers from Dorothy Richardson to Christine Brooke-Rose', *Modern Fiction Studies* 34/3, 353–70.

——and FUCHS, MIRIAM (1989), 'Contexts and Continuities: An Introduction to Women's Experimental Fiction in English', in *Breaking the Sequence: Women's Experimental Fiction* (Princeton, NJ: Princeton UP), 3–51.

HALL, JOHN (1976), 'Christine Brooke-Rose', in James Vinson (ed.), *Contemporary Novelists* (London: St James Press, and New York: St Martin's Press), 182–4.

HAWKINS, SUSAN E. (1989), 'Memory and Discourse: Fictionalizing the Present in *Xorandor*', *Review of Contemporary Fiction* 9/3, 138–43.

HAYMAN, DAVID (1977), 'Some Writers in the Wake of the *Wake*', *TriQuarterly* 38, 3–38.

KAFALENOS, EMMA (1980), 'Textasy: Christine Brooke-Rose's *Thru*', *The International Fiction Review* 7/1, 43–6.

LECERCLE, JEAN-JACQUES (1991), 'Une lecture d'*Amalgamemnon*, de Christine Brooke-Rose', *Tropismes* 5, 263–90.

LEVITT, MORTON P. (1983), 'Christine Brooke-Rose', in Jay L. Halio (ed.), *Dictionary of Literary Biography*, vol. 14, *British Novelists Since 1960* (Detroit: Bruccoli Clark), 124–9.

LITTLE, JUDY (1989), '*Amalgamemnon* and the Politics of Narrative', *Review of Contemporary Fiction* 9/3, 134–7.

MCHALE, BRIAN (n.d.),' "I draw the line as a rule between one solar system and another": The Postmodernism(s) of Christine Brooke-Rose', unpublished essay to be included in his *Constructing Postmodernism* (forthcoming).

MCLAUGHLIN, BRIAN GERARD (1981), 'Structures of Identity: A Reading of the Self-Provoking Fiction of Christine Brooke-Rose, Bryan Stanley Johnson, Eva Figes and Paul West', doctoral thesis, Pennsylvania State University.

MAACK, ANNEGRET (1989), 'Erzähltechniken in Christine Brooke-Roses Romanen', in *Beckett und die Literatur der Gegenwart* Heidelberg: Carl Winter Universitätsverlag), 78–91.

MARTIN, RICHARD (1989*a*), ' "Just words on a page": The Novels of Christine Brooke-Rose', *Review of Contemporary Fiction* 9/3, 110–23.

MARTIN, RICHARD (1989*b*), ' "Stepping Stones into the Dark": Redundancy and Generation in Christine Brooke-Rose's *Amalgamemnon*', in Ellen G. Friedman and Miriam Fuchs (eds.), *Breaking the Sequence: Women's Experimental Fiction* (Princeton, NJ: Princeton UP), 177–87.

MORTON, BRIAN (1984), 'A Glimpse into the Future Tense', *Times Higher Education Supplement* (5 Oct.).

The Oxford Companion to English Literature (1985), 5th edn. Margaret Drabble (ed.) (Oxford: Oxford UP), 136.

RIMMON-KENAN, SHLOMITH (1982), 'Ambiguity and Narrative Levels: Christine Brooke-Rose's *Thru*', *Poetics Today* 3/1, 21–32.

SULEIMAN, SUSAN RUBIN (1989), 'Living Between, or, the Loneliness of the Alleinstehende Frau', *Review of Contemporary Fiction* 9/3, 124–7.

TONGOLA, SILVIA (1983). ' "The Foot": A Pragmalinguistic Analysis', doctoral thesis, Zürich University.

ZAGLI, LUCIA (1983), 'Narratività e metalinguaggio in *Between* di Christine Brooke-Rose', Masters thesis, Oriental Institute of Naples.

Reviews of Brooke-Rose's Novels Cited

ALLEN, WALTER (1957), review of *The Languages of Love*, *New Statesman* (12 Oct.), 469–70.

——(1958), review of *The Sycamore Tree*, *New Statesman* (11 Oct.), 500.

BERGONZI, BERNARD (1961), 'Inanity Fair', *Spectator* (1 Sept.), 297.

CIXOUS, HÉLÈNE (1968), 'Le Langage du déplacement', review of *Between*, *Le Monde* (28 Dec.): vii.

CLUTE, JOHN (1986), review of *Xorandor*, *Interzone* (Autumn), 52.

CRANSTON, MAURICE (1957), review of *The Languages of Love*, *Encounter* (Nov.), 89–90.

DISCH, THOMAS M. (1986), 'Rock of Phages', *New York Times Book Review* (3 Aug.), 10.

FULLER, ROY (1957), review of *The Languages of Love*, *London Magazine* (Dec.), 62, 65.

HALL, JOHN (1970), 'A Novel Theory', *Guardian* (16 Nov.), 9.

HARTLEY, L. P. (1961), review of *The Dear Deceit*, *London Magazine* (Jan.), 73–4.

HOPE, FRANCIS (1961), 'Suffering Fools Sadly', review of *The Middlemen*, *Time and Tide* (7 Sept.), 1,486.

——(1964), 'I, Julian', review of *Out*, *New Statesman* (13 Nov.), 741–2.

KENDALL, ELAINE (1985), 'Battling the Computer in the Cassandra Mode', review of *Amalgamemnon*, *Los Angeles Times* (18 Mar.).

KING, FRANCIS (1975), 'Failed Utopia', review of *Thru*, *Sunday Telegraph* (13 July), 12.

Kirkus Reviews (syndicated column) (1985), review of *Amalgamemnon* (1 Feb.).

MARSHALL, BOB (1984), 'An Egg-head's Christmas List', review of *Amalgamemnon, Bookseller* (24 Nov.), 2,159.

MAYNE, RICHARD (1961), review of *The Middlemen, New Statesman* (8 Sept.), 316.

MORTON, BRIAN (1986), 'Words of the Thinking Rock', review of *Xorandor, Times Literary Supplement* (11 July), 767.

PRICE, R. G. G. (1961), review of *The Middlemen, Punch* (30 Aug.), 332.

QUIGLY, ISABEL (1958), review of *The Sycamore Tree, Encounter* (Nov.), 86.

SEYMOUR-SMITH, MARTIN (1966), 'Heroic Qualities', review of *Such, Spectator* (4 Nov.), 592–3.

Times Literary Supplement (TLS) (1957), 'Fiction II: Larger than Life', review of *The Languages of Love* (18 Oct.), 629.

——(1958), 'Fiction: The Rough with the Smooth', review of *The Sycamore Tree* (3 Oct.), 557.

——(1960), 'Gallery of Rogues', review of *The Dear Deceit*, (21 Oct.), 673.

TURNER, JENNY (1990), 'Global Wordcrunching', review of *Verbivore, City Limits* (22–9 Mar.), 91.

WHITLEY, JOHN (1968). 'Girl in the Glass Booth', review of *Between, Sunday Times* (3 Nov.), 62.

WYNDHAM, FRANCIS (1957), review of *The Languages of Love, Spectator* (11 Oct.), 491.

Other Sources

SCHMIDT, MICHAEL (1990). Personal interview. 13 June.

TREVELYAN, RALEIGH (1979), Letter to Christine Brooke-Rose, 27 Mar., Hamish Hamilton Archives, Bristol University Library, Bristol.

III. LITERARY WORKS CITED

AESCHYLUS, *Agamemnon* (1956), *The Orestian Trilogy*, Philip Vellacott (tr.) (Harmondsworth: Penguin).

BECKETT, SAMUEL (1958), *Malone Dies* (London: Calder and Boyars, 1975).

COTTON, NATHANAEL (1810), 'Visions in Verse IV', in Alexander Chalmers (ed.), *The Works of the English Poets, from Chaucer to Cowper*, xviii, 34–5.

ELIOT, T. S. (1936), *Collected Poems 1909–1935* (London: Faber and Faber).

FOWLES, JOHN (1969), *The French Lieutenant's Woman* (London: Cape).

HERODOTUS, *The Histories* (1954), Aubrey de Selincourt (tr.) (Harmondsworth: Penguin, 1972).

JOHNSON, B. S. (1964), *Albert Angelo* (London: Constable).

O'BRIEN, FLANN (1939), *At Swim-Two-Birds* (Harmondsworth: Penguin, 1975).

PEREC, GEORGES (1969), *La Disparition* (Paris: Denoël).

ROCHE, MAURICE (1972), *Circus* (Paris: Seuil).

IV. GENERAL REFERENCES

ARISTOTLE, *Rhetoric*, in W. Rhys Roberts (tr.), W. D. Ross (ed.), *Works of Aristotle* (Oxford: Clarendon Press, 1924).

ASHCROFT, BILL, GRIFFITHS, GARETH, and TIFFIN, HELEN (1989), *The Empire Writes Back: Theory and Practice in Post-Colonial Literatures* (London and New York: New Accents – Routledge).

BAKHTIN, MIKHAIL M. (1981), *The Dialogic Imagination*, Michael Holquist (ed.), Caryl Emerson and Michael Holquist (tr.) (Austin: University of Texas Press).

——(1984), *Problems of Dostoevsky's Poetics*, Caryl Emerson (ed. and tr.) (Manchester: Manchester UP).

BARTHES, ROLAND (1957), *Mythologies* (Paris: Seuil).

——(1964), 'Eléments de sémiologie', in *L'Aventure sémiologique* (Paris: Seuil, 1985), 17–84.

——(1967), 'Science *versus* Literature', *Times Literary Supplement* (28 Sept.), 897–8.

——(1970*a*), 'L'Ancienne rhétorique: aide-mémoire', in *L'Aventure sémiologique* (Paris: Seuil, 1985), 85–165.

——(1970*b*), *S/Z* (Paris: Seuil).

——(1973), *Le Plaisir du texte* (Paris: Seuil).

——(1984), *Le Bruissement de la langue* (Paris: Seuil).

BAUDRILLARD, JEAN (1970). *La Société de consommation: ses mythes, ses structures* (Paris: Idées-Gallimard, 1985).

——(1981), *Simulacres et simulation* (Paris: Galilée).

BENVENISTE, EMILE (1966), *Problèmes de linguistique générale* (Paris: Gallimard).

BERGONZI, BERNARD (1979), *The Situation of the Novel*, 2nd edn. (London: Macmillan).

BLACK, MAX (1962), *Models and Metaphors: Studies in Language and Philosophy* (Ithaca: Cornell UP).

BLOOM, HAROLD (1973), *The Anxiety of Influence: A Theory of Poetry* (London, Oxford, and New York: Oxford UP).

BOURDIEU, PIERRE (1982), *Ce que parler veut dire: l'économie des échanges linguistiques* (Paris: Fayard).

BRADBURY, MALCOLM (1973), *Possibilities: Essays on the State of the Novel* (London, Oxford, and New York: Oxford UP).

——(1977), Introduction to Malcolm Bradbury (ed.), *The Novel Today: Contemporary Writers on Modern Fiction* (Manchester: Manchester UP–Fontana, and New Jersey: Rowman and Littlefield).

BRADBURY, MALCOLM (1987), *No, Not Bloomsbury* (London: André Deutsch).

BRENNAN, TIMOTHY (1990), 'The National Longing for Form', in Homi K. Bhabha (ed.), *Nation and Narration* (London and New York: Routledge), 44–70.

BRIOSI, SANDRO (1984), 'Retorica, grammatica e fenomenologia della metafora', *Lingua e stile* 19, 189–222.

BRITTON, CELIA (1989), 'The Nouveau Roman and *Tel Quel* Marxism', *Paragraph* 12/1, 65–96.

BROOKS, PETER (1984). *Reading for the Plot: Design and Intention in Narrative* (New York: Vintage-Random House, 1985).

BURNS, ALAN (1981), 'Alan Burns', interview with Charles Sugnet, in Alan Burns and Charles Sugnet (eds.), *The Imagination on Trial: British and American Writers Discuss Their Working Methods* (London and New York: Allison and Busby),161–8.

BUTLER, CHRISTOPHER (1984), *Interpretation, Deconstruction, and Ideology: An Introduction to Some Current Issues in Literary Theory* (Oxford: Clarendon Press).

BUTOR, MICHEL (1960), *Répertoire I* (Paris: Minuit).

——(1967), *Entretiens avec Michel Butor*, Georges Charbonnier (ed.) (Paris: Gallimard).

——(1968), *Répertoire III* (Paris: Minuit).

BYATT, A. S. (1979), 'People in Paper Houses: Attitudes to "Realism" and "Experiment" in English Postwar Fiction', in Malcolm Bradbury and David Palmer (eds.), *The Contemporary English Novel* (London: Edward Arnold), 19–42.

CALVINO, ITALO (1967), 'Cibernetica e fantasmi (Appunti sulla narrativa come processo combinatorio)', *Una Pietra sopra: discorsi di letteratura e società* (Torino: Einaudi, 1980), 164–81.

CAMERON, DEBORAH (1985), *Feminism and Linguistic Theory* (London: Macmillan).

CARTER, IAN (1990), *Ancient Cultures of Conceit: British University Fiction in the Post-War Years* (London and New York: Routledge).

CAUTE, DAVID (1971), *The Illusion: An Essay on Politics, Theatre and the Novel* (London: André Deutsch).

CIXOUS, HÉLÈNE (1975), 'Sorties', in Hélène Cixous and Catherine Clément, *La Jeune née* (Paris: 10/18–Union Générale d'Editions).

COOPER, WILLIAM (1959), 'Reflections on Some Aspects of the Experimental Novel', in John Wain (ed.), *International Literary Annual 2* (London: John Calder), 29–36.

COUTURIER, MAURICE (1991), *Textual Communication: A Print-Based Theory of the Novel* (London and New York: Routledge).

CRANLEY-FRANCIS, ANNE (1990), *Feminist Fiction: Feminist Uses of Generic Fiction* (Oxford: Polity Press).

CULLER, JONATHAN (1988), 'The Call of the Phoneme: Introduction', in Jonathan Culler (ed.), *On Puns: The Foundation of Letters* (Oxford: Blackwell), 1–16.

DEKOVEN, MARIANNE (1989), 'Male Signature, Female Aesthetic: The Gender Politics of Experimental Writing', in Ellen G. Friedman and Miriam Fuchs (eds.), *Breaking the Sequence: Women's Experimental Fiction* (Princeton NJ: Princeton UP), 72–81.

DELEUZE, GILLES (1969), *Logique du sens* (Paris: Minuit).

——and FÉLIX GUATTARI (1972), *Capitalisme et schizophrénie*, vol. 1, *L'Anti-Oedipe* (Paris: Minuit).

DE MAN, PAUL (1979), 'The Epistemology of Metaphor', in Sheldon Sacks (ed.), *On Metaphor* (Chicago and London: University of Chicago Press), 11–28.

DERRIDA, JACQUES (1967), *De la grammatologie* (Paris: Minuit).

——(1972a), *La Dissémination* (Paris: Seuil).

——(1972b), *Marges de la philosophie* (Paris: Minuit).

——(1972c), *Positions* (Paris: Minuit).

DEWALD, CAROLYN (1981), 'Women and Culture in Herodotus' *Histories*', in Helene P. Foley (ed.), *Reflections of Women in Antiquity* (New York, Paris, London, Montreux, and Tokyo: Gordon and Breach), 91–125.

DOYLE, BRIAN (1989), *English and Englishness* (London and New York: New Accents–Routledge).

DUPLESSIS, RACHEL BLAU (1981), 'For the Etruscans', in Elaine Showalter (ed.), *The New Feminist Criticism: Essays on Women, Literature, and Theory* (London: Virago, 1986), 271–91.

EBERT, TERESA L. (1980), 'The Convergences of Postmodern Innovative Fiction and Science Fiction: An Encounter with Samuel R. Delaney's Technotopia', *Poetics Today* 1/4, 91–104.

ECO, UMBERTO (1979), *Lector in fabula: la cooperazione interpretativa nei testi narrativi* (Milan: Bompiani).

ELIOT, T. S. (1932), 'Tradition and the Individual Talent', in *Selected Essays 1917–1932* (London: Faber and Faber).

EMPSON, WILLIAM (1953), *Seven Types of Ambiguity*, 3rd edn. (London: Chatto and Windus).

FEDERMAN, RAYMOND (1975), 'Surfiction: Four Propositions in Form of an Introduction', in Raymond Federman (ed.), *Surfiction: Fiction Now . . . And Tomorrow* (Chicago: Swallow Press), 5–15.

FLORENCE, PENNY (1990), 'The Liberation of Utopia, or Is Science Fiction the Ideal Contemporary Women's Form?', in Linda Anderson (ed.), *Plotting Change: Contemporary Women's Fiction* (London, Melbourne, and Aukland: Edward Arnold), 65–84.

FOUCAULT, MICHEL (1971), *L'Ordre du discours* (Paris: Gallimard).

FOWLER, ROGER (1977), *Linguistics and the Novel* (London and New York: New Accents–Methuen).

FOWLES, JOHN (1974), 'Profile 7: John Fowles', interview with Lorna Sage, *New Review* 1/7, 31–7.

FREUD, SIGMUND (1915), 'The Unconscious', James Strachey (tr.), in *On Metapsychology*, The Pelican Freud Library, vol. 11, James Strachey and Angela Richards (eds.) (Harmondsworth: Penguin), 167–222.

——(1920), 'Beyond the Pleasure Principle', ibid. 261–338.

FRYE, NORTHROP (1957), *The Anatomy of Criticism* (Princeton NJ: Princeton UP).

GENETTE, GÉRARD (1966), *Figures* (Paris: Seuil).

——(1969), *Figures II* (Paris: Seuil).

——(1972), *Figures III* (Paris: Seuil).

——(1982), *Palimpsestes: la littérature au second degré* (Paris: Seuil).

GILBERT, SANDRA M. and GUBAR, SUSAN (1979), *The Madwoman in the Attic: The Woman Writer and the Nineteenth-Century Literary Imagination* (New Haven, Conn., and London: Yale UP, 1984).

GINDIN, JAMES (1962), *Postwar British Fiction: New Accents and Attitudes* (London: Cambridge UP, and Berkeley and Los Angeles: University of California Press).

GOODMAN, NELSON (1969), *Languages of Art: An Approach to a Theory of Symbols* (London: Oxford UP).

GREIMAS, A. J. (1966), *Sémantique structurale: recherche de méthode* (Paris: Larousse, 1986).

——(1970), *Du Sens: essais sémiotiques* (Paris: Seuil).

—— and RASTIER, FRANÇOIS (1968), 'Les Jeux des contraintes sémiotiques', in Greimas (1970), 135–55.

GURR, ANDREW (1981), *Writers in Exile: The Identity of Home in Modern Literature* (Sussex: Harvester, and New Jersey: Humanities).

HALLYN, FERNAND (1975). *Formes métaphoriques dans la poésie lyrique de l'âge baroque en France* (Geneva: Droz).

HANSFORD JOHNSON, BARBARA (1949), 'The Sick-Room Hush Over the English Novel', *Listener* 42, 235–6.

HASSAN, IHAB (1975), 'The New Gnosticism: Speculations on an Aspect of the Postmodern Mind', in *Paracriticisms: Seven Speculations of the Times* (Urbana, Chicago, and London: University of Illinois Press).

——(1982), *The Dismemberment of Orpheus: Toward a Postmodern Literature*, 2nd edn. (Madison, Wis: University of Wisconsin Press).

HAWKES, JOHN (1982), round-table discussion, in Lois Oppenheim (ed.), *Three Decades of the French New Novel* (Urbana and Chicago: University of Illinois Press, 1986), 200–3.

HAYMAN, RONALD (1976), *The Novel Today 1967–1975* (London: Longman).

HEISENBERG, WERNER (1958), *Physics and Philosophy: The Revolution in Modern Science* (New York: Harper).

HENRY, ALBERT (1980), 'Métaphore verbale et métaphore adjective', in Jean Bingen, André Coupez, and Francine Mawet (eds.), *Recherches de* linguistique: hommage à Maurice Leroy (Brussels: Editions de l'Université de Bruxelles), 89–99.

HIRSCH, E. D. (1987), *Cultural Literacy: What Every American Needs to Know* (Boston: Houghton Mifflin).

HRUSHOVSKI, BENJAMIN (1984), 'Poetic Metaphor and Frames of Reference, with Examples from Eliot, Rilke, Mayakovski, Mandelshtam, Pound, Creeley, Amichai, and the *New York Times*', *Poetics Today* 5/2, 5–43.

HUTCHEON, LINDA (1985), *A Theory of Parody: The Teachings of Twentieth-Century Art Forms* (New York and London: Methuen).

——(1988), *A Poetics of Postmodernism: History, Theory, Fiction* (New York and London: Routledge).

INGARDEN, ROMAN (1931), *The Literary Work of Art: An Investigation on the Borderlines of Ontology, Logic, and Theory of Literature*, George G. Grabowicz (tr.) (Evanston, Ill.: Northwestern UP, 1973).

IRIGARAY, LUCE (1966), 'Communications linguistique et spéculaire: modèles génétiques et modèles pathologiques', in *Parler n'est jamais neutre* (Paris: Minuit, 1985), 15–34.

——(1967), 'Approche d'une grammaire de l'énonciation de l'hystérique et de l'obsessionel', ibid. 55–68.

——(1974), *Speculum de l'autre femme* (Paris: Minuit).

——(1977), *Ce sexe qui n'en est pas un* (Paris: Minuit).

ISER, WOLFGANG (1978), *The Act of Reading: A Theory of Aesthetic Response* (London and Henley: Routledge and Kegan Paul).

JAKOBSON, ROMAN, and LÜBBE-GROTHUES, GRETE (1980), 'The Language of Schizophrenia: Hölderlin's Speech and Poetry', in Krystyna Pomorska and Stephen Rudy (eds.), *Verbal Art, Verbal Signs, Verbal Time.* (Oxford: Blackwell, 1985), 133–40.

JAMESON, FREDRIC (1983), 'Postmodernism and Consumer Society', in Hal Foster (ed.), *The Anti-Aesthetic: Essays on Postmodern Culture* (Port Townsend, Wash.: Bay Press), 111–25.

JOHNSON, B. S. (1973), 'Introduction to *Aren't You Too Young to Be Writing Your Memoirs?*', in Malcolm Bradbury (ed.), *The Novel Today: Contemporary Writers on Modern Fiction* (Manchester: Manchester UP–Fontana, and New Jersey: Rowman and Littlefield, 1977), 151–68.

KARL, FREDERICK R. (1962), *A Reader's Guide to the Contemporary English Novel* (London: Thames and Hudson, 1963).

KENYON, OLGA (1988), *Women Novelists Today: A Survey of English Writing in the Seventies and Eighties* (Brighton: Harvester).

KERMODE, FRANK (1958), 'Durrell and Others', in *Puzzles and Epiphanies: Essays and Reviews 1958–1961* (London: Routledge and Kegan Paul, 1962), 214–27.

——(1963), 'The House of Fiction', in Malcolm Bradbury (ed.), *The Novel Today: Contemporary Writers on Modern Fiction* (Manchester: Manchester UP-Fontana, and New Jersey: Rowman and Littlefield, 1977), 111–35.

KITTAY, EVA FEDER (1987), *Metaphor: Its Cognitive Force and Linguistic Structure*, (Oxford: Clarendon Press).

KRISTEVA, JULIA (1969), *Sèméîôtikè* (Paris: Points-Seuil, 1978).

——(1974), *La Révolution du langage poétique: l'avant-garde à la fin du XIXe siécle: Lautréamont et Mallarmé* (Paris: Seuil).

LACAN, JACQUES (1966), *Ecrits* (Paris: Seuil).

LAING, R. D. (1967), 'The Politics of Experience', in *The Politics of Experience and The Bird of Paradise* (Harmondsworth: Penguin), 13–137.

LAING, STEWART (1983), 'The Production of Literature', in Alan Sinfield (ed.), *Society and Literature 1945–1970* (London: Methuen), 121–71.

LAKOFF, GEORGE and JOHNSON, MARK (1980), *Metaphors We Live By* (Chicago and London: University of Chicago Press).

LANHAM, RICHARD A. (1989), 'The Electronic Word: Literary Study and the Digital Revolution', *New Literary History* 20/2, 265–90.

LECERCLE, JEAN-JACQUES (1990), *The Violence of Language* (London and New York: Routledge).

LEE, ALLISON (1989), *Realism and Power: Postmodern British Fiction* (London and New York: Routledge).

LE GUERN, MICHEL (1973), *Sémantique de la métaphore et de la métonymie* (Paris: Larrouse).

LESSING, DORIS (1972), Preface, *The Golden Notebook*, 2nd edn. (London: Michael Joseph, 1982), 7–22.

LÉVI-STRAUSS, CLAUDE (1958), *Anthropologie structurale* (Paris: Plon, 1974).

LEVITT, MORTON P. (1987), *Modernist Survivors: The Contemporary Novel in England, the United States, France, and Latin America* (Columbus, Ohio: Ohio State UP).

LODGE, DAVID (1971), *The Novelist at the Crossroads and Other Essays on Fiction and Criticism* (London: Routledge and Kegan Paul).

——(1977), *The Modes of Modern Writing: Metaphor, Metonymy, and the Typology of Modern Literature* (London: Edward Arnold).

LYOTARD, J.-F. (1979), *La Condition postmoderne* (Paris: Minuit).

McHALE, BRIAN (1987), *Postmodernist Fiction* (New York and London: Methuen).

McLUHAN, H. MARSHALL (1962), *The Gutenberg Galaxy: The Making of Typographic Man* (London: Routledge and Kegan Paul).

MACHEREY, PIERRE (1965), *Pour une théorie de la production littéraire* (Paris: Maspero, 1980).

MADDEN, DAVID W. (1983), 'Alan Burns', in Jay L. Halio (ed.), *Dictionary of Literary Biography*, vol. 14, *British Novelists Since 1960* (Detroit: Bruccoli Clark), 187–94.

MASSIE, ALLAN (1990), *The Novel Today: A Critical Guide to the British Novel 1970–1989* (London and New York: Longman).

MILLER, KARL (ed.) (1968), *Writing in England Today: The Last Fifteen Years* (Harmondsworth: Penguin).

Moi, Toril (1985), *Sexual/Textual Politics: Feminist Literary Theory* (London and New York: New Accents–Methuen).

Mulhern, Francis (1990), 'English Reading', in Homi K. Bhabha (ed.), *Nation and Narration* (London and New York: Routledge), 250–64.

Murdoch, Iris, (1961), 'Against Dryness: A Polemical Sketch', in Malcolm Bradbury (ed.), *The Novel Today: Contemporary Writers on Modern Fiction* (Manchester: Manchester UP–Fontana, and New Jersey: Rowman and Littlefield, 1977), 23–31.

Nash, Cristopher (1987), *World-Games: The Tradition of Anti-Realist Revolt* (London and New York: Methuen).

——(ed.) (1990), *Narrative in Culture: The Uses of Storytelling in the Sciences, Philosophy, and Literature* (London and New York: Routledge).

Nietzsche, Friedrich (1979), 'On Truth and Lies in a Non-Moral Sense', in Daniel Breazeale (tr. and ed.), *Philosophy and Truth: Selections from Nietzsche's Notebooks of the Early 1870s* (Sussex: Harvester, and New Jersey: Humanities Press), 79–97.

Ohmann, Richard (1984), 'The Shaping of a Canon: U.S. Fiction, 1960–1975', in Robert von Hallberg (ed.), *Canons* (Chicago and London: University of Chicago Press), 377–401.

Ong, Walter (1982), *Orality and Literacy: The Technologizing of the Word* (London and New York: New Accents–Methuen).

Palmer, Paulina (1989), *Contemporary Women's Fiction: Narrative Practice and Feminist Theory* (New York and London: Harvester Wheatsheaf).

Parrinder, Patrick (1987), *The Failure of Theory: Essays on Criticism and Contemporary Fiction* (Brighton: Harvester).

Paulson, William (1989), 'Computers, Minds, and Texts: Preliminary Reflections', *New Literary History* 20/2, 291–303.

Perec, Georges (1973), 'Histoire du lipogramme', in OuLiPo (ed.), *La Littérature potentielle (créations re-créations récréations)* (Paris: Idées-Gallimard), 77–93.

Pratt, Terrence W. (1975), *Programming Languages: Design and Implementation* (New Jersey: Prentice-Hall).

Priest, Christopher (1979), 'British Science Fiction', in Patrick Parrinder (ed.), *Science Fiction: A Critical Guide* (London and New York: Longman), 187–202.

Queneau, Raymond (1967), 'Science and Literature', *Times Literary Supplement* (28 Sept.), 863–4.

Quin, Ann (1972), 'Landscape with Three-Cornered Dances', interview with John Hall, *Guardian* (29 Apr.), 8.

Rabinovitz, Rubin (1967), *The Reaction Against Experiment in the English Novel, 1950–1960* (New York and London: Columbia UP).

Ricardou, Jean (1967), *Problèmes du nouveau roman* (Paris: Seuil).

Richards, I. A. (1925), *Principles of Literary Criticism* (London: Kegan Paul, Trench and Trubner, and New York: Harcourt Brace).

RICHARDS, I. A. (1936), *The Philosophy of Rhetoric* (New York and London: Oxford UP).

RICOEUR, PAUL (1975), *La Métaphore vive* (Paris: Seuil).

——(1986), 'Contingence et rationalité dans le récit', in 'Le Roman, le récit et le savoir', *CRIN* 15 (special issue), 131–46.

ROBBE-GRILLET, ALAIN (1955), Letter from Alain Robbe-Grillet to Emile Henriot, 15 June, *Obliques* 16/17 (1978), 88.

——(1963), *Pour un nouveau roman* (Paris: Minuit).

ROGERS, ROBERT (1978), *Metaphor: A Psychoanalytic View* (Berkeley, Los Angeles, and London: University of California Press).

ROSE, MARGARET A. (1979), *Parody/Metafiction: An Analysis of Parody as a Critical Mirror to the Writing and Reception of Fiction* (London: Croom Helm).

SAGE, LORNA (1979), 'Female Fictions: The Women Novelists', in Malcolm Bradbury and David Palmer (eds.), *The Contemporary English Novel* (London: Edward Arnold), 67–88.

SAID, EDWARD (1984), 'Reflections on Exile', *Granta* 13, 157–72.

SARRAUTE, NATHALIE (1956), *L'Ere du soupçon* (Paris: Folio-Gallimard, 1987).

——(1987), *Nathalie Sarraute: qui êtes-vous?* (interviews with Simone Benmussa), Simone Benmussa (ed.) (Lyon: La Manufacture).

SAUSSURE, FERDINAND DE (1915), *Cours de linguistique générale*. Tullio de Mauro (ed.) (Paris: Payot, 1985).

SCHOLES, ROBERT (1967), *The Fabulators*, (New York: Oxford UP).

——(1975), *Structural Fabulation: An Essay on Fiction of the Future* (Notre Dame and London: University of Notre Dame Press).

——(1979), *Fabulation and Metafiction* (Urbana, Chicago, and London: University of Illinois Press).

SIMON, CLAUDE (1972), 'La Fiction mot à mot', *Nouveau roman: hier, aujourdui*, vol 2 (Paris: 10/18-Union Générale d'Editions).

SOLLERS, PHILIPPE (1968), *Logiques* (Paris: Seuil).

SPENDER, STEPHEN (1962), 'Moderns and Contemporaries', *Listener* 68, 555–6.

SPIVAK, GAYATRI CHAKRAVORTY (1988), *In Other Worlds: Essays in Cultural Politics* (New York and London: Routledge).

STANFORD, DEREK (1963), *Muriel Spark: A Biography and Critical Study* (Fontwell: Centaur Press).

STERN, J. P. (1973), *On Realism* (London: Routledge and Kegan Paul).

STEVENSON, RANDALL (1986), *The British Novel Since the Thirties: An Introduction* (London: B. T. Batsford).

STEVICK, PHILIP P. (1989), 'Voices in the Head: Style and Consciousness in the Fiction of Ann Quin', in Ellen G. Friedman and Miriam Fuchs (eds.), *Breaking the Sequence: Women's Experimental Fiction* (Princeton NJ: Princeton UP), 231–9.

STEWART, IAN (1987), *The Problems of Mathematics* (Oxford and New York: Oxford UP).

SUGNET, CHARLES (1981), 'Introduction' to Alan Burns and Charles Sugnet (eds.), *The Imagination on Trial: British and American Writers Discuss Their Working Methods* (London and New York: Allison and Busby), 2–13.

SULEIMAN, SUSAN RUBIN (1980), 'Introduction: Varieties of Audience-Oriented Criticism', in Susan R. Suleiman and Inge Crosman (eds.), *The Reader in the Text: Essays on Audience and Interpretation* (Princeton NJ: Princeton UP), 3–45.

——(1990), *Subversive Intent: Gender, Politics, and the Avant-Garde* (Cambridge, Mass. and London: Harvard UP).

SUTHERLAND, J. A. (1978), *Fiction and the Fiction Industry* (London: Athlone-University of London, and New Jersey: Humanities Press).

SUVIN, DARKO (1979), *Metamorphoses of Science Fiction: On the Poetics and History of a Literary Genre* (New Haven, Conn., and London: Yale UP).

SWINDEN, PATRICK (1984), *The English Novel of History and Society, 1940–1980* (London and Basingstoke: Macmillan).

TAMBA-MECZ, IRÈNE (1981), *Le Sens figuré: vers une théorie de l'énonciation figurative* (Paris: Presses Universitaires de France).

TEL QUEL (1968), *Théorie d'ensemble* (Paris: Seuil).

TODD, JANET (1989), *Dictionary of British Women Writers* (London: Routledge).

TODOROV, TZVETAN (1971), *Poétique de la prose* (Paris: Seuil).

——(1978), *Les Genres du discours* (Paris: Seuil).

TURKLE, SHERRY (1988), 'Artificial Intelligence and Psychoanalysis: A New Alliance', *Daedalus*, special issue, 241–68.

WATT, IAN (1957), *The Rise of the Novel: Studies in Defoe, Richardson and Fielding* (London: Chatto and Windus, 1960).

WAUGH, PATRICIA (1984), *Metafiction: The Theory and Practice of Self-Conscious Fiction* (London and New York: New Accents–Methuen).

——(1989). *Feminine Fictions: Revisiting the Postmodern* (New York and London: Routlege).

WEIGHTMAN, JOHN (1965), 'The Writer in France', *The Author* 76/1, 1–6.

WILDE, ALAN (1981), *Horizons of Assent: Modernism, Postmodernism, and the Ironic Imagination* (Baltimore and London: Johns Hopkins UP).

WILSON, ANGUS (1958), 'Diversity and Depth', *Times Literary Supplement* (15 Aug.), viii.

——(1968), 'Books of the Year', *Observer* (22 Dec.), 17.

ZAVARZADEH, MAS'UD (1976), *The Mythopoeic Reality: The Postwar American Nonfiction Novel* (Urbana, Chicago, and London: University of Illinois Press).

Index